A Practitioner's Guide to Wills

Fourmat Publishing

A Practitioner's Guide to Wills

by
Meryl Thomas, BA, LL.M

1992
Fourmat Publishing
London

ISBN 1 85190 165 5

First published 1992

A catalogue record for this book is available from the British Library.

Printed in Great Britain by
Billing & Sons Ltd, Worcester

© 1992 Meryl Thomas
Published by Fourmat Publishing
133 Upper Street, London N1 1QP

Preface

"Few things show the human character in a more ridiculous light than the circumstance of will-making. It is the latest opportunity we have of exercising the natural perversity of the disposition, and we take care to make a good use of it. We husband it with jealousy, put it off as long as we can, and then use every precaution that the world shall be no gainer by our deaths. This last act of our lives seldom belies the former tenor of them for stupidity, caprice, and unmeaning spite. All that we seem to think of is to manage matters so (in settling accounts with those who are so unmannerly as to survive us) as to do as little good, and to plague and disappoint as many people, as possible." William Hazlitt, *Table-Talk*.

This book, as its title suggests, is intended to be a comprehensive guide to the drafting of wills. In addition to the selection of precedents and draft wills which have been included, the text also examines the major areas of law which are likely to be relevant to the practitioner. As the book is intended as a practical guide rather than an academic text, references to authorities have been kept to a minimum.

Although it is outside the scope of this book to deal at length with the intricacies of tax planning, the more fundamental implications of the current tax regime are considered in the final chapter.

Unless otherwise indicated, throughout the text and precedents, references to the male are intended to include the female and *vice versa*, and no sexist connotation should be inferred.

Whilst it is hoped that the precedents and draft clauses provided will be of assistance to the practitioner, they are intended to be of general guidance only and may need modifying to suit the requirements of individual situations. In no circumstances will any liability be accepted by or on behalf of the author or the publishers for any loss of any kind suffered in whole or in part as a result of the reliance by any person upon any of the clauses or precedents contained in this book.

It is not possible to mention everyone who has assisted in the preparation of this book, but the following deserve particular thanks. First, my husband Bruce Leyland who has helped greatly, particularly in the drafting of the precedents; also Sharron Alldred, Kathryn Bates and Valerie Simpson for their secretarial assistance; and third Brian Dowrick, my research assistant, for his invaluable work.

The law is as stated on 11 March 1992.

Meryl Thomas

Contents

page

Table of Cases

page

page

List of Precedents

page

Chapter 21: Perpetuities and accumulation

Chapter 22: Construction of wills

Chapter 23: Failure of gifts and intestacy

Introduction

Before drafting a client's will, a solicitor must enquire into all the testator's circumstances, including his family, assets and liabilities. The solicitor must also be sure that the client is not under any incapacity (such as mental illness or minority) which would prevent the making of a valid will.

The solicitor must enquire about his client's marital status and the composition of his family. Any intended provisions must be looked at in the light of the Inheritance (Provision for Family and Dependants) Act 1975, and the testator must be advised of the effects of the Act and the applications that could be made under it.

If the testator is unmarried, then the effect of future marriage or remarriage should be made clear to him. If the testator intends to be married in the near future then special provision may be needed in the will to prevent revocation of the whole or part of the will on that remarriage.

Apart from the testator's duties to provide for his family and dependants, the solicitor must also ascertain whether his client has any contractual obligations or other duties requiring him to make certain dispositions under his will.

The solicitor must be fully aware of the size and nature of the estate. He must also find out whether the client has any power of appointment or disposition to be exercised by the will. Further, the solicitor should find out what recent lifetime gifts have been made as these may affect the inheritance tax position, and some *inter vivos* gifts may be liable to be brought into hotchpot.

The solicitor should also find out the size and nature of the testator's debts and liabilities so that these can be taken into account.

If the testator has a business, or is a partner in a firm or a director of a company, special provision may have to be made in the will, and the partnership deed or the articles and memorandum of association of the company must be inspected before the will is drafted to check that the provisions of the will and such documents are not inconsistent.

Once full instructions have been taken the solicitor should take great care to ensure the will complies with the instructions. Once drafted, the provisions should be fully explained to the testator before the will is executed, to ensure that he both knows and approves of the will's contents. Although section 20 of the Administration of Justice Act 1982 allows rectification of a will where mistakes have arisen by reason of a clerical error or a misunderstanding of instructions, the section does not enable every mistake to be corrected.

The solicitor's duty does not end when the will is drafted; he must ensure that it is properly and validly executed. Not only does the solicitor have a contractual duty to his client but he also owes a duty of care to potential beneficiaries – see *Ross* v *Caunters* [1980] Ch 297. In this case Megarry VC held that a solicitor was negligent where he:

(i)   failed to warn a testator that the spouse of a beneficiary should not witness a will;

(ii) failed to check whether the will was properly attested when it was returned to him;

(iii) failed to observe that the attesting witness was the spouse of a beneficiary; and

(iv) failed to draw this to the testator's attention.

The solicitor should draw his client's attention to the effect of dealing with property (such as the doctrines of ademption and lapse). Property passing outside of the will (such as joint property, the proceeds of insurance policies and payments from pension funds) should also be discussed. Tax aspects should be looked at and discussed in relation to the particular circumstances of the client and his family.

The form of the will drafted is largely a matter of choice for the solicitor, although the formalities under the Wills Act 1837 must always be complied with. There are certain conventions that are usually followed, such as the lack of punctuation in the text. Words of

command such as "I GIVE" or "I APPOINT" are usually put into cap-
itals. The usual structure of a will is as follows:

1. opening words;
2. revocation clause;
3. appointment of executors, trustees etc;
4. specific gifts (if any);
5. general legacies (if any);
6. a gift of residue;
7. extension of executors' and trustees' powers (if appropriate);
8. attestation clause.

Most wills can be prepared from a selection of standard clauses modified to suit the needs of the individual client and it is hoped that this
book provides a basis of precedents to work from.

Chapter 1

The nature of a will

1. Definition

A will is an expression by a person of his wishes which is intended to take effect only at his death. It is ambulatory in nature which means that it has no effect until the testator dies, and does not therefore limit the testator's rights of ownership or his right to make *inter vivos* dispositions of the property contained in the will. Until the testator's death the will is no more than a declaration of his intention and may be revoked or varied at any time until death.

Although a document which is intended to operate as a will need not describe itself as such in order to be valid, any professionally drafted document should expressly state that it is a will. If the document is intended to be supplementary to a will it should state, usually at the beginning, that it is a codicil to a will of the testator. The usual forms of commencement are:

C.1.1   Forms of commencement of will
    This is the last Will of me [testator] of [address]
or
C.1.2   I [testator] of [address] hereby revoke all former testamentary dispo-

sitions made by me and declare this to be my last will.

The usual form of commencement for a codicil is:

C.1.3 Form of commencement of codicil

I [testator] of [address] declare this to be a [first] codicil to my will dated the ...... day of .....

The commencement clause should include the testator's full name and address so that he may be identified clearly.

2. A will distinguished from other concepts

It is important to distinguish a will from other legal devices which can be used effectively to dispose of property:

(a) Settlements inter vivos

A testator may leave his realty to a beneficiary by means of a will, but a similar result may be achieved by conveying the property *inter vivos* to trustees to hold for himself (the settlor) for life with the remainder to the beneficiary. If the beneficiary survives the settlor, the effect of the settlement will be similar, in many respects, to a gift contained in a will. However, on the creation of the settlement, the beneficiary receives an interest in remainder with the result that if the beneficiary predeceases the settlor, then provided the settlor has not revoked the settlement, the beneficiary's interest will form part of his (the beneficiary's) estate.

(b) Nomination

This is a direction to a person (A) who holds a fund for another person (B) to pay the fund in the event of B's death to a person nominated by B to take the fund. Nominations operate either by statute or by means of an occupational pension scheme. The former case covers property in, for example, a Provident Society, up to the current limit of £5,000. In order to be valid, the nomination must be:
  (i)   made in writing; and
  (ii) made by a person who is sixteen or over; and
  (iii) attested by one witness.

2

In the latter case the rules of the pension scheme may provide that if an employee dies during the course of his employment without having retired, the amount of his contributions paid to the fund may be paid to any person nominated in writing by the employee. In the absence of any such nomination the fund is paid directly to the personal representatives of the deceased employee and forms part of his estate. A nomination, however, does not in any way operate as part of the will – see *Baird* v *Baird* [1990] 2 All ER 300 – and is therefore not subject to the rules for the creation of a valid will (see Chapter 3). Similarly the property which is the subject matter of the nomination is not caught by the provisions of the Inheritance (Provision for Family and Dependants) Act 1975, and is not subject to inheritance tax.

(c) Donatio mortis causa

This has been described as a gift of an "amphibious nature" (see Buckley J in *Re Beaumont* [1902] 1 Ch 889, 892) because it is neither entirely *inter vivos* nor entirely testamentary. It is a gift made *inter vivos* which is conditional upon, and which takes effect upon, death. It is in no way governed by the provisions relating to properly executed wills, nor is it governed by the rules relating to the effective disposition of *inter vivos* gifts, but it is subject, in general, to the rules relating to satisfaction and ademption (see Chapter 19).

It is important to note that inheritance tax is payable on any property which is the subject matter of a *donatio mortis causa*, since it forms part of the donor's estate on death.

According to Lord Russell CJ in *Cain* v *Moon* [1896] 2 QB 283, three essential requirements must be fulfilled in order for there to be a valid *donatio mortis causa:*

(i)   the gift must be made by the donor in contemplation, although not necessarily in expectation, of death;

(ii) the gift must be conditional on death, so that if the donor recovers from the contemplated cause of death, the gift is revoked;

(iii) before the donor dies he must part with dominion over the subject matter of the gift, that is, the subject matter must have been delivered to the donee.

In addition to these requirements the subject matter of the gift must be such that it is capable of passing as a *donatio mortis causa*. Most personalty is capable of this. Since the recent Court of Appeal decision in *Sen* v *Headley* [1991] 2 All ER 636, it seems that realty is also capable of being the subject matter of a valid *donatio mortis causa* if there is constructive delivery of the deeds, but this case is (at March 1992) on appeal to the House of Lords and may be reversed. A cheque or promissory note drawn by a third party can be the subject matter of a *donatio mortis causa*, but a cheque drawn by the deceased cannot since such a cheque is an order to the deceased's bank and is automatically revoked on death. There are conflicting opinions as to whether stocks and shares can be the valid subject of a *donatio mortis causa*. The case of *Re Weston* [1902] 1 Ch 680 seems to suggest that they cannot, but *Staniland* v *Willott* (1852) 3 Mac & G 664 suggests otherwise.

Finally, it is important to note that a valid *donatio mortis causa* cannot be revoked by a will (see *Jones* v *Selby* (1710) Prec Ch 300).

3. Contracts to make a will

A promisor can, if he wishes, execute a contract to make a will. The contract may contain clauses relating to the content of the will to ensure, for example, that particular property is given by the will to the promisee. A contract merely to make a will is discharged by the execution of the will. If this is not done the promisee is in theory entitled to be placed in the same position as if the will had been made, but the problem is that the promisee has no knowledge of what property, if any, he would have received under the will, if made. In any event such a contract does not imply that the testator will not revoke a will made pursuant to the contract.

If the contract contains terms as to specified property that is to pass to the promisee, and the promisor alienates that property during his lifetime to a third party, then the promisee may sue the promisor (or his estate) for damages, or obtain a declaration of his right to the property, or obtain an injunction to prevent the alienation.

Contracts not to revoke a will can also be executed and are also valid. The court will not intervene to prevent the revocation of the will itself, but it will enforce the terms of the contract and grant an injunction and/or damages where the promisor seeks to alienate property in contravention of the agreement – see *Synge* v *Synge* [1894] 1 QB 466 and *Hammersley* v *De Biel* (1845) 12 Cl & Fin 45. Such a contract is not breached where revocation occurs by operation of law but is only breached by the acts of the promisor. However, the promisor may remain bound by the contract to ensure that the property concerned passes to the promisee on death and may therefore be obliged to execute a further will to give effect to the agreement.

In order for there to be a valid contract to make a will, or a valid contract not to revoke a will, there must be present the same basic elements as with any other contract:

(a) an intention on the part of the promisor to enter into a contractual relationship;

(b) offer and acceptance;

(c) certainty of subject matter;

(d) consideration or execution in the form of a covenant.

Where the contract is to make a will involving the disposition of land then, if executed after 27 September 1989, it falls within the provisions of s 2 of the Law of Property (Miscellaneous Provisions) Act 1989 and must be made in writing. Before this, such a contract had to comply with s 40 of the Law of Property Act 1925, which said that contracts for the sale of land were enforceable only if there was a note or memorandum in writing of the contract, signed by the deceased or some person authorised by him. The will itself could constitute such a note or memorandum. Where there was no note or memorandum in writing, the contract was nevertheless enforceable under the equitable doctrine of part performance. This cannot now be so since s 2 requires the actual contract to be in writing.

4. Joint and mutual wills

Two or more persons may wish to execute the same document as the will of both or all of them in order to attempt in one transaction to dispose of property belonging to each of them, jointly or separately.

Such a document constitutes a joint will and is treated as the separate will of both or all of them. On the death of each and every person the will is admitted to probate provided that it remains unrevoked. Each is free to revoke or vary the will at any time, whether or not the other person is still alive, and any declaration in a joint will which says it is to be irrevocable does not prevent the testator from subsequently revoking it (see *Re Duddell* [1932] 1 Ch 585). It is important to remember, however, that the mere fact that two wills are executed in a similar manner is not sufficient to establish a joint will. Such a will is generally used only in two situations. The first is to exercise a joint power of appointment, and the second is where there is an intention to make mutual wills.

A mutual will (see Appendix A for a precedent) is made where two or more persons execute wills, usually in the same terms, conferring reciprocal benefits on one another, following an agreement between them to make such wills and not to revoke them without the consent of the other. Such wills can be contained in a single document, but it is more usual and advisable to use separate documents. The mere execution of mutual wills does not of itself imply an agreement not to revoke. Such an agreement must be expressed. If two wills, though similarly worded, are not intended to be mutual wills in the technical sense, then it is advisable expressly to state this at the end of the revocation clause. This clause may take the following form:

C.1.4 Clause negating mutual wills

Notwithstanding that my husband [wife] is making a will in similar terms to this will we have agreed that these our said wills are not mutual wills and that each of us shall be free to revoke his or her will at any time whether before or after the death of the other and shall not be under any obligation or trust to dispose of any of his or her property in accordance with the terms of the said wills.

Mutual wills are most commonly executed between husband and wife and normally take one of two forms. The first creates between the husband and wife reciprocal life interests with a remainder over to their child or children. The second form provides for absolute gifts between the husband and wife with alternative provisions, for example, a gift over to a child, in the event of the other person's predeceasing.

Mutual wills can be made by any two or more persons. It is important to remember that the execution of mutual wills severs a joint tenancy. For mutual wills to be valid they must be made pursuant to an agreement to make mutual wills and not to revoke them once made. This agreement may be incorporated into the will by recital or otherwise, or it may be proved by extrinsic evidence, but it is advisable that such an agreement be incorporated into the recitals. It can be oral or written, but in so far as the agreement relates to land, it must be in writing (see *Humphreys* v *Green* (1882) 10 QBD 148). The court has been willing to infer an agreement from the conduct of the parties, the circumstances and the terms of the will – see *Dufour* v *Pereira* (1769) 1 Dick 419. The mere simultaneity and similarity of wills are not sufficient *per se* to establish the necessary agreement. In the case of *Re Hagger* [1930] 2 Ch 190 a husband and wife made a joint mutual will which contained a declaration by them that it should not be altered or revoked except by their mutual agreement. It was implicit in this declaration that the parties agreed the survivor should be bound by the arrangement. The requirement can also be satisfied by an agreement to leave property by a will. In *Re Green* [1951] Ch 148 a husband and wife made mutual wills which recited an agreement between them that, if the survivor had the use of the other's property for life without any liability to account, the survivor would provide by will for the carrying out of the wishes expressed in the other's will.

The following is an example of an agreement that mutual wills are to be irrevocable:

C.1.5   Mutual wills – agreement not to revoke

Whereas my sister [husband] [wife] and I have agreed with one another to execute wills of the same date and in similar terms and have further agreed that such respective wills shall not hereafter be revoked or altered either during our joint lives [or so long as we remain married] or by the survivor of us [if surviving as the lawful spouse of the other] I relying upon such agreement HEREBY GIVE all my property whatsoever and wheresoever [including any property over which I may have a general power of appointment or disposition by will] to my trustees UPON TRUST to sell call in and con-

vert the same into money with power to postpone the said sale calling in and conversion thereof for so long as they shall in their absolute discretion think fit without being liable for loss and to hold the
proceeds of such sale calling in and conversion and my ready money
upon the following trusts:
(add trusts)

Once one of the parties dies, the arrangement becomes irrevocable, at
least if the survivor accepts the benefits that are conferred on him by
the other's will, and it seems doubtful that acceptance is formally necessary – see *Stone* v *Hoskins* [1905] P 194, 197. Until the first party
dies, however, either may withdraw from the arrangement despite an
agreement not to revoke.

The effect of the whole arrangement is that the survivor holds the
property concerned on a constructive trust for the beneficiaries named
in the wills. If the survivor alters his will the personal representatives
of the latter will take the property subject to the earlier trusts. It is
important to know what property falls within the boundaries of the
trust. The will itself should define this and may bind part or the whole
of each person's residuary estate. If the will is not clear on this point
then there are four possibilities:

(a) the trust attaches to the property which the survivor receives
     from the estate of the first to die; or
(b) the trust attaches to all the property that the survivor owned at
     the time of the first death; or
(c) the trust attaches to all the property which the survivor owned at
     his death; or
(d) the trust attaches to all the property which the survivor owned at
     any time since the first death.

The trust must include the property in (a) but the position is more difficult with regard to the survivor's property. In *Re Hagger* [1930] 2
Ch 190 it was said that all the property which the survivor had at the
time of the first death would also be subject to the trust.

With regard to (c) and (d), there appears to be a divergence of opinion. It was said in *Paul* v *Paul* (1882) 20 Ch D 742 that the agreement
acts like a covenant to settle after-acquired property, and the property
becomes subject to the trust on its becoming vested in the trustee. If
this is correct, the effect of mutual wills is to reduce the position of

the survivor to that of a mere life tenant in respect of all his property. In the case of *Re Cleaver* [1981] 1 WLR 939, however, Nourse J adopted the view that the survivor could enjoy the property as an absolute owner in his lifetime "subject to a fiduciary duty which ... crystallised on his death and disabled him only from voluntary dispositions *inter vivos*". It is submitted that the correct view is probably that the trust attaches itself to the property in (a) and (b).

5. Property which can validly be disposed of by will

A testator can dispose of any property vested in him at the time of his death provided his interest in the property does not cease on death. Thus a mere life interest (but not an interest *per autre vie*) or an unsevered joint tenancy cannot be disposed of by means of a will and the will itself cannot act to sever the joint tenancy. Tenants in common can bequeath their shares in the proceeds of the sale of land and their interests in other property. Incorporeal hereditaments may be devised by a will except where they are inseparable from the tenement. If they are devised to the owner of the servient tenement then clearly they are extinguished.

An ordinary covenant against the assignment of a leasehold interest without consent does not apply to a specific or general bequest of the leasehold – *Doe d. Goodbehere v Bevan* (1815) 3 M&S 353, 360.

A testator may dispose of moneys payable under an assurance policy which he effected on his own life in whatever manner he wishes, unless the policy provides otherwise.

A testator is at liberty to dispose of shares in a company under his will subject to the articles of the company concerned, which may restrict or preclude the disposal of shares – s 7 Companies Act 1985.

All contingent and future interests in property can be disposed of by will, whether or not they are vested in the testator at the time of his death.

Where the testator has agreed upon the sale or purchase of his interest in property, that interest may still be devised by will but subject to the contract.

Whether a *chose in action* can be bequeathed in a will depends on the nature of the *chose* ; it must be one that is capable of assignment. Where the *chose* amounts to a contract for personal services, or a mere right of litigation, or is one where assignment is prohibited by statute (for example, certain types of salary or pension), it cannot be bequeathed in a will. Other types of *chose in action* can be bequeathed, but the gift of a debt does not entitle the legatee to sue in his own right. Such a right is vested in the personal representatives.

Along with the subject matter of any gift there impliedly passes as accessory to the main gift all the rights and benefits that are necessary for the reasonable enjoyment of the gift.

Chapter 2

Testamentary capacity

A will made by a person of full capacity is not revoked merely by the fact that he subsequently becomes incapable of making a will; conversely, a will made by a person who is incapable of so doing does not become valid merely by the fact that the incapacity ceases, unless the will is re-executed by the testator when of full capacity.

1. Minors

Wills executed before 1 January 1970 are governed by s 7 of the Wills Act 1837 which says that no will (except for those within the special provisions affecting soldiers in actual military service and mariners or seamen at sea – see Chapter 3) made by a person under the age of twenty-one years is valid. However, for a will executed on or after 1 January 1970 the testator need be aged only eighteen years or over – Family Law Reform Act 1969, s 3(1).

2. Persons of unsound mind

The testator must have full testamentary capacity and must know and approve of the contents of the will at the time he gives instructions for the drafting and when it is drawn up. He need not understand the precise legal machinery, as long as he understands the broad effects of the will. The classic statement of the test of a person's mental capacity can be found in the judgment of Cockburn CJ in the case of *Banks v Goodfellow* (1870) LR 5 QB 549, 565:

> "It is essential ... that a testator shall understand the nature of the act and its effects; shall understand the extent of the property of which he is disposing; shall be able to comprehend and appreciate the claims to which he ought to give effect; and, with a view to the latter object, that no disorder of the mind shall poison his affections, pervert his sense of right, or prevent the exercise of his natural faculties – that no insane delusion shall influence his will in disposing of his property and bring about a disposal of it which, if the mind had been sound, would not have been made."

The testator must have "a memory to recall the several persons who may be fitting objects of the testator's bounty, and an understanding to comprehend their relationship to himself and their claims upon him", *per* Sir J Hannen in *Boughton v Knight* (1873) 3 P&D 64, 65-66. A will is not invalid merely because the testator is motivated by frivolous or bad motives and spite. Eccentricity or mere foolishness is again insufficient to show want of capacity to make a will, although what amounts to mere eccentricity in one person may amount to incapacity in another – *Mudway v Croft* (1843) 3 Curt 671.

(a) Delusions

A testator lacks testamentary capacity if at the time of making the will he suffers from delusions which in any way influence or are capable of influencing the provisions of his will. A delusion is a belief in the existence of something in which no rational person could believe. Sir J Hannen in *Boughton v Knight* (above, 68) said that the jury must ask themselves: "Can I understand how any man in possession of his senses could have believed such and such a thing? ... if the answer you give is, I cannot understand it, then ... you should say the man is not sane." A delusion is not necessarily incompatible with the ability to act rationally, and it is a question of fact whether the delusion actually affected the disposition.

Cockburn CJ in *Banks* v *Goodfellow* (above, 565) said:
"If the human instincts and affections, or the moral sense, become
perverted by mental disease; if insane suspicion, or aversion, take
the place of natural affection; if reason and judgement are lost, and
the mind becomes a prey to insane delusions calculated to interfere
with and disturb its functions, and to lead to a testamentary disposition, due only to their baneful influence – in such a case it is obvious that the condition of the testamentary power fails, and that a
will made under such circumstances ought not to stand."
Thus for delusions to be a cause of incapacity the intelligence must be
so adversely affected that the testator does not appreciate the testamentary act in all its bearings.

(b) Drink and drugs
The use of alcohol or drugs by the testator is not, *per se,* proof of
incapacity.

(c) Insanity
In questions relating to insanity, the legal burden of proof always lies
upon the person propounding the will to prove that the testator had
testamentary capacity at the time the will was made. If a duly executed will is rational on the face of it, there is a presumption that the testator had testamentary capacity. This may be rebutted by evidence to
the contrary. Where it can be shown that the testator suffered from
serious mental illness during a period before the execution of the will,
a presumption arises that the illness continued and the testator lacked
testamentary capacity. Such a presumption may be rebutted if it can
be shown that the testator made the will during a lucid interval or
after he recovered from the illness.

If there is any doubt about an intending testator's mental capacity,
then, to prevent a later challenge to the will, it is a wise precaution to
have a medical practitioner present at the time of execution, and he
should either sign as a witness to the will or be referred to in the attestation clause.

(d) Wills made by the court

Section 96(1)(e) of the Mental Health Act 1983 says that the Court of Protection has a power to make a will on behalf of an adult mental patient where it believes that the patient is incapable of making a will for himself. Such a will should be signed by the authorised person with the name of the patient and with his own name, in the presence or two or more witnesses present at the same time, and these witnesses should attest and subscribe in the usual way. The will is then authenticated with the official seal of the Court of Protection. The form of commencement for such a will can take the following form:

C.2.1   Form of commencement of will made under Mental Health Act 1983

I [testator] of [address] hereby revoke all former testamentary dispositions made by me and declare this to be my last will which is executed for me by [name of authorised person] of [address] [s]he being the person authorised to execute it by an Order made on [date] by the Court of Protection pursuant to Section 96(1)(e) of the Mental Health Act 1983.

The court when exercising its jurisdiction takes the position of the testator in a hypothetical lucid interval and makes the will that the patient is likely to have made, taking a broad view of any claims upon his estate.

The power of the court can also be invoked to remedy an injustice caused by the effect of ademption on a specific legacy, or to avoid an undesired intestacy – see *Re Davey* [1980] 3 All ER 342.

3. Intention

It is important that the testator has the intention or the "*animus testandi*" to make a will. The test is whether by his act, the testator intends to make a disposition of his property which is to take effect on his death, whether or not the testator knows at that time that the disposition is in law a will.

Where the transaction has been effected by a document which has been executed in a manner satisfying the requirements of the Wills

Act 1837 (see Chapter 3), but it is unclear whether it is to be a will, extrinsic evidence will be admitted by the court to decide the issue.

4. Knowledge and approval

Before a will is admitted to probate the court must be satisfied that the testator knew and approved of the contents at the time he signed it. Usually, proof of testamentary capacity and due execution suffice to establish knowledge and approval, but in certain cases the court may require further evidence. These cases include where the person who prepared the will is also to receive a benefit under it (see page 18) and where the testator is deaf and dumb or illiterate or blind.

Where a testator instructs an expert draftsman to give effect to his intentions he must accept the language used by the draftsman even if he does not fully understand the terms used. The case of *Parker* v *Felgate* (1883) 8 PD 171 extended this principle and said that a will prepared in accordance with the instructions given when the testator fully understood the effect and contents of them is valid even if at the time of execution the testator does not in fact have that understanding for whatever reason (including incapacity through mental illness), provided:

(a) the testator had testamentary capacity at the time he gave the solicitor instructions to prepare his will; and
(b) the will was prepared in accordance with such instructions; and
(c) at the time the will was executed the testator could recall having given instructions for a will to be prepared and believed the will had been prepared in compliance with those instructions.

Where the testator has read his will, or where it has been read over to him before execution, or where the contents of the will have been brought to the testator's attention in any other way and the will has been executed, this gives rise to a rebuttable presumption that the testator knew and approved of the contents of the document.

5. Mistake

There are three possible mistakes which may occur:
  (a) the wrong document may be executed;
  (b) the testator may mistakenly believe certain circumstances or facts exist, and these affect his motives for the provisions of the will;
  (c) the testator may be mistaken as to the effect of a will, or of one or more of its provisions.

Where a document is executed by mistake, it will not be admitted to probate. If the testator intended certain words to be used in the will, and they are, but the testator is mistaken as to their legal effect, the will is nevertheless admitted to probate.

There are three limited powers which courts have to alter the words in a will:
  (a) A court of probate may omit from the will any words which the testator did not know of and approve. However, the court will refuse to omit part of the will from probate if the effect of the remainder is altered – see *Re Horrocks* [1939] P 198. If a testator died before 1983, the court, when admitting the will to probate, had no power to add any words which the testator intended. It had power to omit words from the will and it was immaterial that the effect of this might indeed render a clause in the will ambiguous or even meaningless.
  (b) Where the testator dies after 31 December 1982, s 20 of the Administration of Justice Act 1982 empowers a court of equity to order that a will be rectified so as to carry out the intention of the testator. This can be done only if the court is satisfied that the will fails to carry out the testator's intentions because of either:
     • a clerical error; or
     • a failure to understand his instructions.
  If a court rectifies a will under s 20 then it may in fact add to the will words that were intended by the testator. If, however, the will does not carry out the testator's intentions for some other reason, s 20 does not apply.
  An application for rectification must be made not later than six

months from the date on which a grant of probate or letters of administration to the deceased's estate is first taken out, although the court does have a discretion to extend this time limit.

(c) A court of construction can construe the will as if certain words were inserted, omitted or changed, provided it is clear from the will that an error has been made in the wording and it is clear what the substance of the intended wording was (see Chapter 22 for a further discussion on this point).

6. Force, fear, fraud or undue influence

If a will is made as a consequence of force, fear, fraud or undue influence, it will not be regarded as the act of the testator and will not be admitted to probate. The burden of proof is on the person who alleges that a will has been made in such circumstances, and there are no presumptions to assist in discharging this burden.

(a) Force and fear
If a testator made a will as a result of having been injured or threatened with injury then the will is not admitted to probate.

(b) Fraud
Fraud is something which misleads the testator. Lord Langdale said in *Giles* v *Giles* (1836) 1 Keen 685, 692, "a legacy given to a person in a character which the legatee does not fill, and by the fraudulent assumption of which character the testator has been deceived, will not take effect". Fraud includes making false representations about the character of others in order to induce the testator to make or revoke gifts, or to exclude persons from a proposed will.

(c) Undue influence
Undue influence is something that overpowers the volition of the testator. It is permissible to persuade a testator, but not to coerce him. It may be difficult in some situations to distinguish between persuasion and undue influence; provided the testator retained real freedom of

choice a court will not normally interfere. If, on the other hand, the testator surrendered to intolerable pressure the court will intervene. The court is more inclined to find undue influence where the testator is physically or mentally weak. The mere proof of the relationship of parent and child, confessor and penitent, guardian and ward, husband and wife, doctor and patient, or tutor and pupil, does not of itself raise a presumption of undue influence sufficient to vitiate a will.

(d) Will prepared by a beneficiary

Where a person who prepared a will for a testator is one of the beneficiaries of the will, a suspicion of undue influence arises and must be dispelled by the person propounding the will. The degree of suspicion varies according to the circumstances of the case.

It should be noted that solicitors are subject to the rules of conduct laid down by the Council of the Law Society:

"Where a client intends to make a gift *inter vivos* or by will to his solicitor, or to the solicitor's partner, or a member of staff or to the families of any of them and the gift is of a significant amount, either in itself or having regard to the size of the client's estate and the reasonable expectations of prospective beneficiaries, the solicitor must advise the client to be independently advised as to that gift and if the client declines, must refuse to act."

It is not sufficient for the will merely to be attested by an independent solicitor. There is, however, nothing unprofessional in a solicitor's preparing a will which contains a token legacy to the solicitor as a mark of regard and appreciation. A testator may wish to give property to a solicitor to be held on a secret trust for specified beneficiaries, the solicitor receiving no personal benefit. The solicitor is free to prepare such a will but the Council advises that the instructions from the client be preserved and the terms of the trust be embodied in a written document signed or initialled by the testator.

A solicitor is also perfectly entitled, with his client's approval, to include a charging clause in a will, authorising himself to charge for services performed in connection with the administration of the estate (or of any trust arising under the will). See Chapter 20 for specimen charging clauses.

Chapter 3

Formal requirements for the creation of a will

1. General

Section 9 of the Wills Act 1837, as substituted by s 17 of the Administration of Justice Act 1982, provides that in order for a will or any form of testamentary disposition to be valid:

"(a) it [must be] in writing, and signed by the testator, or by some other person in his presence and by his direction; and

(b) it [must] appear that the testator intended by his signature to give effect to the will; and

(c) the signature [must be] made or acknowledged by the testator in the presence of two or more witnesses present at the same time; and

(d) each witness [must] either –

(i) attest and sign the will; or

(ii) acknowledge his signature, in the presence of the testator (but not necessarily in the presence of any other witness),

but no form of attestation shall be necessary."

This amended section applies to cases where the testator dies after 31 December 1982. Where the testator died before 1 January 1983, the original s 9 of the Wills Act 1837, as amended by the Wills Act Amendment Act 1852, applies.

2. Writing

No will is valid unless it is made in writing, although there is an exception in the case of members of the forces on actual military service and mariners at sea (see page 27).

It may be written in any language and on any material by any means. Where a will is written partly in pencil and partly in ink there is a presumption that the pencil writing is deliberative and will not be admitted to probate unless the court decides it represents the testator's definite intention.

3. Signature

(a) Form of signature
In general, any mark, sign or signature made by the testator on his will is a valid signature, provided it was intended to be a signature. However, the usual signature of the testator should be signed so as to avoid any doubt about validity.

Initials (*Re Savory's Goods* (1851) 15 Jur 1042); a stamped signature (*Re Jenkins* (1863) 3 Sw & Tr 93); a mark such as a cross; an inked thumb mark (*Re Finn's Estate* (1935) 105 LJP 36); a mark of any shape (*In the estate of Holtam* (1913) 108 LT 732); an unfinished signature (*In the Goods of Chalcraft* [1948] P 222); or a signature in pencil (*Bateman* v *Pennington* (1840) 3 Moo PC 223) have all been held to be sufficient to amount to a valid signature provided the testator intended them to be such.

(b) Signature on the testator's behalf
A person other than the testator may sign on the latter's behalf provided the signature is made in the presence of and by the direction of the testator. The person so signing may be one of the witnesses although he need not be. He may sign either in his own name or in the name of the testator, although it is advisable to do so in his own name and write that he is signing on behalf of the testator, in his presence and by his direction. The testator must be present when the signature is made and must in some way indicate to the witnesses that the signa-

ture has been put there at his request.

(c) Signature by a blind or illiterate testator

Rule 13 of the Non-Contentious Probate Rules 1987 (SI 1987 No 2024) provides:

> "Before admitting to proof a will which appears to have been signed by a blind or illiterate testator or by another person by direction of the testator, or which for any other reason raises doubt as to the testator having had knowledge of the contents of the will at the time of its execution, the registrar shall satisfy himself that the testator had such knowledge."

(d) Position of signature

The original s 9 required that the signature be "at the foot or end" of the will and this was strictly interpreted, invalidating a number of wills which did not comply with it. The Wills Act Amendment Act 1852 was then passed to extend the meaning of the term "foot or end", and as a result the court could in certain circumstances admit part of a document to probate while excluding other parts which appeared physically after the signature.

The amended s 9 repeals the 1852 Act. Where the testator died on or after 1 January 1983, s 9 no longer requires the signature to be at the foot or end of the will. It is sufficient that "it appears that the testator intended by his signature to give effect to the will". The new s 9 contemplates the signature validating all or none of the will.

A signature on a separate page attached to the beginning or end of the will will probably satisfy the requirement of s 9.

Where the testator has enclosed the will in an envelope and signed the envelope, it is thought that, provided the signature was intended to give effect to the will, this is sufficient. If, however, the signature is made merely to identify the contents of the envelope this is insufficient.

(e) Acknowledgement of signature in the presence of at least two witnesses

The testator must sign the will or acknowledge his signature in the presence of *two* or more witnesses present *at the same time* who must then sign or acknowledge their signatures in the testator's presence. The witnesses must both remain until the testator's signature is complete. If the testator has not signed in the simultaneous presence of both witnesses then he must acknowledge his signature in their *joint presence*.

The acknowledgement must be made by words or by conduct, but the witnesses must at the time of the acknowledgement see, or have the opportunity of seeing, the signature of the testator. If the signature is concealed there is, therefore, no valid acknowledgement. They need not know, however, that the document is a will, nor need they look at the signature itself. The signature may be made by the testator or by another for him.

4. Attestation

Section 9 requires that each witness must either attest and sign the will, or acknowledge his signature in the presence of the testator. Before 1983 a witness who had signed before the testator was not able to acknowledge his signature and the will would fail unless that witness signed again after the testator. After 1 January 1983 the invalidity caused by the testator's signing in the presence of one witness who signs, the testator then acknowledging his signature in the presence of both witnesses and the second witness signing, can be remedied by the first witness's acknowledging his prior signature after the testator acknowledges his, with the second witness then signing.

Both attesting witnesses must be present at the same time and both must attest and subscribe, or acknowledge after the testator's signature has been made or acknowledged in their presence. Nevertheless it is not essential that they sign in each other's presence. Their signatures may appear anywhere on the will and need not be next to or after the testator's signature.

There is no special form of attestation clause but the usual forms of testimonium and attestation clauses are as follows:

C.3.1   Attestation clause

IN WITNESS whereof I have hereunto set my hand this ...... day of ...... 19 ...

Signed by the above-named [testator] as his
last will in the presence of us present at the
same time who at his request in his presence } [Signature]
and in the presence of each other have hereunto subscribed our names as witnesses

[Signatures, addresses and descriptions of two witnesses]

C.3.2   Attestation clause – short form

AS WITNESS my hand this ...... day of ...... 19 ...

Signed by the testator in our joint presence } [Signature]
and then by us in his

[Signatures, addresses and descriptions of two witnesses]

C.3.3   Form of testimonium and attestation clause to a codicil

IN WITNESS whereof I have hereunto set my hand this ...... day of ...... 19 ...

Signed by the above-named [testator] as a
codicil to his will made on the ...... day of
...... 19 ... in the presence of us present at the } [Signature]
same time who at his request in his presence
and in the presence of each other have hereunto subscribed our names as witnesses

[Signatures, addresses and descriptions of two witnesses]

C.3.4   Attestation clause where the will has been altered

Signed by the above-named [testator] as his
last will in the presence of us present at the
same time who at his request in his presence
and in the presence of each other have here- } [Signature]
unto subscribed our names as witnesses the
alteration [or erasure or interlineation] [in
line......] on page ...... hereof having been
made previously hereto.

[Signatures, addresses and descriptions of two witnesses]

C.3.5 Attestation clause where the testator acknowledges a signature which he has made previously

Signed by [the above-named [testator]] [[person signing] with the name of the above-named [testator] in his presence and by his direction] and acknowledged by him as his last will in the presence of us present at the same time who at his request in his presence and in the presence of each other have hereunto subscribed our names as witnesses

[Signature]

[Signatures, addresses and descriptions of two witnesses]

C.3.6 Attestation clause where the testator signs with his mark

Signed by the above-named [testator] with his mark as his last will (the same having been previously read over to him by [name] [me the undersigned [name]] when he seemed thoroughly to understand the same) in the presence of us present at the same time who at his request in his presence and in the presence of each other have hereunto subscribed our names as witnesses

[Testator's mark]

[Signatures, addresses and descriptions of two witnesses]

C.3.7 Attestation clause where another signs on behalf of the testator

Signed by [person signing] with the name of the above-named [testator] as his last will (the same having been previously read over to him by [name] [me the undersigned [name]] when he seemed thoroughly to understand the same) in his presence and by his direction and in the presence of us present at the same time who at the request of the said [testator] in the presence of him and of each other have hereunto subscribed our names as witnesses

[Signature]

[Signatures, addresses and descriptions of two witnesses]

C.3.8   Attestation clause where the testator is blind

This will having first been read over to the
above-named [testator] (who is blind) [in
our presence] by me the undersigned
[name] in the presence also of me the
undersigned [name] when the said [testator]
appeared thoroughly to understand the same   [Signature]
and to approve the contents thereof was
signed by the said [testator] as his last will
in the presence of us present at the same
time who at his request in his presence and
in the presence of each other have hereunto
subscribed our names as witnesses
[Signatures, addresses and descriptions of two witnesses]

**C.3.9   Attestation clause where the testator has an imperfect
knowledge of English**

This will having first been read over to the
said [testator] (who understands the French
language but has an imperfect knowledge of
and cannot read the English language) by
me the undersigned [first witness] in
English and having been truly interpreted to
the said [testator] by me the undersigned
[second witness] [who understands both the
English and French languages] [both of
whom the said [witnesses] understand both   [Signature]
the English and French languages] which
reading and interpretation were both done in
our presence when the said [testator]
appeared thoroughly to understand this will
and to approve the contents thereof was
signed by the said [testator] with his mark as
his last will in the presence of us present at
the same time who at his request in his presence and in the presence of each other have
hereunto subscribed our names as witnesses

[Signatures, addresses and descriptions of two witnesses]

C.3.10 Testimonium and attestation clause of a will made pursuant to an order of the Court of Protection

IN WITNESS whereof the said [name of authorised person] has signed the name of the above-named [testator] and his own name this [date].

Signed by the said [authorised person] with the name of the said [testator] and by him with his own name both signatures being made in our presence and then signed by us in the presence of the said [authorised person] } [Signature made by authorised person in testator's name] by [Signature of authorised person in his own name]

[Signatures, addresses and descriptions of two witnesses]

5. Capacity of witnesses

There are no particular rules about who may act as a witness. The only test seems to be whether they are capable of attesting at the time they sign. Thus a minor may witness a will provided he is not too young to understand the significance of his act. Someone who is blind cannot act as a witness since he is incapable of seeing the signature. A person who is drunk or of unsound mind would also be incapable of attesting.

In choosing witnesses a solicitor should have regard to the fact that the person chosen may be required to give evidence of due execution, and therefore persons who are old or who may be difficult to trace should be avoided. A beneficiary under the will or a beneficiary's spouse should not be chosen since, although their signatures are perfectly valid, they will lose their legacy – s 15 Wills Act 1837.

There are, however, several restrictions to the rule in s 15. This rule does not apply:

(a) to an informal will made by a privileged testator, since such a will does not require witnessing;

(b) in the case of a testator dying after 29 May 1968, the attestation of the will by beneficiaries or their spouses is to be disregarded if the will has been duly executed without taking any beneficiary's signature into account – Wills Act 1968;

(c) where the beneficiary or his spouse signed the will not as an attesting witness but in some other capacity. There is, however, a rebuttable presumption that any person, except the testator, whose signature appears at the end of a will signed the will as an attesting witness;

(d) to a beneficiary who marries an attesting witness after the will has been executed. Section 15 applies only to a beneficiary who is the spouse of an attesting witness at the time the will was executed;

(e) to gifts to attesting witnesses as trustees, including trustees of a secret trust;

(f) if the gift to the beneficiary is contained in a will or a codicil which was not attested by the beneficiary or his spouse, but some other document was so attested;

(g) if the gift to the beneficiary is contained in a document which was attested by the beneficiary or his spouse, but the document was confirmed by a will or codicil not so attested.

6. Privileged wills

The formal requirements for the execution of a valid will are waived for a testator who has privileged status. Such a will can be made in any form and may even be an oral statement provided it shows an intention to dispose of property in the event of the testator's death. The testator need not know that he is making a will. Such a will is valid even if made by a minor. It should be noted that since no attestation by witnesses is required, a gift to a witness in a soldier's, sailor's or airman's will is effective. Since such a will requires no formalities for its execution, it requires none for its revocation – see *Re Gossage's Estate* [1921] P 194. A privileged will is revoked by a subsequent marriage – *Re Wardrop's Estate* [1917] P 54.

The privilege extends to soldiers in actual military service and to mariners or seamen at sea. The term "soldier" includes members of the RAF and naval or marine personnel serving on land. The meaning of the term "actual military service" is not certain, but includes activities closely connected with warfare, whether or not war has been declared and whether or not the testator has actually arrived at the scene of fighting. A soldier stationed in Northern Ireland as part of the armed forces deployed there at the request of the civil authorities to assist in the maintenance of law and order has been held to be in actual military service – *Re Jones* [1981] Fam 7. The fact that there was not an actual state of war or that the enemy was not a uniformed force engaged in regular warfare was irrelevant.

The term "being at sea" again cannot be defined precisely, but this privilege is wider in its scope than the former category. In *Re Rapley* [1983] 3 All ER 248 it was said that the privilege can be invoked if the following conditions are met:

(a) the testator was serving or employed in, or by, the Royal Navy or the Merchant Navy, on service of whatever nature, that could be regarded as sea-service;

(b) the testator must be "on maritime service" in the sense that he is:

- at the time of making the will in a post as ship's officer; or
- at the time of making the will is a member of a particular ship's company serving in that ship or on shore leave, or on long leave ashore; or
- being employed by the owners of a fleet of ships and having been discharged from one such, is already under orders to join another ship in that fleet.

The privilege does not apply to the will of a seaman made whilst on shore leave, at a time when he is not a member of the crew of a particular ship and when he has not received orders to join a ship.

7. Incorporation of unattested documents

It is usually preferable to contain all the provisions of a will in one properly executed document; any alterations may be made by codicils to the original will or by the execution of a fresh will. However, an unattested document can, if desired, be incorporated into a will and admitted to probate as part of the will provided the following conditions are satisfied:

(a) the unattested document must be in existence at the time the will is executed or at the time the will is republished by codicil. This is a question of fact;

(b) the unattested document must be referred to in the will as being in existence at the time of execution. This means that a will which states "I leave £1,000 to each of the persons named in my notebook called 'My Notebook 1987' to be found in my desk drawer" will satisfy this condition, whereas one that says "I leave £1,000 to each of the persons named in my notebook which I shall write before my death" does not satisfy the condition. The notebook will not be admitted to probate even if it is written before the will was executed, as the will refers to its coming into existence at a later date.

If a will is republished by a codicil (see Chapter 7), this may have the effect of incorporating an unattested document which is in existence at the time of execution of the codicil and is referred to as being in existence in either the will or the codicil;

(c) the unattested document must be clearly identified in the will.

C.3.11 Gift by reference to a document already in existence

I give my watches jewellery trinkets and other articles of personal use and ornament to [name] upon trust to distribute the same to the persons if living and in the manner set out in a list dated ...... which I have already prepared and signed and which will be found with this my will at my death and in so far as there may be any such articles at the date of my death which are not subject to any directions contained in the said list I give the same to [name] absolutely.

Chapter 4

Beneficiaries

See also Chapter 2 (page 17) on undue influence, and, for the position of attesting witnesses, Chapter 3.

1. General

Any legatee in a will must always be clearly described; otherwise the gift, unless charitable (see page 42), will be void.

2. Gift to a beneficiary who predeceases the testator

Where the beneficiary under a will is either dead at the time the will is made, or dies after the will is executed but before the death of the testator, then the gift will, in general, be invalid and lapse. The will may provide for such an eventuality, for example:

C.4.1   Clause as to the application of a lapsed share of residue
I DIRECT that if any gift of any share of residue shall lapse where such lapse in the absence of this provision would give rise to an intestacy or partial intestacy then such lapsed share shall be primari-

ly applied in or towards the payment of my debts funeral and testamentary expenses and pecuniary legacies hereby or by any codicil hereto bequeathed first recourse to be had to the said lapsed share before any other property hereby or by any codicil hereto bequeathed or devised.

Note: see the Administration of Estates Act 1925, Sch 1, Part II as to the order of application of assets where the estate is solvent.

The doctrine of lapse cannot be excluded from a will – *Re Ladd* [1932] 2 Ch 219, but a gift may be worded so that the subject matter passes to some other beneficiary if the original beneficiary predeceases the testator. The testator may provide that in the event of the death of the beneficiary the property will pass to the beneficiary's personal representatives to be held as part of his estate; or the testator may include a gift over to the beneficiary's children:

C.4.2   Gift over to personal representatives

I DECLARE that if [name] shall die during my lifetime (or after my death but before my executors have given effect to the gift to him [her]) the share of residue [legacy of ......] hereby given to him [her] shall not lapse but shall in that event pass to his [her] personal representatives as part of his [her] estate.

Note: If the beneficiary dies before the testator there will not be a charge to inheritance tax on the gift as part of the beneficiary's estate as well as part of the testator's estate, since the beneficiary will not be entitled to anything at his death.

C.4.3   Gift to beneficiary's children

I DECLARE that if [name] my [son] [daughter] shall die in my lifetime [leaving issue living at my death or then en ventre but born afterwards] the share of residue hereby given to my said son [daughter] shall not lapse but shall pass to such of his [her] children who are alive at the date of my death and who attain the age of [eighteen] years or marry under that age and if more than one in equal shares per stirpes by way of direct gift and shall not at any time form part of the estate of [name] my [son] [daughter] so that the said share shall not be subject to his [her] debts or to inheritance tax.

The doctrine of lapse has no application where the testator makes a gift to two or more persons as joint tenants, but will apply where the beneficiaries take as tenants in common. In the case of a settled share the doctrine of lapse can be avoided by a declaration against lapse:

C.4.4   Declaration against lapse in the case of a settled share

I DECLARE that if any daughter [son] of mine be already dead or dies before me without leaving issue then the share of residue hereby given to her [him] whether original or accruing shall be held by my trustees upon trusts similar in all respects to those trusts which would have arisen if such daughter [son] had died immediately after me.

(a) Class gifts and lapse

In the case of class gifts, the members of the class are not generally ascertained until after the testator's death. For this reason any person who would have formed part of the class but who dies before the testator will not be included as a member of the class and thus the doctrine of lapse has no application. A gift may still be a class gift even if some particular member is named in the gift, for example a gift to "my children including [or excluding] A" – *Shaw* v *M'Mahon* (1843) 4 Dr & War 431.

It is important to note the distinction between class gifts and gifts to a distinct group of individuals. A gift to a number of defined individuals, such as named sisters as tenants in common in equal shares would not be a class gift where the share of each is distinct and quantifiable, regardless of which of the individuals survive the testator. The doctrine of lapse would apply if one of the sisters predeceased the testator. A gift to such of the testator's children as survive him in equal shares would create a class gift and the doctrine of lapse would apply only if there are no children of the testator alive at his death.

C.4.5   Declaration against lapse in the case of a class gift of residue

...... ALWAYS PROVIDED THAT if any person would have been entitled to a vested interest in my residuary estate had he or she been living at the date of my death but that person dies before me then I GIVE such share as would have passed to such person directly to that person's personal representatives as part of his or her estate as if such person had died immediately following my death.

(b) Exceptions to the doctrine of lapse
There are three situations where the doctrine of lapse will not operate:
- (i)   gifts in discharge of a moral obligation;
- (ii) under s 32 of the Wills Act 1837;
- (iii) under s 33 of the Wills Act 1837.

(i) Gifts in discharge of a moral obligation: The doctrine of lapse does not apply to gifts made in order to discharge a moral obligation. The precise ambit of the common law exception is uncertain but it applies, *inter alia*, to a gift in discharge of a debt which is statute-barred, and to a direction that creditors of a deceased beneficiary be paid. It may be that the rule extends only to directions to pay debts and not to other forms of moral obligation.

(ii) Section 32 Wills Act 1837: Subsection (1) of this section provides that a gift of entailed property will not lapse if at the testator's death there are any issue living who are capable of taking under the entail. This section can be excluded by contrary intention.

(iii) Section 33 Wills Act 1837: This section (as substituted by the Administration of Justice Act 1982) applies where a testator dies after 31 December 1982 and provides that where:
- a will contains a devise or bequest to a child or remoter descendant of the testator; and
- the intended beneficiary dies before the testator, leaving issue; and
- the issue of the intended beneficiary are living at the testator's death,

then, unless there is a contrary intention in the will, the devise or bequest shall take effect as a devise or bequest to the issue living at the testator's death.

Section 33(3) provides that such issue take "according to their stock, in equal shares if more than one, any gift or share which their parent would have taken", and no issue shall take where a parent is living at the testator's death and so capable of taking.

Section 33 will apply to contingent gifts but it is not clear whether a substituted beneficiary would have to satisfy that same contingency. It is extremely important when drafting any contingent gift to make the position of any substituted beneficiary clear by means of an express provision as to whether or not any substitutional gift is subject to the contingency.

Subsection (2) of s 33 deals with class gifts. It provides that where:

- a will contains a devise or bequest to a class of person consisting of children or remoter descendants of the testator; and
- a member of the class dies before the testator, leaving issue; and
- the issue of that member are living at the testator's death,

then, unless there is a contrary intention in the will, the devise or bequest shall take effect as if the class included the issue of its deceased member living at the testator's death. The issue take according to their stock, in equal shares if more than one, the share which their parents would have taken, and no issue whose parent is living at the time of testator's death shall take – s 33(3).

Section 33(4) provides that for the purpose of s 33 the illegitimacy of any person is to be disregarded and a child *en ventre sa mère* is living for the purpose of the section.

Section 33 applies only where a gift is made to a child or remoter descendant of the testator. In all other cases a substitutional gift will take effect only if expressly provided for in a will. For avoidance of doubt and in order clearly to express the testator's intentions a substitutional gift should, as a matter of practice, always be made the subject of an express provision, notwithstanding s 33. (See also Chapter 16 for substitutional gifts.)

C.4.6 Declaration excluding s 33 of the Wills Act 1837

Section 33 of the Wills Act 1837 (as substituted by section 19 of the Administration of Justice Act 1982) shall not apply to any of the foregoing trusts.

(c) Presumption where uncertainty as to which survived

Because of the effect of the doctrine of lapse it may be necessary to establish whether the testator or the beneficiary died first. Section 184 of the Law of Property Act 1925 provides that:

"In all cases where, after the commencement of this Act, two or more persons have died in circumstances rendering it uncertain which of them survived the other or others, such deaths shall (subject to any order of the court), for all purposes affecting the title to property, be presumed to have occurred in order of seniority, and accordingly the younger shall be deemed to have survived the elder."

Consequently, the younger will be deemed to inherit the elder's property, which will then pass under the terms of the younger's will or intestacy.

This section applies whether the deaths occurred in a common disaster (*commorientes*) or separately.

The statutory presumption where the order of deaths is uncertain does not apply between spouses if the elder spouse dies intestate – s 1(4) Intestate Estates Act 1952. In such a situation, when the elder spouse's estate is being administered the younger spouse is presumed not to have survived the elder intestate spouse. When the estate of the younger spouse is being administered, s 184 applies in its usual way. To avoid property passing through two estates, it is wise to include a survivorship clause in the will (see Chapter 16).

C.4.7 Contingent gift of property which carries immediate income during survivorship period

I GIVE [property] to [donee] absolutely provided that he survives me for [twenty-eight days] and if he shall fail to survive me for the said [twenty-eight days] then he shall be treated as if he had predeceased me and income from the said [property] arising after my death and prior to the death of [donee] shall not belong to him and in that event [I GIVE the said [property] including the intermediate income thereof to [alternative donee]] [the said [property] including the intermediate income thereof shall form part of my residuary estate]].

C.4.8 "Omnibus" survivorship provision against commorientes extending to all gifts in the will

No person shall take any benefit under the provisions of this my will UNLESS they shall survive me for [four calendar months] and if any person shall fail to survive me for that period then each and every such person shall be treated for all purposes connected with the devolution of my estate [[including] [but not including] section 33 of the Wills Act 1837] as if he had predeceased me and my estate and the intermediate income thereof shall devolve accordingly and shall not belong to him but shall form part of my residuary estate.

Note: The period in brackets must not exceed six months.

The Inheritance Tax Act 1984, s 4(2) provides that "where it cannot be known which of two or more persons who have died survived the other or others they shall be assumed to have died at the same instant". This provision in effect avoids a double charge to tax. If an elder person leaves property to a younger person it is taxed as part of the elder's estate, and the younger is not deemed to have survived for tax purposes. Thus the property is not taxed as part of his estate.

3. Unlawful killing

It is a rule of public policy that a person must not be allowed to benefit from his crime. An intended beneficiary found guilty of the murder or manslaughter of the testator, generally cannot receive a benefit under the testator's will (or intestacy), although it has been said in *Re K* [1985] Ch 85, that the rule does not apply to all manslaughters, only to those where there has been violence or a threat of violence. The rule includes all unlawful killings, such as causing death by dangerous driving. Motive and moral guilt seem to be irrelevant, except where unsoundness of mind or justifiable homicide is proved. Where an intended beneficiary is disqualified by the rule the gift devolves as if that beneficiary had died immediately before the testator – *Re Crippen's Estate* [1911] P 108. If the beneficiary is a member of a class to receive a benefit under the will then he is excluded from the class as if he predeceased the testator, and the remainder of those eligible will take. The effect of the forfeiture rule is to sever a joint tenancy so that the beneficial interest vests in the personal representatives of the deceased and the survivor as tenants in common.

(a) Relief from forfeiture

The Forfeiture Act 1982 allows the person who has killed the testator to apply to the court to modify the rule of public policy in so far as it affects him. An application must generally be made within three months of the conviction – s 2(3) Forfeiture Act 1982. However, where the conviction was for murder the court has no powers to modify the effect of the rule. In all other cases the court may, if it thinks fit to do so, allow the applicant and any person claiming through him to take:

(i)   under the will;
(ii) on intestacy;
(iii) under a nomination;
(iv) under a *donatio mortis causa;*
(v)   the deceased's share of jointly owned property;
(vi) other property held in trust.

(b) Family provision and forfeiture

It is expressly provided that the forfeiture rule is not to be taken as precluding any person from making an application under the Inheritance (Provision for Family and Dependants) Act 1975. However, in the case of *Re Royse* [1985] Fam 22, a woman who was convicted of unlawfully killing her husband and who was disinherited by the forfeiture rule was not able to make an application under the 1975 Act, since the absence of reasonable financial provision could not be attributed to the deceased's will or intestacy, but to the rule of public policy. An application can be made only if the requirements of the 1975 Act are complied with (see Chapter 24).

4. Gifts for the upkeep and maintenance of graves

Gifts for the upkeep and maintenance of graves can take effect only as trusts of imperfect obligation and are void if worded so as to last for an indefinite period. They must be limited to the perpetuity period (see Chapter 21). This effectively means that they can continue for a period of twenty-one years only and the alternative eighty year period which is provided for by the Perpetuities and Accumulations Act

1964 would appear not to be applicable – see s 15(4), Perpetuities and Accumulations Act 1964. A bequest to trustees to provide for the upkeep of graves "so far as they can legally do so and in any manner they may in their discretion arrange", is a valid form of wording – *Re Hooper* [1932] 1 Ch 38. The testator should be advised that the trustees in a trust of imperfect obligation are not obliged to comply with the wishes of the testator and a resulting trust arises if the trustees do not carry out the terms of the trust.

C.4.9 Gift for the upkeep of a grave limited in perpetuity

I GIVE to my trustees the sum of £ .... upon trust to invest the same as they in their absolute discretion think fit and during the period of twenty-one years from my death (which period shall be the perpetuity period applicable to the disposition hereby effected) to apply the income thereof for the upkeep of the grave and gravestone of [name] at [place] to maintain the same in good order and repair and to keep any lettering on the said gravestone legible causing the same to be re-cut from time to time when necessary for that purpose.

A "condition" requiring the perpetual maintenance of a grave or gravestone can be attached to a gift to charity A, with a gift over to charity B if charity A should fail to fulfil the condition – *Christ's Hospital* v *Grainger* (1845) 1 Mac & G 460. However, the "condition" must be discretionary in its nature in order to be upheld. If the gift over is not to a charity, but to an individual, the gift is subject to the perpetuity rule. If the gift over falls outside the perpetuity period the original charitable legatee takes free from the condition – *Re Cooper's Conveyance* [1956] 3 All ER 28. The original gift may impose only a moral obligation on the trustees.

C.4.10 Gift for the upkeep of a grave avoiding the perpetuity rule using *Christ's Hospital* v *Grainger*

(1) I GIVE to [charity A] the sum of £ .... upon trust to invest the same in such manner as the trustees shall think fit to apply the income thereof to the general purposes of [charity A] [or name particular purposes] so long as [charity A] shall maintain [description of grave] as the same has been maintained during my lifetime and [upon [charity A] failing so to maintain the grave I GIVE the said sum of £ .... to [charity B]] [if before the expiration of twenty-one

years from the death of the last survivor of all the descendants living and actually born at the date of my death of his late Majesty King George V the said [charity A] shall fail so to maintain the said grave then I GIVE the said sum of £ .... to [name of individual] absolutely].

Note: The "royal lives clause" extends the vesting period but does not circumvent the perpetuity period.

(2) I DECLARE that neglect to tend and replant the grave for a period of [two] years shall constitute a failure to maintain the same and that allowing more than [one third] of the lettering of the tombstone on the said grave to become illegible for the same period shall also constitute such a failure.

(3) The receipt of the person professing to be the treasurer or other proper officer of either [charity A] or [charity B] as the case may be shall be a sufficient discharge to my trustees.

Alternatively, the gift can be made as a gift for the upkeep of a church or whole churchyard (which would amount to a charitable gift) and such a gift remains charitable notwithstanding the addition of some precatory request for the maintenance of a particular tomb or grave:

C.4.11 Gift for the upkeep of a grave avoiding the perpetuity rule by means of a precatory request

(1) I bequeath to the vicar and churchwarden of the parish church of ...... and their successors the sum of £..... upon trust to invest the same and during the period of twenty-one years from my death (which period shall be the perpetuity period applicable to this gift) to apply the income thereof for the purpose of maintaining [description of grave] in good order and repair and in keeping the lettering on any gravestone or to be erected thereon legible and causing the same to be recut from time to time when necessary for that purpose and to apply the balance of the said income as shall not be required for such purpose in keeping the said graveyard in good order and repair.

(2) After the expiration of the said period of twenty-one years the said vicar and churchwarden and their successors shall hold the said sum and investments representing the same upon trust to apply the income thereof in keeping the said graveyard in good order and repair AND I request but without imposing any legal obligation on them that they will maintain the [description of grave] in the manner hereinbefore described.

Under the Parish Councils and Burial Authorities (Miscellaneous Provisions) Act 1970 a burial authority or a local authority may agree with a person, on the payment of a sum by him, to maintain a grave, tomb, vault or any memorial in a burial ground or crematorium provided it is maintained by the authority, or any monument or other memorial to any person within the area of the authority to which the authority has a right to access – s 1. The maximum period of such an agreement is 100 years from the date of the agreement, and a testator can direct his executors to enter into such an agreement.

C.4.12 Gift for the upkeep of a grave using the provision of the Parish Councils and Burial Authorities (Miscellaneous Provisions) Act 1970

If the burial authority or local authority which provides or maintains the burial ground where my body is buried is willing to make an agreement (whether pursuant to the provisions of the Parish Councils and Burial Authorities (Miscellaneous Provisions) Act 1970 or any statutory modification or re-enactment thereof or under those of any local Act or other enabling power) with my executors for the maintenance of my grave and of the tombstone or other memorial placed upon it then I direct my executors to make an agreement with the authority providing for such maintenance to be carried out for the longest period for which the authority is prepared to undertake it and to pay from my estate the sum required by the authority as consideration therefor and any other costs which may be reasonably incurred in implementing the provisions of this clause.

5. Gifts to animals

A gift for the maintenance of a particular animal or animals is a valid gift, but again creates a trust of imperfect obligation and as such is restricted in duration to twenty-one years. Some gifts to animals are valid charitable gifts if they are shown to be for purposes beneficial to the community (see page 48).

C.4.13 Gift for the maintenance of a particular animal

I GIVE to my trustees the sum of £.... upon trust to invest the same as they in their absolute discretion think fit and to apply the income thereof for the upkeep and maintenance of my [dog] [other animal, describing it] for the duration of its life or for the period of twenty-one years from the date of my death whichever period shall be the shorter and after the death of my [dog] [other animal] or after the expiration of the period of twenty-one years whichever shall first happen the gift shall fall into and form part of my residuary estate.

6. Gifts to societies and clubs

A gift may be made to a society or club, but where the society or club is not charitable the gift must comply with the perpetuity rule. The rule can be avoided, however, if the members are left free to dispose of the gift as they think fit – see *Re Clarke* [1901] 2 Ch 110.

Special problems arise if the society or club is non-charitable and unincorporated. Such an institution is not a legal person, and with the exception of trade unions (see Trade Union and Labour Relations Act 1974, s 2) cannot hold property in its own right *qua* society. The validity of gifts to such institutions will depend upon the construction of the gift by the courts. An absolute gift to a non-charitable unincorporated society has been held to be a gift to the members of the society at the time of the gift as joint tenants. This gave every member the right to sever his share and take the value of it – *Re Drummond* [1914] 2 Ch 90. A different view was taken by Cross J in *Neville Estates Ltd* v *Madden* [1962] Ch 832 where such a gift was construed as a gift to the members of the association at the date of the gift, not as joint tenants, but subject to their contractual rights and liabilities towards each other as members of the association. As such, no individual member would be entitled to sever his share and take the value. If he were to cease to be a member, the benefit of his share would accrue to the remaining members. If, however. a gift is worded (or the rules provide) so that it is held in trust for, or applied for, the purposes of the society, then it will fail unless the society is charitable – *Leahy* v *A G for New South Wales* [1959] AC 457. Nevertheless, in the case of *Re Denley's Trust Deed* [1969] 1 Ch 373, a deed conferring on employees a right to use and enjoy land as a sports ground was upheld because the rule against the enforceability of non-charitable purpose trusts was confined to those which were abstract or impersonal in nature where there was no beneficiary. Provided a trust is in fact for the benefit of individuals then it is valid notwithstanding that it is expressed to be for a purpose. This reasoning was applied in the case of *Re Lipinski's Will Trusts* [1976] Ch 235, where a gift was left to an unincorporated non-charitable association to be used solely for constructing new buildings.

7. Gifts to charities

A charity may receive the benefit of a gift in a will by means of a charitable trust. No specific form of language is required but the intention of the testator to give the property to charity must be clearly expressed and imperative in nature. Precatory words have even been held to be sufficient – see *AG* v *Davies* (1802) 9 Ves 535. It is also sufficient if the gift provides "for such charities as my executors shall select" since it is only necessary to show a certainty of intention to apply the property for charitable purposes.

Charitable gifts receive concessionary treatment over other trusts in terms of enforcement, perpetuity, certainty and taxation, and are exempt from inheritance tax (IHT) – Inheritance Tax Act 1984, s 23.

In order for a gift to be charitable three criteria must be met:

(a) the gift must be of a charitable nature within the spirit of the preamble to the Statute of Elizabeth I as interpreted by the courts and extended by statute;

(b) the gift must promote a public benefit of a nature recognised by the courts as a public benefit;

(c) the purpose of the trust must be wholly and exclusively charitable.

(a) Charitable nature

The charitable purposes mentioned in the Statute of Elizabeth I have become anachronistic and in *Income Tax Special Purpose Commissioners* v *Pemsel* [1891] AC 531, Lord MacNaghten categorised four groups of charitable trust, those:

(i)   for the relief of poverty;
(ii) for the advancement of education;
(iii) for the advancement of religion;
(iv) for other purposes beneficial to the community, not falling within the preceding heads.

C.4.14 General gift to charitable institution

I GIVE the sum of £ .... to [charity] and declare that the receipt of the treasurer or other proper officer for the time being thereof shall be a sufficient discharge to my trustees.

Note: It is no longer necessary to include the words "free of inheritance tax" since the £100,000 limit on the exemption for gifts made on or within one year of death has been removed.

C.4.15 Legacy to several charitable institutions

I GIVE to each of the following charitable institutions the amounts set forth below the receipt of the treasurer or other proper officer for the time being of each said institution being a sufficient discharge to my trustees:

To [charity A] the sum of £ .....
To [charity B] the sum of £ .....

C.4.16 Gift of land to charity

I GIVE to [charity] absolutely my freehold property [description] and I direct my trustees to vest the same in or cause the same to be vested in the trustees of [charity] to be held by them for the general purposes of the charity.

C.4.17 Gift to charity to be selected by the trustees

I GIVE the sum of £ ..... to my trustees upon trust for such charitable object or objects or for such charitable purpose or purposes as my trustees may in their absolute discretion select and I DECLARE that the receipt of the treasurer or other proper officer for the time being of any charity to which my trustees may allocate any sums hereunder shall be a sufficient discharge to my trustees.

(i) Gifts for the relief of poverty: Poverty is a relative term and is not confined to the destitute in society – *Re Coulthurst* [1951] 1 All ER 774, *IRC* v *Baddeley* [1955] 1 All ER 525. The gift may be general or

it may be confined to some particular section of the public defined by reference to a place, a religion or otherwise. The gift must be made by way of bounty, not bargain, but there is no objection to the beneficiaries being required to contribute to the cost of the benefit – *Joseph Rowntree Memorial Trust Housing Association* v *AG* [1983] 1 All ER 288.

The original wording of the preamble of the statute of Elizabeth I, which says gifts for the "relief of aged, impotent and poor" are charitable, initially led to debate over whether the words could be read disjunctively. Recent case law, however, has clarified the matter and it is accepted that the words can be read disjunctively. Thus poverty is not an essential element in gifts to aged persons – *Joseph Rowntree Memorial Trust Housing Association* v *AG* (above).

(ii) Gifts for the advancement of education: Charitable gifts for the advancement of education extend to all kinds of educational services, and the courts have upheld as charitable, *inter alia,* gifts to libraries; gifts to facilitate a chess tournament for schoolboys; the provision of a field day for a Sunday school; and a gift to the Boy Scouts Association. There is, however, a strict requirement that the gift must benefit a section of the public or be of a public nature. A trust to promote a particular sport does not, *per se*, qualify under this head, unless the gift is one to an educational institution for the purpose of improving or promoting its sporting facilities – *Re Mariette* [1915] 2 Ch 284 (see page 48).

C.4.18 Gift to a school for the provision of playing fields

I GIVE to the Governors of ...... School the sum of £..... for the purchase by them of an area or areas of land to be used for the playing of games and for the sporting activities and other events of the school and its pupils and for similar purposes.

C.4.19 Gift to a school for the endorsement of a prize for sport

I GIVE to the Governors of ...... School the sum of £..... to be invested by them as they see fit the income therefrom to be applied in the provision of a prize or trophy for the winners of [the one hundred metres relay] at the school's annual sports day.

(iii) Gifts for the advancement of religion: In *Bowman* v *Secular Society Ltd* [1917] AC 406 Lord Parker suggested that any form of monotheistic theism would be recognised as religion. Religion requires a spiritual belief, a faith, a recognition of some higher unseen power which is entitled to worship. Any religion is better than none in the eyes of the law and different creeds have not been distinguished. Religious gifts have included gifts for the provision and support the clergy, building and maintenance of religious buildings, and the provision of graveyards and burial places. It has been held, however, that a gift for missionary work is not charitable on the ground that the description is so wide as to include non-charitable purposes; see *Scott* v *Brownrigg* (1881) LR 9 Ir 246. In this case, however, as with many other phrases like "for God's work", "for the service of God", "for his work in the parish" the court will often find circumstances to indicate that the purposes are intended to be limited to charitable religious purposes – *Re Moon's Will Trusts* [1948] 1 All ER 300.

C.4.20 Gift for religious purposes in a particular parish

I GIVE to the churchwardens [vicar] [Parochial Church Council] for the time being of [name of parish] the sum of £ .... to be held together with the income thereof UPON TRUST for such religious purposes (including but not limited to the building or repair of buildings in the parish used for religious purposes) as the said churchwardens [or as appropriate] shall in their absolute discretion think fit and I DIRECT that the said churchwardens [or other] shall be entitled to apply both the capital and income of the fund to any such purposes notwithstanding that the whole of the capital sum is thereby expended and I FURTHER DECLARE that the receipt of the said churchwardens [or any two of them] shall be a sufficient discharge to my trustees in all respects.

C.4.21 Gift to a religious community

I GIVE the sum of £ .... to the Mother Superior for the time being of the Convent of ...... at ...... to be applied together with any income thereof for the general purposes of the convent and I DIRECT THAT the receipt of the Mother Superior or the person acting as such shall be a sufficient discharge to my trustees in all respects.

C.4.22 Gift to parish priest for the offering of masses for the dead

I GIVE the sum of £ .... to the priest in charge of ...... Church at ...... to be applied in the offering of masses in public for the repose of the soul[s] of ...... and I DECLARE that the receipt of the priest in charge of the church at the time of the payment of the said sum shall be a sufficient discharge to my trustees.

Note: The validity of such gifts as charitable has been re-affirmed in *Re Hetherington* [1989] 2 All ER 129.

C.4.23 Gift to Church of England Board of Finance

[I GIVE the sum of £ .... to] [My Trustees shall hold my residuary estate upon trust for] the Central Board of Finance of the Church of England of Church House, Great Smith Street, London SW1 for [such ecclesiastical charitable purposes as the Board shall in its absolute discretion decide] [specify particular objects] and I DECLARE that the receipt of the secretary for the time being of the Board shall be a full and sufficient discharge to my trustees.

C.4.24 Gift to vicar for poor of a parish

I GIVE to the vicar [or rector] for the time being of the Parish of ...... near ...... in the County of ...... the sum of £.... to be applied by him as he shall in his absolute discretion think fit for the benefit of the poor of the said parish and the receipt of the said vicar [rector] shall be a full discharge to my trustees for the said sum and my trustees shall not be bound to enquire as to the application thereof.

(iv) Other purposes beneficial to the community: The first three heads are by their nature charitable, but gifts within the fourth head must be shown to have a purpose that is beneficial in a way which the law regards as charitable. Whether the donor thinks the gift charitable is irrelevant.

Examples of gifts that have been held to be charitable under the fourth head include:

- gifts to benefit the sick and in support of hospitals;
- gifts for the welfare of animals generally;
- gifts to promote the efficiency of the armed forces or emergency services;
- locality trusts.

C.4.25 Gift to a hospital

SUBJECT TO the conditions set out in clause [two] hereof

(1) I GIVE the sum of £ ...... to [...... Health Authority for the benefit of ...... Hospital] [the trustees for the time being of ...... Hospital] to be invested by the [Management Committee] [Board] [trustees] of that hospital in any investments authorised hereunder or by statute for the investment of trust funds with full power to transpose the same as the said [Committee] [Board] [trustees] think[s] fit into others of a like nature to be held UPON TRUST to apply the income therefrom for any one or more of the following purposes [list purposes desired]:

(i) for the provision of facilities services or equipment or otherwise for the improvement of the general welfare of the staff of the said ...... Hospital;

(ii) for the assistance of the patients or former patients of the said ...... Hospital in whatever manner including gifts of clothing or additional medical or surgical appliances to them on leaving the said ...... Hospital;

(iii) for the provision of accommodation for the use of relatives of critically ill patients;

(iv) for the purpose of any research [or name a particular branch of research] carried on at the said ...... Hospital;

[(2) The above gift hereinbefore contained is made subject to and conditional upon the said authority undertaking to name and maintain a bed in the said Hospital to be known as the ...... Bed.]

[(3) I desire that the gift shall be known as the ...... Fund]

(4) I DECLARE that a receipt signed by the [treasurer or other proper officer of the said authority] [any two of the trustees of the said hospital] shall be sufficient discharge to my trustees in all respects.

Note: The appropriate health authority to receive the gift will be the area health authority except where there are special trustees for the hospital.

Political trusts: Trusts of a political nature are not charitable. Slade J said in the case of *McGovern* v *AG* [1982] Ch 321 that a trust is to be classified as "political" where there is a direct or principal purpose:

• to further the interests of a political party; or
• to procure changes in the laws of this or another country; or
• to procure a reversal of governmental policies in this country; or

- to procure a reversal of governmental policy or of particular decisions of governmental authorities in a foreign country.

Provided the main objects of the trust are charitable in nature, a secondary political purpose, incidental to the main objects, will be irrelevant.

Despite the failure of political trusts as charities, gifts to political parties are nevertheless exempt from inheritance tax – s 24(1) IHTA 1984, provided that the political party is a qualifying political party. This is one where, at the general election immediately preceding the transfer, either two members of the party were elected to the House of Commons, or one member was elected and no fewer than 150,000 votes were cast in favour of that party. The current political parties that qualify for this exemption are Conservative, Labour, Liberal Democrat, Official Ulster Unionist, Plaid Cymru, Scottish Nationalist, Social Democrat and Ulster Democratic Unionist, Social Democratic and Labour Party.

The £100,000 limit on such gifts was removed by s 137 of the Finance Act 1988 for gifts made on or after 15 March 1988.

Social, recreational and sporting trusts: A gift to provide sporting facilities is not charitable, unless, as has been seen (page 44), it is to provide facilities for pupils of schools, universities or institutes of higher education.

A further exception to the general rule is contained in the Recreational Charities Act 1958 under which such a gift shall be deemed to be charitable if it is to provide or assist in the provision of facilities for recreation or other leisure-time activities where those facilities are provided in the interests of social welfare. The facilities must be provided to improve conditions of life for persons who can be shown to have need of those facilities due to their youth, age, deformity or disability, poverty or social and economic circumstance, or they must be available to members or female members of the general public.

(b) Public benefit

A gift can be charitable only if it is for public benefit, but this requirement differs from category to category. With regard to gifts for the relief of poverty, the test for public benefit is very wide, and some trusts or gifts have been upheld as charitable even though limited in their application to some small group of individuals ascertained by reference to some personal nexus (for example, of blood or contract).

In any gift for the advancement of education, the need for public benefit will not be satisfied where the beneficiaries are to be ascertained merely by reference to a personal tie, as in the case of the relations of a particular person, or the employees of a particular firm. However, where there is a public element, the trust may be charitable even though such people benefit – *Re Koettgen's Will Trusts* [1954] Ch 252. Here a trust was said to be charitable where it was to promote commercial education amongst such members of the public who could not afford it, with a direction that a preference be given to the families of employees of a named company up to a maximum of 75 per cent of the income.

Trusts for the advancement of religion must also be beneficial to the public – *Gilmour* v *Coats* [1949] AC 426, as must trusts under the fourth head.

(c) Purposes wholly or exclusively charitable
For a charitable trust to be valid it is required to have as its object the furtherance of purposes which are wholly and exclusively charitable.

Care should be taken when drafting to avoid such phrases as "charitable *or* deserving", "charitable *or* benevolent" and "charitable *or* other objects" since such gifts could be applied for a purpose which is not charitable.

If, however, a gift is drafted so that it is to have "charitable and benevolent" or "charitable and philanthropic" objects, then the terms do not necessarily invalidate the gift. The charitable purpose remains clear, although the type of charity may be restricted.

There are exceptions to the general rule:
(i) where one gift is expressed to be for both charitable and noncharitable purposes and a *power* is given to the trustees to divide the gift between the purposes, as in *Re Douglas* (1887) 35 Ch D 472, the court will hold that the gift is good: " ... the mere addition to the general charitable purposes of certain definite objects

does not make the gift bad because one of the objects is itself not a charity" (at page 486);

(ii) where the primary purpose of the gift is charitable, but the gift is not exclusively charitable, the courts may overlook the non-charitable part, but the charitable purpose must have a greater weight than the non-charitable purposes – see *Re Coxen* [1948] Ch 747;

(iii) under the Charitable Trusts (Validation) Act 1954 which perfects trusts made *before* December 1952. Where a trust is drafted in terms which could result in the property's being used exclusively either for charitable purposes, or for non-charitable purposes, retrospective validation may be possible provided that the invalid terms of the trust would have been considered valid had their object been exclusively charitable – s 2(1).

Discrimination: Section 34 of the Race Relations Act 1976 makes express provision in relation to charities and charitable instruments. The Act deals only with discrimination on the grounds of colour. Any provision in the charitable instrument which provides for conferring benefits on persons of a class defined by reference to colour has effect as if such reference to colour were disregarded and the benefits are conferred on the persons of the class which results. Where the original class is defined by reference to colour only, the gift will take effect in favour of persons generally.

The Sex Discrimination Act 1975 does not affect provisions in a charitable instrument conferring benefits on persons of one sex only.

The cy-près doctrine: The cy-près doctrine comes into operation where a testator demonstrating a general charitable intention creates a charitable trust, the objects of which are neither possible nor practicable. The trust may be saved by the doctrine and the court may, at its discretion, apply the intended subject matter of the trust to a purpose which resembles the original purpose as nearly as possible.

Before the Charities Act 1960 the application of the cy-près doctrine was confined to cases where it was either impossible or impracticable to carry out the testator's intentions. As a result of the Act, it is no longer necessary to decide matters of impossibility or impracticability. A cy-près application is permitted where the settlor has a clear charitable intention, and (s 13(1)):

"(a) where the original purposes, in whole or in part, –
  (i) have been as far as may be fulfilled; or
  (ii) cannot be carried out, or not according to the directions given and to the spirit of the gift; or
(b) where the original purposes provide a use for part only of the property available by virtue of the gift; or
(c) where the property available by virtue of the gift and other property applicable for similar purposes can be more effectively used in conjunction, and to that end can suitably, regard being had to the spirit of the gift, be made applicable to common purposes; or
(d) where the original purposes were laid down by reference to an area which then was but has since ceased to be a unit for some other purpose, or by reference to a class of persons or to an area which has for any reason since ceased to be suitable, regard being had to the spirit of the gift, or to be practical in administering the gift; or
(e) where the original purposes, in whole or in part, have, since they were laid down, –
  (i) been adequately provided for by other means; or
  (ii) ceased, as being useless or harmful to the community or for other reasons, to be in law charitable;
  (iii) ceased in any other way to provide a suitable and effective method of using the property available by virtue of the gift, regard being had to the spirit of the gift."

Charities wrongly named or having ceased to exist: Provided it can be shown from the wording of the disposition that a testator intended to benefit a charitable purpose, the gift need not fail even if the institution has never existed or cannot be identified. Where the beneficiary is an institution which has ceased to exist in the testator's lifetime, whether before or after the execution of the will, the gift lapses unless a general charitable intention is apparent. There is no lapse where there has simply been a change of name or an amalgamation with another institution. If the charity ceases to exist after the death of the testator but before payment, the gift still takes effect.

C.4.26 Clause to prevent the lapse of a gift to a body in the event of a change of name or amalgamation

I DECLARE that if before my death (or after my death but before my trustees have given effect to the gift in question) any charitable [or other] body to which a gift is made in this my will or any codicil hereto has changed its name or has amalgamated with or transferred all its assets to any other [charitable] body then my trustees shall give effect to the gift as if it has been made (in the first case) to the body in its changed name or (in the second case) to the body which results from such amalgamation or to which the transfer has been made.

C.4.27 General provision against lapse of charitable gifts

Where any provision within this my will or any codicil hereto names any institution society or other body whether incorporated or not as an intended beneficiary and that beneficiary is stated to be a charity or the intended gift is stated to be for a charitable purpose and where the said intended beneficiary is found never to have existed or to have ceased to exist or to have changed its name or constitution either by amalgamation with another body or otherwise prior to my death then in such an event the benefit of such gifts for each such intended beneficiary shall instead be given to such charitable body or bodies or applied to such charitable purpose or purposes as my trustees shall in their absolute discretion think fit.

Rule against perpetuities: Charities form an exception to the general rule against perpetuities. A gift to one charity with a gift over to another charity upon a certain event is valid even if that event occurs at any time beyond the perpetuity period. The rule that a gift which purports to give income from property for an unlimited period is void has no application to a gift for a charitable purpose.

Chapter 5

Beneficiaries identified by description or relationship

1. Introduction

Where a beneficiary in a will is referred to not by name but by description of relationship to the testator, such as "my wife" or "my servant", then, unless a contrary intention is expressed in the will, it is the person who satisfies that description at the time the will is made who will be entitled to the gift – *Re Whorwood* (1887) 34 Ch D 446.

A person who is ascertained to be a beneficiary under a description continues to be entitled even if he ceases to fit the description, unless a contrary intention is shown by the will or codicil.

2. Relationship by blood and affinity

Where a relationship is specified in a will it is presumed that the only persons to take are the relations by blood, not those by affinity or marriage, unless a contrary intention is expressed or there are no blood relations in existence.

A description by relationship *prima facie* includes not only people of the whole blood, but also of the half blood – see *Re Hammersley*

(1886) 2 TLR 459 – unless a contrary intention is evident. The words "my own brothers and sisters" were said to exclude those of the half blood – *Re Dowson* (1909) 101 LTR 671.

Where a particular relationship is specified by the testator, relations of the exact degree only are presumed to benefit. Thus, if the testator refers to nieces it is presumed he means nieces and not great-nieces. Again this presumption may be rebutted by the context or a contrary intention.

The term "cousins" generally includes only first cousins; the term "first cousins or cousins germain" does not include the descendants of first cousins; the term "second cousins" does not include first cousins once removed; and the term "half cousins" includes first cousins once removed and second cousins.

3. Legitimate relations

From 4 April 1988 the Family Law Reform Act 1987 governs the property entitlement of illegitimate persons. Section 1 of the Act provides that, unless a contrary intention appears, in instruments made after 4 April 1988, references to any relationship between two persons shall be construed without regard to whether or not the father and mother of either of them, or any person through whom the relationship is deduced, have or had been married to each other at any time.

4. Survivors

A gift may be made to such of a particular group of beneficiaries as survive the testator. Where the gift is immediate in nature, any beneficiary who outlives the testator will become entitled to his share of the property on the testator's death.

However, where the gift does not take immediate effect, the beneficiary's interest in the property will not vest immediately upon the death of the testator. For example, where a gift is expressed to be "to A for life, with remainder to such of his children as survive him", only such of A's children who are living at the date of A's death will take, despite the fact that other of A's children may have survived the testator.

5. Husband and wife

Where a testator expresses a gift to be "to my wife" and he is married at the date the will is executed, there is a *prima facie* presumption that he is referring to his existing wife and not to any subsequent wife. One should, however, remember that a marriage following a will generally revokes it. A reference to the "wife" of any other person would be a reference to the wife existing at the time the will is created unless a contrary intention is shown (for example, the wife for the time being), or that other person is unmarried at the date of the will, in which case the first person to answer the description will take.

A decree absolute dissolves the marriage and the parties cannot then be described as husband and wife.

The generally accepted definition of the term "widow" is the surviving legal wife until her death or remarriage. Where the testator is divorced his ex-wife will not therefore become his widow, although a person not legally married has been held to be a widow – see *Re Wagstaff* [1908] 1 Ch 162, but compare *Re Lynch* [1943] 1 All ER 168. If a widow remarries, then the period of widowhood will cease, provided the subsequent marriage is not annulled. A wife was held not to be entitled to an annuity payable "so long as she shall continue my widow" where, after the date of the will, the testator's own marriage was declared null and void – *Re Boddington* (1884) 25 Ch D 685.

Where a partner is described as a "wife", the gift will not fail merely because there was an invalid marriage, whether or not the parties knew of the invalidity. The gift will remain valid provided the testator is not deceived for the purposes of the gift.

Generally, the term "wife" applies *mutatis mutandis* in the case of a "husband".

6. Children

Where a gift is to "children" of the testator, the term is presumed to include immediate descendants, but not grandchildren or remoter issue. If the testator has adopted children they will be included in a gift to his children generally, unless a contrary intention is expressed. If the child was adopted by a married couple then he will be treated in law as a child of that marriage. If the adopter is not in fact married, the child will be treated in law as if born to the adopter in wedlock.

A child *en ventre sa mère* is also included in the description of children born or living at a particular date if it is to the child's own benefit that he should be included.

C.5.1   General clause for a child en ventre

Any reference to a child or children in this will or any codicil hereto SHALL INCLUDE any person en ventre sa mere at the date of my death or at such time as may be referred to therein provided that such person be born alive thereafter and I DECLARE that any such person shall be deemed to be living at that date [ALWAYS PROVIDED THAT this clause shall not operate where the effect would be to cut down or reduce any entailed interest which such child would have taken under my will or any codicil hereto but for the existence of this clause.]

If the word "begotten" is used in a will it includes both children already begotten and those to be begotten in the future. The context, however, may displace this meaning – see *Locke* v *Dunlop* (1888) 39 Ch D 387.

If the child is a minor it should be remembered that he cannot "hold" a legal estate in land, nor give a good receipt for a legacy unless, in the latter case, the will expressly provides for such.

7. Descendants

The term "descendants", when used in a will, generally includes anyone who is descended from a particular individual, however the descent is traced, although it does not include collateral relations, unless the will specifically defines the terms and indicates that it should do so.

Whenever drafting gifts to the testator's children (or remoter issue), it should be borne in mind that s 33 of the Wills Act 1837 (as amended) provides a statutory substitution clause in certain circumstances (see page 33 *et seq* and page 162).

C.5.2   Devise for the benefit of testator's children or the children of another with substituted gift to the issue of deceased children

I DEVISE all my interest in any real property whatsoever and wheresoever situated to my trustees UPON TRUST to sell the same and to hold the net proceeds of sale both as to capital and income and the net rents and profits until sale on trust for [all and every one of my children or child (if only one)] [the children or child (if only one) of ...... deceased] who attain the age of [eighteen] [twenty-one] years or marry under that age and if more than one in equal shares as tenants in common PROVIDED THAT if any child of [mine] [the said ......] has died or shall die in my lifetime leaving issue living at my death who attain the age of [eighteen] [twenty-one] or marry under that age such issue shall stand in the place of such deceased child and take per stirpes and equally between them if more than one the share of the proceeds of sale which such deceased child would have taken if he or she had survived me and attained a vested interest but so that no issue shall take whose parent is alive at my death and so capable of taking [ALWAYS PROVIDED THAT this gift shall take effect and be construed as if section 15(1) of the Family Law Reform Act 1987 had not been enacted].

Note: But for the words in square brackets the references to children and issue would be deemed to include references to illegitimate children and issue.

C.5.3   Trust for children of testator living at his death and issue of deceased children then living

IN TRUST in equal shares (if more than one) for all my children living at my death who attain the age of [eighteen] [twenty-one] years or marry under that age and for all or any of the issue living at my death who attain the age of [eighteen] [twenty-one] years or marry under that age of any child of mine who fails to survive me and attain the age of [eighteen] [twenty-one] years and who dies leaving issue such issue to take through all degrees according to their stocks in equal shares (if more than one) the share which their parent would have taken if living at my death and so that no issue shall take whose parent is living at my death and so capable of taking.

C.5.4 Trust for children of testator with provision for share of any deceased child leaving issue to pass to the child's personal representatives

IN TRUST for my children living at my death who attain the age of [eighteen] [twenty-one] years and for such of my children who shall die leaving issue living at my death before attaining the age of [eighteen] [twenty-one] years whether such child shall die during my lifetime or otherwise and if more than one in equal shares as tenants in common PROVIDED THAT the share of any child who fails to survive me leaving issue as aforesaid shall pass to his or her personal representatives as part of that child's estate as if the child had survived me.

Note: A share passing to the representatives of a deceased child becomes liable to the payment of the debts of that child. A direct gift to the child's issue may therefore be more expedient.

C.5.5 Trust for children in unequal shares

IN TRUST as to three equal seventh parts for my son [name] absolutely as to two other equal seventh parts for my daughter [name] if and when she attains the age of [eighteen] [twenty-one] years and as to the remaining two equal seventh parts in trust in equal shares for my grandchildren ...... and ...... if and when they shall respectively attain the age of [eighteen] [twenty-one] years or marry under that age [add gift over of shares which fail to vest].

C.5.6 Trust for children of quantified amounts

IN TRUST as to £[5000] or investments of that value for my son [name] if and when he attains the age of [eighteen] [twenty-one] years or marries under that age and as to £[5000] or investments of that value for my daughter [name] if and when he attains the age of [eighteen] [twenty-one] years or marries under that age and as to the residue (if any) for my son [name] absolutely.

Note: Provision should be made directing the trustees how investments are to be valued for this purpose.

C.5.7 **Trust for two persons as tenants in common on attaining twenty-one, with a gift over on the death of either to the other of them**

IN TRUST for [name] and [name] if and when they shall respectively attain the age of twenty-one years in equal shares as tenants in common but so that if either of them is already dead or shall die in my lifetime or before reaching the age of twenty-one years as aforesaid I bequeath the share [of residue] hereinbefore bequeathed to the one so dying to the other of them if and when [he] shall attain the age of twenty-one years ALWAYS PROVIDED THAT if both [name] and [name] shall fail to take a vested interest hereunder for any reason I bequeath the said [property] (add gift over).

C.5.8 **Trust for wife and children equally**

IN TRUST for such of my wife [name] and my children as survive me in equal shares as tenants in common.

C.5.9 **Trust for brothers and sisters and children of deceased brothers and sisters**

IN TRUST for such of my brothers and sisters as are living at the date of my death and the children then living of any then deceased brother or sister of mine who attains the age of [eighteen] [twenty-one] years or being female marries under that age if more than one in equal shares as tenants in common but so that the children of any such deceased brother or sister shall take equally between them as tenants in common only the share their parent would have taken had he or she survived me.

8. Issue

The word issue, when used in its strict sense, means "descendants in every degree". The meaning may, however, be restricted by the wording of the will. For example, where the testator refers first to issue but later speaks of the gift in question as a gift to children, or where the testator speaks of the "issue of such issue", the meaning will be restricted to "children". The same will result where the property is directed to be settled on a person and his "issue".

9. Next of kin

This expression is usually used to refer to the nearest relative of kin. However, the term "statutory next of kin" refers to the persons who would be entitled to succeed to the property on intestacy in the same manner and for such shares and amounts as they would have taken under the intestacy rules.

Where there is more than one person in the same degree of kinship each will rank equally and may take subject to contrary intention.

10. Heir

The word "heir" has largely lost its significance since 1925. Before then, the heir succeeded by right to the real property of an ancestor on intestacy. The word could be a word of purchase, indicating the particular person to take an interest; or a word of limitation, indicating the nature of estate which the person took. It is still relevant in connection with the creation of an entailed interest (see page 137), or where a person gives land by his will to his heir so that the interest will pass under the old rules governing the descent of real estate.

If land is given without words of limitation, for example "to A", A simply acquires all that the testator has to give. It is not necessary to use any words of limitation if A is to receive the fee simple although it is customary, for example, to say "to A in fee simple". Occasionally even now an alternative form, namely, "to A and his heirs", is used. Before 1882 the words "and his heirs" were necessary at common law in order to show that A had an estate capable of continuing after his death and of descending to his heirs if he died intestate. The words "and his heirs" are words of limitation and not words of purchase.

The requirements for the entailed interest after 1925 have been made stricter and since 1925 the words of limitation must include the words "and his heirs of his body" or "in fee tail" or "in tail".

11. Holders of an office

Where a donee is described by reference only to his office he will take the gift in his personal capacity unless the context and circumstances show that the holder for the time being was the intended donee. In the latter case the gift will be construed as a gift for the office or the association in which the office is held.

12. Precatory words

A testator may give a legacy to some person, often a trusted friend or relative, expressing a hope or wish that the legatee will apply the gift to a particular purpose, for example "£10,000 to my wife in the hope that she will provide for Aunt Matilda". Such a gift takes effect as an absolute gift to the legatee and the legatee will have only a moral obligation to fulfil the testator's wishes and cannot be impeached if she elects to take the gift herself for her own purposes. If anything more than a wish, hope or desire is expressed there is a danger of creating a half-secret trust and therefore it is necessary expressly to provide that no trust or legal obligation is intended:

C.5.10 Clause creating precatory "trust"
I GIVE to [name] absolutely the sum of [£2000] absolutely and I request without imposing any trust condition or legal obligation whatsoever on the said [name] that he gives such sums to such persons as are described in any memorandum by me with my solicitor at .... PROVIDED ALWAYS that no such memorandum or expression of my wishes shall have any testamentary effect nor shall it create any trust right liability or obligation or be deemed to form any condition in relation to the gift herein.

13. Secret trusts

A testator may wish to keep concealed the exact nature of a disposition he is making and not to set out the gift in a document such as a will, since such documents are open to public inspection.

A way in which publicity may be avoided is by the creation of a secret trust, the terms of which are not defined in the will. The testator must communicate the terms of the trust to the intended trustee, and there must be an intention to impose an obligation on the donee which the donee accepts. Where the trust is referred to but not defined in the will (a half secret trust), it is enforceable, but only if:

(a) it is described in the will as having been defined and communicated to the trustees prior to, or contemporaneously with, the execution of the will; and

(b) it is also proved that it was so defined and communicated to, and accepted by, some, even if not all, the trustees.

If in a will the reference to the undefined trusts is not restricted to trusts defined and communicated prior to or contemporaneously with the execution of the will, the trusts are unenforceable, because a testator cannot confer on himself the power of making future testamentary dispositions, by naming trustees and leaving the details of the trusts to be supplied afterwards.

Chapter 6

Revocation and alteration of a will

1. Revocation

A will is always revocable during the testator's lifetime, and a will or codicil can be revoked by:

    (a) marriage;

    (b) destruction;

    (c) execution of another valid will or codicil; or

    (d) duly executed writing declaring an intention to revoke the will.

The legal burden of proof of revocation falls on the person alleging that the will has been revoked.

(a) Marriage

Section 18 of the Wills Act 1837, as substituted by the Administration of Justice Act 1982, provides that for wills executed after 1 January 1983, the marriage of a testator automatically revokes any will made before the marriage (although a void marriage will not revoke a will). There are, however, three exceptions to this rule:

    (i)   Section 18(3) provides "Where it appears from a will that at the time it was made the testator was expecting to be married to a particular person and that he intended that the will should not be revoked by the marriage, the will shall not be revoked by his marriage to that person." It must "appear from the will" that the testator is expecting to marry a particular person at the time of execution, so that an express statement to that effect should be included. The will would still be revoked if the testator in fact marries another person. In the absence of such a statement it is thought that references to "my fiancée" or "my future wife" would suffice, and such reference would include any fiancée at the time the will was executed. It must also "appear from the will" that the testator intended the will should not be revoked by the marriage. The Act is silent as to how such an intention should be manifested, but an express statement to that effect would suffice and should be included.

C.6.1 **Clause declaring the testator's expectation to marry an intending spouse – prevention of revocation**
I declare that I make this will expecting to be married to [name of intended spouse] and that I intend that this will shall not be revoked by my marriage to the said [intended spouse].

(ii) Section 18(4) provides "Where it appears from a will that at the time it was made the testator was expecting to be married to a particular person and that he intended that a *disposition in the will* should not be revoked by his marriage to that person,–
   (a) that disposition shall take effect notwithstanding the marriage; and
   (b) any other disposition in the will shall take effect also, unless it appears from the will that the testator intended the disposition to be revoked by the marriage."
The testator's intention should again be expressly stated in the will. Similarly, if some of the provisions are to be revoked by the marriage then that intention must be apparent from the will. Where a provision has been included expressly saving a disposition from revocation by marriage the remaining dispositions are *prima facie* preserved by s 18(4), and if this is not intended a suitable provision should be added, either to the will or to each disposition:

C.6.2 Clause extending s 18(4) Wills Act 1837

I declare that unless otherwise stated herein all dispositions contained in this will or any codicil hereto shall be revoked by the celebration of my forthcoming marriage to [name].

Section 18(3) saves the whole of a will made in contemplation of marriage, but s 18(4) saves only "dispositions". Thus in the latter case any appointment clauses and similar administrative clauses (except powers of appointment) will be revoked by the subsequent marriage, notwithstanding the provisions of the subsection.

(iii) Section 18(2) provides that the exercise of a power of appointment by will (see Chapter 17) remains effective notwithstanding a subsequent marriage. This provision operates regardless of any intention of the testator to marry at the time the will is made. However, s 18(2) has no application where the subject matter of the appointment would pass to the testator's personal representatives in default of appointment.

(b) Destruction

Under s 20 of the Wills Act 1837 a will may be revoked by an act of "burning, tearing or otherwise destroying the same by the testator, or by some person in his presence and by his direction, with the intention of revoking the same." Two distinct elements are involved:

- an act of destruction; and
- an intention to revoke.

Neither alone is sufficient.

Destruction must be actual, not symbolic, and must be complete. Destruction of part of a will may be sufficient to revoke the whole will if the part destroyed is sufficiently vital (for example, the signature of the testator and of the attesting witnesses). However, the danger is that the part actually destroyed may be relatively unimportant, and the act of destruction may be construed as revocation of only that part actually destroyed.

Writing on the will or crossing out words will not generally be sufficient to revoke the will, but may have that effect if the signatures of both the attesting witnesses and the testator are rendered illegible or barely legible – *Re Adams* [1990] 2 All ER 97.

Any act of revocation by the testator must be as complete as the testator himself intended and if he is stopped for any reason before the will has been destroyed as intended, then the revocation will not be effective – see *Doe d. Perkes* v *Perkes* (1820) 3 B & Ald 489.

To establish the intention to revoke, the act of destruction must be carried out by the testator himself or another person in his presence and by his direction. If the will is destroyed accidentally or without the testator's authority, or if the testator is not present at the time of destruction, then the will is not revoked and the destruction cannot be ratified at a later date. If the testator then wishes to revoke the will he must do so by a written instrument. Destruction by a person of unsound mind does not revoke the will. Furthermore, if the testator destroys a will believing it to be invalid then there can be no intention to revoke a valid will and therefore no revocation.

Two rebuttable presumptions may apply in the following situations: *(i) A will missing at death:* Where a will cannot be found after the testator's death but it is known to have been in the testator's possession, a presumption arises that the will has been destroyed by the testator with the intention of revoking it. The presumption is rebuttable by evidence of non-revocation, including evidence showing the testator's intention to adhere to the will, provided that evidence is clear.

(ii) A will found mutilated at death: A will found in the testator's possession at his death, which is torn or mutilated, is presumed to have been destroyed by the testator with the intention of revoking it in whole or in part. This presumption may again be rebutted by evidence to the contrary.

(c) Execution of another valid will or codicil

Section 20 of the Wills Act 1837 says that the whole or any part of a will may be revoked by another duly executed will or codicil. The clearest way in which a later will can revoke an earlier one is by the inclusion of an express revocation clause:

C.6.3 Revocation clauses

I [testator] of [address] hereby revoke all former testamentary dispositions made by me.

C.6.4   I [testator] of [address] hereby revoke a will dated the ...... day of

...... and all other testamentary dispositions made by me and declare that it is my intention to die intestate.

A clause such as C.6.3 above should always be included in a new will and normally operates to revoke all previous testamentary instruments.

There are rare occasions when such a clause does not revoke all previous testamentary instruments, and an example of this is found in the case of *Re Wayland* [1951] 2 All ER 1041. Here a testator made two wills, the first dealing with his property in Belgium, made under Belgian law; and the second, subsequent, will was made in England and contained the revocation clause, but said "this will is intended to deal only with my estate in England". The court took the view that the revocation clause in the latter will had been restricted to testamentary dispositions relating to the testator's estate in England and admitted both the Belgian and the English wills to probate.

A revocation clause will also be excluded from a will if it was included without the testator's knowledge and approval, but not if the testator was mistaken only as to its effect.

A revocation clause in a conditional will has no effect if the condition remains unfulfilled, as the will itself is inoperative. Similarly, the revocation clause itself may be conditional and if that condition is not satisfied the clause will have no effect.

A later will or codicil impliedly revokes a prior will or codicil if and in so far as the later will contains provisions which are inconsistent with those in the former. The provisions in the earlier will which are neither inconsistent with nor replaced by the later will remain inoperative.

(d) Intention to revoke declared in duly executed writing
Section 20 of the Wills Act 1837 says that the whole or any part of a will may be revoked by "some writing declaring an intention to revoke the same" and executed in the same manner as a will.

2. Divorce and revocation

Section 18(1) of the Wills Act 1837 (as substituted by s 18(2) of the Administration of Justice Act 1982) provides that the divorce or annulment of a marriage of the testator will have two major effects on any will made by him before the divorce or annulment:

(a) the will will take effect as if any appointment of the former spouse as executor or trustee of the will were omitted. The provision is subject to contrary intention being shown in the will;

(b) any devise or bequest made by the will in favour of the former spouse lapses after the divorce or decree of nullity. This again is subject to a contrary intention.

These provisions apply only where the testator dies after 31 December 1982. Before this, divorce or nullity had no effect.

Where there is no provision in the will for a substitutional gift, the former spouse's lapsed share passes into residue or, if the gift over was of residue, it will pass as on intestacy. The case of *Re Sinclair* [1985] Ch 446 illustrated the need for carefully worded substitution clauses. Here property was left to the testator's former wife subject to a survivorship clause, with a gift over to the Imperial Cancer Research Fund should she fail to outlive the testator by one month. On the divorce of the testator the gift to the former spouse lapsed. The former spouse outlived the testator by over one month but was no longer entitled to the gift. However, there was no provision for the property to pass to the Cancer Research Fund in these circumstances and thus the conditional gift also failed, resulting in an intestacy.

To prevent such a result, any gift to a spouse by will which is to contain a substitutional gift should use the words "if this gift shall fail for any reason ......".

Where the former spouse is to receive a life interest under the will, the divorce or annulment accelerates the interest of the remainderman as if the life tenant had died at the time of the divorce or annulment.

It should be noted that a decree of judicial separation has no effect in relation to dispositions made under the will.

The rights of a former spouse under the Inheritance (Provision for Family and Dependants) Act 1975 are not affected by s 18A.

3. Revocation by a privileged testator

As has been said, a privileged testator can make a will free of many of the formal requirements of s 9 of the Wills Act 1837. He may also revoke the will in an informal manner, whether or not that will was made formally.

Where a privileged testator loses his privileged status he must generally make any desired revocation formally. However, the Family Law Reform Act 1969, s 3 allows a minor who has made a privileged will to revoke that will while still a minor, notwithstanding that his privileged status has been lost. In this case the revocation must be either by destruction, or by the execution of a formal attested document of revocation.

4. Conditional revocation

Where a testator destroys his will with the intention of revoking it, it must be determined whether the intended revocation was to be absolute or conditional. This is a question of fact, and extrinsic evidence is admissible as proof of that intention.

It may be the testator's intention to substitute one gift for another, perhaps by changing the amount of the original gift. If he revokes or alters his existing will with the intention of making a substituted provision then it is presumed that the initial revocation is intended to be conditional upon the validity of the substituted provision.

This presumption is known as the doctrine of "dependent relative revocation" and will apply also where the testator revokes a will or a provision in a will giving property to one person, with the intention of replacing the first provision with another provision in favour of a second person. Provided that it can be shown that the intention to revoke was conditional, then the original gift will stand where the substituted gift is invalid or ineffectual. Such a conditional intention may be inferred if it can be shown that the testator would rather have left the gift to the first person than have the gift fail entirely.

For example, where a testator destroyed a will in favour of his wife in the mistaken belief that she would be entitled to all his property on an intestacy, whereas she was in fact entitled to part only, it was held that the revocation of the will was conditional upon the testator's widow being entitled to the whole estate on intestacy. The will therefore remained valid – *Re Southerden* [1925] P 177.

5. Alteration

The general rule is that any alteration to the will made after its execution should be re-executed by the testator and initialled by two witnesses, or made by a duly executed codicil to the will.

The Wills Act 1837 s 21 provides:

"no obliteration, interlineation or other alteration made in any will after the execution thereof shall be valid or have any effect, except so far as the words or effect of the will before such alteration shall not be apparent, unless such alteration shall be executed in like manner as hereinbefore is required for the execution of the will ...".

Where there is an alteration which is apparent on the face of the will, a rebuttable presumption arises that the alteration has been made after the execution of the will. For this reason any apparent alteration should be referred to in the attestation clause as already made at the time of execution (see precedent C.3.4, page 23) and any alteration should be executed in order to avoid uncertainty.

Alterations that are deliberative in nature and not intended to form part of the final will will be excluded from probate. If a will is written partly in ink and partly in pencil, a rebuttable presumption arises that the parts in pencil are deliberative only. If the will is made on a type-written form and partly completed in ink it is presumed to be in a final form if duly executed. Similarly, in a hand-written will a correction that corrects an otherwise unintelligible clause or sentence and which is made in the same ink and handwriting as the rest of the will is sufficient to rebut the presumption of later alteration.

Not surprisingly, special rules apply to the alteration of privileged wills and the presumption is that any informal alterations made to the will by the testator are made while the testator is still privileged and the will and alterations are therefore valid.

If there is any doubt about an alteration which comes to the testator's attention, or that of his solicitor, it may be clarified by means of a codicil in the following form:

C.6.5 Codicil clarifying an alteration to a will

I [testator] of [address] declare this to be a codicil to my will dated the ...... day of ......

WHEREAS in my said will at line ...... on page ...... and at line ...... on page ...... words ...... and ...... and the figure ...... are crossed out and words ...... and ...... and the figure ...... have been substituted by interlineations and such alterations were not executed on the said will by myself and the attesting witnesses nor referred to in the attestation clause

1. Now I hereby declare that the said alterations were made prior to the execution of my said will and I direct that my said will shall be read and construed subject to the said alterations and as if the said substituted words were the original words written in my said will.

2. In all other respects I confirm my said will.

[testimonium and attestation clause].

Where words have been crossed out or partly obliterated without the alteration being attested, then:

(a) if the original wording is "apparent" those words are admitted to probate. "Apparent" means decipherable by ordinary means such as holding the document up to the light;

(b) where the original wording is not apparent due to the attempted alteration, those words are excluded from probate provided the obliteration was made by the testator with an intention to revoke the words deleted.

If the testator had no such intention, or if the alteration was made by some other person, then extrinsic evidence (for example, from solicitor's instructions or copies or infra-red photographs) is permitted to prove the original wording.

Where the testator made the obliteration with a conditional intention to revoke, the court will admit the original wording to probate under the principle of dependent relative revocation (see above) provided that wording can be proved by extrinsic evidence.

Chapter 7

Codicils, revival and republication

1. Codicils

A codicil is a testamentary instrument made supplemental to an existing will in order to add to, alter or revoke the original provisions, without revoking the whole. It is most useful to effect minor alterations to a complicated will. Major alterations may be better made by the execution of an entirely fresh will, revoking the existing one, as this will be easier to draft.

A codicil takes the same form as a will and is subject to the legal formalities under s 9 of the Wills Act 1837. It must recite the will to which it is supplemental and must be executed and attested in the same manner as a will, although it is not necessary for the witnesses of the codicil to be the same as those of the will.

The codicil should recite any changes in the testator's circumstances, including any change in the testator's name, a marriage or divorce. The body of the codicil should recite the provisions of the original will that are to be amended or revoked, and should then set out in detail the exact alterations to be made and any new provisions to be added to the will.

The codicil should specifically state that the remainder of the will is confirmed in all other respects.

2. Revival

Where a will or codicil has been revoked but not destroyed it may be revived by the testator, either by re-execution of the original document or by the execution of a further codicil expressing an intention to revive the original will and any subsequent codicils to it – Wills Act 1837, s 22.

C.7.1   **Will reviving a former will and codicils thereto which have been revoked**

I [testator] of [address] hereby declare this to be my last will.

WHEREAS I made a will dated ...... day of ...... [and executed ...... with [two] codicil[s] thereto dated [respectively] the ...... day of ...... [and the ...... day of......]] which will [and codicil[s]] I duly revoked on or about the ...... day of ......

NOW I hereby revive and confirm the said will dated the ...... day of ...... [and the said codicil[s] thereto] and hereby revoke all testamentary dispositions made by me other than the said will dated the ...... day of ...... [and the said codicil[s] thereto]

[Testimonium and attestation clause]

C.7.2   **Codicil to revive will following the testator's second marriage substituting the name of his second wife for that of his first, and extending the provisions in favour of his children of the second marriage**

I [testator] of [address] declare this to be a [first] codicil to my will dated the ...... day of ......

WHEREAS

(1) My wife [name] referred to in my said will has since died and I have married [name]

(2) By clause [8] of my said will I gave my residuary estate to my trustees to hold the same in trust for my late wife [name] for life with a gift over on her death to my children and issue.

1. NOW I HEREBY DECLARE that the name of my wife [name] shall be substituted for the name of my late wife [name] in clause [8] of my said will aforesaid and the same shall be read and construed accordingly [and I FURTHER DECLARE that any reference to "child", "children" or "issue" in any provision of my said will shall include as well any child children or issue of mine by my first marriage].

> 2. In all other respects I confirm and revive my said will and declare that for all purposes my said will as hereby modified shall operate and take effect as if it had been made on the date of this codicil and after my marriage with my wife [name].
> [Testimonium and attestation clause]

Once a will has been revived it takes effect as if executed on the date of its revival – Wills Act 1837, s 34.

Where one will has been revoked by a subsequent will it is not revived when the later will is revoked. To revive the first will a codicil should be used which shows an intention to revive the revoked will. The intention must:

> "appear on the face of the codicil, either by express words referring to a will as revoked and importing an intention to revive the same, or by a disposition of the testator's property inconsistent with any other intention, or by some other expression conveying to the mind of the Court, with reasonable certainty, the existence of the intention in question (*In the Goods of Steele* (1868) LR 1 P&D 575, 578).

In construing a codicil the usual rules on the admission of extrinsic evidence apply.

3. Republication

Whereas revival operates to bring a revoked will or codicil back into effect, republication *confirms* an unrevoked will.

There are only two methods by which a will or codicil may be republished. Firstly, the document may be formally re-executed. Alternatively, a codicil referring to the previous will or codicil may be executed.

A codicil need not expressly confirm the contents of a previous will; the will is republished at the date of the codicil if it is referred to, as it is assumed the testator considered the will at that time. This is termed "constructive republication".

A republished will speaks from the date of republication, subject to any amendments and additions in any codicil. However, where the effect of the republication would be to defeat the intention of the testator in respect of a provision in the previous will or codicil, then the doctrine of republication will not apply to that gift.

Republication by codicil or re-execution may save a gift originally given to an attesting witness or his spouse, provided the witnesses of the codicil are not the same as those of the original will.

Republication may save certain gifts in the original will from lapsing, as the construction may be altered. Where, for example, a gift in the will refers to "the wife of my cousin Harvey" and Harvey's wife then dies the gift to her will lapse. If, however, the testator republished the will after the death of Harvey's wife and knowing of her death, then the gift will pass to the next wife of Harvey should he remarry – for a similar situation see *Re Hardyman* [1925] Ch 287.

If, on the other hand, the gift had been to a named wife of Harvey and that wife had died, then the gift would lapse and could not be saved by the subsequent republication.

For republication and ademption see Chapter 19.

Chapter 8

Executors and trustees

1. Appointment of executors

An executor is appointed, usually by will, to "stand in the shoes" of the testator, administering his estate according to the law and the provisions of the will. He is not an agent of the deceased – *Rickless* v *United Artists* [1988] QB 40.

An express provision should be included in the main body of the will appointing a named executor, or more than one if desired. If the executors are also to be the trustees, then at least two should be appointed.

C.8.1   Clause appointing sole executor
I appoint [name] of [address] to be the sole executor of this my will.

C.8.2   Appointment of executors
I appoint [name] of [address] and [name] of [address] to be the executors of this my will.

C.8.3   Appointment of two people as executors and trustees
I appoint [name] of [address] and [name] of [address] (hereinafter referred to as my trustees which expression shall include the trustees for the time being hereof) to be the executors and trustees of this my

will [and the trustees hereof for the purposes of the Settled Land Act 1925].

Note: The words in the last set of square brackets are required only where the provisions of the will are such that land becomes settled land within the Settled Land Act 1925. Their inclusion is not so important since the Settled Land Act 1925 s 30(3) makes the personal representatives trustees until other trustees are appointed if none is appointed by the will and there are none by virtue of the provisions of the earlier part of that section.

No more than four executors may take out a grant of probate at one time in respect of part of an estate – Supreme Court Act 1981, s 114. Where there are more than four executors appointed then some may "stand in reserve".

An executor should be named in the will and not referred to by description of his office. The person must be clearly identified or the appointment will be void for uncertainty; see for example *In the Goods of Baylis* (1862) 2 Sw & Tr 613, where an appointment of "any two of my sons" was void for uncertainty. However, where the will shows a clear intention that a particular individual or particular person should act in the estate and perform the functions of an executor then he has implied authority to act as "executor according to the tenor of the will". An executor impliedly appointed in this way may act alongside executors expressly appointed. The authority to act derives from the will itself and not the grant of probate, which merely confirms the appointment and affords evidence to the executor to prove his office.

Conditional appointments of executors, for example conditional on the named executor's attaining the age of eighteen, are permissible, but should be used only in special circumstances – *Re Langford's Goods* (1867) LR 1 P & D 458.

C.8.4   Appointment of wife while a widow and two sons (one under age at date of the will) to be executors and trustees

I appoint my wife [name] [so long as she shall remain my widow] and my son [name] if and when he shall attain the age of eighteen years and also my son [name] to be the executors and trustees of this my will [and the trustees thereof for the purposes of the Settled Land

Act 1925 hereinafter referred to as my trustees which expression shall include the trustees for the time being hereof.]

2. Who can be an executor

Any person may be named as an executor in the will, but care should be taken to choose someone who will be both willing and able to take up the office. Neither a minor nor a person of unsound mind will be granted probate and where such a person is appointed as sole executor a grant of administration with the will annexed may instead be given to the guardian of the appointed executor, or to another person on his behalf.

Where it is desired to appoint a firm of solicitors as executors, careful wording should be used. Where a firm of solicitors is appointed the appointment is presumed to be an appointment of all the individual partners in the firm at the date of the death. Provision should also be made against a change of name or amalgamation with another firm:

C.8.5 Appointment of firm of solicitors as executor

I appoint the partners at the date of my death in the firm of [name] [or the firm which at that date has succeeded to and carries on its practice] of [address] to be the executors and trustees of this my will [and I express the wish that two and only two of them shall prove my will and act initially in its trust]
[Insert charging clause; see page 203.]

Where a trust corporation is to be appointed as executor, either alone or jointly with others, the corporation's own appointment clause should be used in order to ensure the appointment is accepted.

C.8.6 Appointment of a bank as executor and trustee together with individuals

1. I appoint the .... Bank plc and [name] of [address] and [name] of [address] (hereinafter called my trustees which expression shall include the trustees for the time being hereof) to be the executors and trustees of this my will.
2. [Add the bank's standard clauses which will include a remuneration clause]

Note: It must be ascertained whether the trustee department of the bank is a separate company, and if it is it must be referred to by that name.

C.8.7 Appointment of a bank as sole executor and trustee

1. I appoint ...... Bank plc to be the sole executor and trustee of this my will [and the trustee thereof for the purposes of the Settled Land Act 1925].

2. [Clauses required by the bank]

The Public Trustee may be appointed executor, either alone or jointly with others. Such an appointment is rarely called for but may be necessary where there is difficulty in finding someone who is able and willing to act. The Public Trustee can refuse to act and will not generally act in estates involving the carrying on of a business for an indefinite period, nor may he undertake a trust where the whole of the trust property is devoted to religious or charitable purposes. The Public Trustee Act 1906 also forbids the Public Trustee from acting in certain types of estate.

C.8.8 Appointment of the Public Trustee as sole executor and trustee

I appoint the Public Trustee to be the sole executor and trustee of this my will [and the trustee hereof for the purposes of the Settled Land Act 1925].

Note: See Public Trustee (Fees) (Amendment) Order 1988, SI 1988 No 571.

Where an estate contains unpublished works worth a considerable amount and it is considered that someone of special experience should deal with that part of the estate, then a special literary editor may be appointed. However, because of the need for a special grant in such a situation, and the added administrative difficulties, the appointment of such trustees should be avoided if possible. It would not be necessary, for example, simply to collect the royalties from unpublished works.

C.8.9 Appointment of literary executors

(1) I APPOINT [name] of [address] and [name] of [address] (hereinafter referred to as my trustees) to be the executors and trustees of this my will except in relation to that part of my estate hereby given to my literary executors as hereinafter mentioned.

(2) I APPOINT [name] of [address] and [name] of [address] (here-inafter called my literary executors) to act as executors of this my will to administer only that part of my estate as is hereinafter given to them [and I DIRECT that the expenses of extracting a limited grant of probate in respect of the part of my estate so given to them and all taxes payable in respect of that part of my estate shall be borne by and payable out of [my residuary estate] [the part of my estate so given on a first charge thereon.]]

A person named as an executor may renounce that office at any time before he first accepts it. Acceptance need not be formal, and may be shown by the executor's:

(a) taking out a grant of probate; or

(b) acting as executor.

A named executor may renounce the appointment even after swearing the oath and applying for a grant, provided the grant has not been made at the time of renunciation and provided he has not acted as an executor at that time in relation to the estate.

Where it is sought to show that an executor has taken up the office as a result of his actions, all the circumstances of the case will be looked at. Merely dealing with assets as the agent of another executor is not sufficient to imply acceptance, neither will it be implied from trivial administrative acts.

Since 1925 the legal estate in a settlement of land is vested in the tenant for life or any other person entitled by statute to exercise the powers of a tenant for life. A settled land grant will be needed only when the legal estate is vested in a sole or sole surviving tenant for life, and the land is to continue to be settled after his death. In the case where the land ceases to be settled on the death of the tenant for life, it passes under the ordinary grant to the personal representatives.

Where the land will continue to be settled there are two situations to examine. The first is where there are trustees of the settlement at the date of the death of the tenant for life. In default of any express appointment, which should be made only at the request of the testator, the existing trustees are deemed to be the special executors with regard to settled land – Administration of Estates Act 1925, s 22.

C.8.10 Appointment of special executors

I appoint as my special executors in regard to such settled land of which at my death I shall be the tenant for life or the person having the powers of a tenant for life and which continues to be settled land after my death the respective persons who shall at the time of my death be the trustees for the purpose of the Settled Land Act 1925 of the settlements in which the same is comprised.

The second situation is where there are no trustees of the settlement at the date of the death of the tenant for life. Where the trustees are appointed after the death of the tenant for life they are not special executors under the statute and could therefore obtain only a grant of administration with the will annexed, limited to the settled land.

3. Renunciation

An executor who has not accepted the office is free to renounce probate. The renunciation should be in writing and filed in court.

C.8.11 Renunciation of executorship

In the High Court of Justice
Family Division
The Principal [or The...... District] Probate Registry
In the Estate of [name of deceased] deceased
WHEREAS [deceased's name] late of [deceased's last address], deceased, died on the ...... day of ......, at ......, having made and duly executed his last will and testament dated the ...... day of ...... and thereof appointed [name] his sole executor; now I the said [name] do hereby declare that I have not intermeddled in the estate of the said deceased and will not hereafter intermeddle therein with the intent of defrauding creditors, and I hereby renounce all my rights and title to the probate and execution of the said will.
[Signature of executor]
Signed by the said [name]
this ...... day of ......, in the presence of ....,
Signature of witness:
Address:

Once the executor has renounced his office he cannot reclaim it without the leave of the court.

4. Appointment of trustees

It is usual to appoint the same people as both executors and trustees, although the duties and functions of each office are very different. The trustee's duty is to manage the trusts of the will for as long as they continue, whereas the executor's duty is to gather in and liquidate the assets of the estate and distribute them. Where the executors are to transfer property to the trustees but both offices are held by the same people, the transfer of personalty to them is notional; in the case of land, an assent must be executed in order to pass legal title.

The definition of "trustee" in the Trustee Act 1925 includes a personal representative where the context so admits – s 68(17) – and the provisions of that Act therefore apply to both executors and trustees unless otherwise provided.

If there are no specific trusts expressed in the will, the estate will be held on trust for the beneficiaries according to their rights and interests under the will. Otherwise the property will be held according to the specific trusts expressed.

Where the executors and trustees are different people the executors will first liquidate the estate, paying such debts as there may be. They will then vest the property in the trustees, either by delivery, or, in case of realty, by assent.

Where there has been no express provision appointing trustees in the will, or where the appointment has failed to take effect for any reason, or the appointed executors have renounced their office, an intending administrator of the estate must apply for a grant of letters of administration with the will annexed. As from the time of their appointment, such administrators become trustees – Administration of Estates Act 1925, s 33. This provision caused some difficulties which were resolved in *Re Yerburgh* [1928] WN 208, which decided that administrators with the will annexed are in fact personal representatives until the estate is cleared, when they become trustees.

This has important consequences as it affects the interests of the beneficiaries during the administration, the powers of the administrators under s 39 of the Administration of Estates Act 1925, and the power to act severally or give receipts for purchase money on the sale of the land.

C.8.12 Deed of disclaimer by trustee named in a will

WHEREAS by a will dated [date] the late [testator] appointed me to be the trustee [and executor] of the said will.

BY THIS DEED I [disclaiming trustee] of [address] hereby disclaim all estates and interests in the real and personal estate of the said [testator] devolving to me as trustee [and executor] of the said will and the trusts and powers thereby reposed in me whether solely or jointly with some other person or persons ALWAYS PROVIDED THAT this disclaimer shall not operate to disclaim or release any beneficial interest to which I am now or may become entitled under the said will save where such benefit was conferred upon myself solely in consequence of my appointment as trustee for acting in the said trusts.

IN WITNESS etc

[Signature of disclaiming trustee].

C.8.13 Clause to define trustees

I DECLARE that for all purposes of this my will the expression "my trustees" shall (where the context admits) be construed and taken to mean the trustees for the time being hereof whether original or substituted and if there be no such trustee shall include such persons as are willing to be bound to exercise and perform any power or trust hereby or by any statute conferred upon my trustees and who are authorised by statute so to do.

5. Guardians

It is important for a testator with young children to consider whom he would wish to care for them after his death. Where there is no parent alive who can assume parental responsibility for the child then the court can appoint a guardian – s 5(1)(a) Children Act 1989. The testator may wish to cater for the possibility that his spouse does not survive him, and to appoint a guardian to assume parental responsibility on his death. Such an appointment may be made by two or more persons acting jointly – s 5(10) Children Act 1989. The appointment may, but need not, be contained in a will or a deed. If it is not contained in a will then it must be made in writing, dated and signed by or at the direction of the person making the appointment, in his presence, and in the presence of two witnesses who each attest the signature.

Care should be taken to ensure any intended guardian is aware of the appointment and willing and able to act. The will should also make provision for the maintenance of children. The easiest way to do this is by means of a trust fund. The guardian may be appointed trustee of the trust fund for ease of administration. The trust should contain powers for spending income and capital on the maintenance, education and advancement or other benefit of the child although the need for such provisions is in some ways obviated by ss 31 and 32 of the Trustee Act 1925.

C.8.14 Appointment of guardians conditional upon the testator or testatrix surviving his or her spouse

[If my wife [husband] dies before me] I appoint [name] of [address] [and [name] or [address]] to be the guardian[s] of any of my children who have not attained the age of eighteen [and I direct that they shall bring up such children [as members of the Church of England] [in the Roman Catholic faith] [as Moslems]].

C.8.15 Appointment of guardian to act with testator's wife during her life, and after her death to act with persons to be appointed by her

I appoint [name] of [address] to be guardian of any child or children of mine who may be minors at the date of my death to act jointly with my said wife during her life and after her death to act either alone or jointly with such persons as my said wife may appoint.

Chapter 9

The disposal of the body

1. Directions as to burial

A testator may want to express his wishes concerning the disposal of his body in his will. He should be advised to inform his relatives of his wishes as well as including them in the will, since the will may not be read until after the testator's funeral.

C.9.1 Direction as to place of burial and tombstone

I DIRECT that my body be buried [in my family grave] in the ...... Cemetery [in Section ...... Grave no ......] AND I FURTHER DIRECT that my executors shall expend a sum not exceeding £ ...... upon the erection of a suitably inscribed tombstone upon the said grave.

Note: A direction as to the burial of the body cannot be enforced since a person has no property in his body after death – *Williams* v *Williams* (1882) 20 Ch D 659.

C.9.2 Direction as to cremation

I desire that my body be cremated [in the crematorium at ......] and that my ashes be kept at ...... [or scattered on consecrated ground at ......]

Note: Cremation must take place at a recognised crematorium.

C.9.3   Direction not to cremate a body
I DIRECT that my body shall not be cremated.

Note: It is not unlawful to cremate a body where there is such a direction.

C.9.4   Direction as to necessary expenses
I desire there should be no flowers at my funeral or on my grave and that mourning shall not be worn by my relatives and no expense incurred beyond that which is necessary.

Note: This direction is merely indicative of the testator's desire.

C.9.5   Power for executor to incur expense in respect of directions
[State the directions to the executor and continue as follows] and I HEREBY authorise my executor to spend such sums as he shall in his absolute discretion consider reasonable in carrying out the above directions and his decision as to what is reasonable shall be final and binding upon all beneficiaries under this my will.

2. Anatomical research and organ transplantation

A testator may if he wishes give his body to a medical school or a hospital. The two Acts that govern such a disposition are the Human Tissue Act 1961 ("HTA 1961") and the Anatomy Act 1984. The former Act contains the main provisions governing gifts of the body and of parts of the body for "therapeutic purposes and purposes of medical education and research", which include transplantation and research. The latter Act contains provisions governing gifts of bodies for anatomical research purposes only. No statutory form of wording is required, only a written statement indicating that the testator intends to bequeath his body or part of it for such a purpose. The statement may, but need not, be contained in a will. The deceased can make the request orally but only during his last illness and in the presence of two or more witnesses – s 1(1) HTA 1961.

Where parts of the body are to be used for transplant purposes it is better to indicate that intention in a statement separate from the will, and to notify the relatives, since the organs must be removed shortly after death before the will is read. The statement can be contained in a standard form available from the hospital. Such forms should be completed in triplicate and one left with the next of kin, one annexed to the will and one left with the family doctor.

Where the testator wishes his body to be used for anatomical research then the necessary consent forms should be obtained from the anatomy department of the nearest medical school. A copy of the completed forms should be returned to the department.

There is no guarantee that a bequest of this type can be carried out. If a *post mortem* has been performed on the body then it may be impossible to preserve it and so the body would be unsuitable for anatomical examination or transplant purposes.

C.9.6 Direction for anatomical examination and corneal grafting

1. I desire that after my death my body may be made available [to ......] for such anatomical examination and research or transplantation of any part or parts as may be thought fit provided that such examination is in accordance with the provisions of the Anatomy Act 1984 [and I DIRECT that the institution receiving my body shall have it cremated in due course].

2. I hereby request that my body or any part thereof as is suitable shall be used for such therapeutic purposes or for the purposes of medical education or research as [institution] thinks fit.

Note: The surviving spouse or nearest relative can require interment without examination of the body. The institution receiving the body is responsible for ensuring that it is decently cremated or buried in consecrated ground or in a public burial ground being used for persons of the religious persuasion of the deceased.

C.9.7 Clause providing for use of testator's body for therapeutic purposes, but not for medical education or research

(a) I desire that after my death any part or parts of my body which may be suitable for any therapeutic purpose (including corneal grafting in the case of my eyes and transplantation in the case of any other parts of my body) shall be removed in order that they may be used for such purposes.

(b) For the avoidance of doubt I declare that the foregoing provisions shall not authorise the use of my body or any part of it for medical education or research and I express my desire that neither my body nor any part of it should be used for such purposes.

(c) I desire that after the removal of such parts of my body as may be removed under the provisions hereinbefore set out the remainder shall be cremated by any hospital or other institution which has custody of my body after such removal has been completed.

Where a deceased person has in his lifetime made a statement in accordance with s 1(1) HTA 1961, requesting the use of any parts of his body, or a specified part or parts, for one or more uses under that section then "the person lawfully in possession of the body" may authorise the removal of such parts for use in accordance with the request unless the request has been withdrawn by the deceased. If the person has died in hospital then the health authority is in possession of the body whilst it is still on hospital premises (until executors or relatives claim the body).

A DHSS Code of Practice issued in 1979 says that two doctors must certify brain death of the potential donor; one doctor must be a consultant of at least five years' standing, or his deputy, with experience in these cases. Neither doctor should be a member of the transplant team.

The relatives of the deceased, including the next of kin, cannot themselves countermand the deceased's request and cannot prevent the removal or examination of parts of the body in accordance with the request. Section 1(1) does not impose any duty upon the person lawfully in possession of the body to consult relatives or consider any objections by them, although it is customary for near relatives to be consulted.

The removal of any part of the body must be effected by a fully registered medical practitioner, who must have satisfied himself by personal examination of the body that life is extinct – s 1(4) HTA 1961.

Section 1(2) HTA 1961 deals with the situation where no express request has been made about the use of the body after death. In such circumstances:

"the person lawfully in possession of the body of a deceased person may authorise the removal of any part from the body for use for the said purposes if, having made such reasonable enquiry as may be practicable, he has no reason to believe:-

(a) that the deceased had expressed an objection to his body being so dealt with after his death, and had not withdrawn it or

(b) that the surviving spouse or any surviving relative of the deceased objects to the body being so dealt with."

Thus, where the deceased has not himself requested or consented to the use of any parts of his body for research or medical or therapeutic purposes, the decision to object rests with the surviving relatives, and the person lawfully in possession of the body has a duty to make enquiries both as to whether or not the relatives object to the use of the body parts, and as to whether or not the deceased himself expressed an objection.

If a person positively objects to his body being used for these purposes he should inform his relatives so that they are aware of his view, and he should sign a written statement of objection which may either be included in his will or kept with it.

Chapter 10

Wills involving foreign property or domicil

See Appendix A for a precedent of a complete will disposing of English and foreign property.

1. General

Before considering wills involving foreign property, or made by a testator who has a foreign domicil, the classification of property into movables and immovables must be considered. The term "immovables" roughly corresponds with the English classification of realty, comprising all estates and interests in freehold land, including those subject to a trust for sale, and leasehold land and rentcharges, and annuities payable out of rents and profits of land. The term "movables" has a meaning broadly similar to that of "personalty".

2. Movables

A will that has been drafted in England by a testator who is domiciled in England at the date of his death, is governed by English law in all respects except with regard to the disposition of immovables situated outside England. If, on the other hand, a testator dies domiciled abroad but leaves assets in England, a grant of probate must be taken out in England and the estate administered according to English law, but all questions concerning beneficial succession under the will are dealt with according to the law of the testator's domicil at death.

The rules governing testamentary dispositions are best dealt with according to the issue involved:

(a) Capacity

When drafting a will with an international element it should be remembered that the capacity of a testator to make a will is determined by the law of the domicil. Problems can arise where the testator has changed his domicil after making his will and there is an element of disagreement as to whether the governing law is that of the domicil at the date of death or at the time the will was made. Most writers appear to believe the law at the testator's death should govern the situation.

Whether or not a legatee has capacity to take a gift under a will is determined by either the law of the legatee's domicil, or the law of the testator's domicil – see *Re Schnapper* [1928] Ch 420 – whichever is more favourable to the legatee.

(b) Formal validity

It was thought at one time that the formal requirements for validity were those of the law of the country where the testator was domiciled at the date of his death. The Wills Act 1963, which applies to the wills of testators dying after 1 January 1964, provides in s 1 that "a will shall be treated as properly executed" if its execution conforms with the internal law in force in any one of the following territories:

(i)   the territory where the will was executed. This is so irrespective of the duration of the testator's visit to the territory;

(ii) the territory where the testator was domiciled either at the time of making the will or at death;

(iii) the territory where the testator was habitually resident either at the time of making the will or at death;

(iv) the state of which the testator, either at the time of making the will or at death, was a national.

Following the UK's ratification of the Washington Convention on International Wills (1973) a will is formally valid in all the contracting states if it complies with the formalities provided for by the Convention. The domicil and the nationality of the testator are no longer relevant, nor is the place where the will was made, nor the location of the assets of the estate. Under the Convention the will must be made in writing and the main formalities are that it must be signed and acknowledged by the testator in the presence of two witnesses and an "authorised person". The "authorised person" (a solicitor or notary public if the will is made in England) must complete a form of certificate authenticating the will and confirming that it has been properly executed. The certificate is then annexed to the will.

(c) Essential validity
Issues of "essential validity" include whether or not a gift to an attesting witness is valid; whether a gift infringes rules on perpetuity periods; and whether the testator has fulfilled a requirement to leave part of his property to his wife and children. Whether or not a gift or will has "essential validity" or "material validity" depends upon whether or not the testator has complied with all the requirements of the relevant law.

In respect of movable property the relevant law is that of the country in which the testator is domiciled at the time of his death.

Mere compliance with the formalities required by the Wills Act 1963 does not necessarily make valid either individual gifts or the whole will. That Act only provides proof that the document in question is a will and therefore admissible to probate. An obvious example of this distinction is where the testator is a British subject who dies domiciled in France, having made a will in England according to English law. Probate will be granted provided the formalities of English law have been complied with when executing the will. But under French law the testator would be required to make provision for his children under his will, and if the will does not contain such a provision, some or all of it may be ineffective. The will would take effect subject to the French law, which may result in intestacy. If only part of the estate fails, then the remainder may pass under the will, although any bequest will then be reduced *pro rata*. See *Re Groos*

[1915] 1 Ch 572; *Re Annesley* [1926] Ch 692 and *Re Ross* [1930] 1 Ch 377.

(d) Construction

Where the provisions of a will are unclear or incomplete in their effect, then the court must intervene to determine what, given the proper construction of the will, was intended by the testator.

The court will usually attempt to determine the law with which the testator was most familiar and, in the absence of a contrary intention being manifested by the will, that law will be used in relation to questions of construction. It is presumed that the testator had that law in mind when the will was drafted. The law usually in the mind of the testator is the law of his domicil at the time the will was made.

(e) Revocation

The rules relating to revocation vary under different legal systems and the choice of law is determined by the method of revocation:

(i) *Revocation by a later will:* A will purporting to revoke an earlier will is formally valid and effective if it satisfies the requirements of any one of the laws by which, under the Wills Act 1963, its formal validity is determinable, or if it complies with the requirements of any one of the laws qualified to govern the formal validity of the earlier will.

(ii) *Revocation by destruction of the will:* The Wills Act 1963 deals only with revocation by a testamentary instrument, and not by destruction. If, when the act of revocation by destruction was performed, the domicil was different from that when the will was executed, the common law principle of domicil will operate and the legal effect of the act of destruction falls to be determined at the time of its performance.

(iii) *Revocation by marriage:* The rule of revocation by marriage under the English legal system is not commonly adopted by other systems. If a person makes a will, marries, and later dies leaving movables in another country, the effect of the marriage on the will may need to be determined. Whether or not the relevant law is that of the domicil at the date of the marriage or at the date of the death depends upon whether the rule itself is matrimonial or testamentary in nature. If matrimonial then the domicil at the time of the *marriage* will be applied. Otherwise the domicil at death will apply. The matter was settled in the case of *Re Martin* [1900] P 211, where it was decided that revocation by marriage was essentially a doctrine connected with the relationship of marriage and therefore matrimonial.

3. Immovables

(a) Capacity
In the case of testamentary succession to immovables the *lex situs* governs questions of capacity.

(b) Formal validity
The Wills Act 1963 has considerably extended the common law position in relation to immovables. Previously, a will relating to immovables was subject to the formal requirements of the *lex situs*. Under the 1963 Act the will is valid if it complies with any one of the laws specified in s 1 (above). The *lex situs* is defined for the purpose of the Act to mean "the internal law in force in the territory where the property was situated" (s 2(1)(b)), and the doctrine of *renvoi* appears to have been excluded by the reference to the "internal law" of the *lex situs*.

(c) Essential validity
The material or essential validity of a gift of immovables by will is again governed by the *lex situs*.

(d) Construction
Provisions in a will concerning immovables will be construed according to the system of law intended by the testator. This is presumed to be the law of his domicil at the time the will was made, but the presumption may be rebutted by adducing evidence from the language of the will to prove that he made his dispositions with reference to some other legal system. If, however, the interest that arises from such construction is not permitted or not recognised by the *lex situs,* then that

law must nevertheless prevail.

(e) Election

The question of election by a beneficiary is discussed more fully later (see page 187). It arises where a testator leaves property to a beneficiary, but also makes a provision in his will disposing of some property already belonging to that beneficiary to another. The beneficiary must elect whether to accept the gift to him under the will, in which case he must adopt the gift of his own property to the other person; or he can elect to keep his own property, in which case the gift of the testator's property in the will does not take effect, or takes effect subject to a deduction in respect of the property the beneficiary elects to withhold.

Where the testator's property is situated in more than one country, the question whether or not the beneficiary is put to his election is determined according to the *testator's* domicil. The courts of that domicil will not be able directly to enforce the disposition where land is held abroad, but they can force the beneficiary to compensate any person suffering loss in respect of the property that was to be given to him, and that compensation will be made out of the movable property which the beneficiary is to take under the will.

(f) Revocation

Broadly speaking, a will in relation to immovables may be revoked in the same way as one concerning movables. Thus it may be revoked by a later will or a testamentary document showing an intention to revoke. The effect of an act of revocation by destruction or obliteration will be determined by reference to the *lex situs*.

In the case of revocation by a subsequent marriage, reference should be made to the law of the domicil at marriage and not the *lex situs*, despite a view to the contrary in *Re Caithness* (1891) 7 TLR 354, since the Australian decision of *Re Micallef's Estate* [1977] 2 NSWLR 929 seems to have found more support.

4. Powers of appointment exercised by will

For a detailed discussion of powers in English law see Chapter 17.

(a) Nature of a power
The nature of a power, that is, whether it is special or general, is a matter of construction to be determined according to the law governing the instrument creating it.

(b) Capacity
Capacity to exercise a testamentary power is determined by the law of the appointor's domicil. The instrument which creates the power (not the one by which the power is exercised) is the governing instrument and the appointee takes under the instrument, and not under the will of the appointor.

It appears that an appointor must have capacity under the law of his domicil in order validly to exercise a general power of appointment. In the case of a special power, however, the appointor is treated as an agent acting under the terms of the governing instrument, and the exercise of that power is valid if the appointor is capable either under the law of his domicil or under the law that governs the instrument of creation.

(c) Formal validity
The situation may well arise in which a testamentary appointment is given, under an English instrument, to a person who either makes his will abroad, or dies while domiciled in another country.

In such a case, a will exercising that power of appointment is treated as properly executed in respect of the exercise of that power if it complies with the requirements of one of the specified legal systems under the Wills Act 1963, s 2(1)(d).

The governing law will therefore be determined according to the place where the will was executed or the nationality, domicil or habitual residence of the testator or, in the case of immovables, the *lex situs*.

A will exercising a power of appointment is also duly executed for these purposes if its execution is in the manner prescribed by the law governing the essential validity of the instrument creating the power.

It should also be noted that under s 2(2) of the Wills Act 1963, the testamentary exercise of a power of appointment is not formally invalid by reason only of a failure to observe a formality required by the instrument of creation.

(d) Essential validity

The effect of an appointment under a special power will be subject to the law governing the instrument creating the power.

The effect in respect of a general power relating to movables depends upon the circumstances and is a matter of construction. If the settled property was treated by the donee as his own, the operation and effect of the will exercising the power are determined by the law of the donee's domicil at death. If the settled property, though subject to a general power of appointment, has been kept separate from the donee's own property and the funds remain distinct, then the same law applies to the will making the appointment as would apply in the case of the special power, and that will is to be governed by the law governing the instrument of creation.

Where there is a general power of appointment in respect of immovables the *lex situs* will govern the essential validity of the will exercising that power.

(e) Construction

Whether or not a power of appointment is special or general, the construction is governed by the legal system in the mind of the appointor when the power was created. If there is no expressed intention in the instrument of creation, the intended law will be presumed to be the law of the domicil where that instrument was executed.

Where the appointor (or testator) indicates the intended legal system which is to apply, then such an indication is conclusive, even where the nominated legal system does not recognise the concept of powers.

(f) Revocation

The domicil of the donee will govern the revocation of a power of appointment over movables.

A power of appointment over movables or immovables may be revoked by a properly executed will (which will be valid if it complies with the law governing the legal validity of the power under s 2(1) Wills Act 1963), provided there is another power of appointment drafted in its place.

Where a will is revocable by marriage under the law of the domicil of the testator at the time of such a marriage, then a power under the will may be revoked, but this will not necessarily be the case in England as powers of appointment are saved from revocation by marriage under s 18(2) of the Wills Act 1837 "unless the property so appointed would in default of appointment pass to [the testator's] personal representatives."

5. Inheritance tax

Unless an estate contains no UK property and the testator has no permanent ties with the UK, then inheritance tax provisions cannot be avoided. Even where a person is not actually domiciled in the UK he will be deemed to be domiciled here for inheritance tax purposes if:

(a) he was domiciled in the UK on or after 10 December 1974 and within three years immediately preceding the time at which his domicil is to be determined for IHT purposes; or

(b) he was resident in the UK on or after 10 December 1974 and in not less than seventeen of the twenty years of assessment ending with the year of assessment in which his domicil falls to be determined for IHT purposes (s 267 Inheritance Tax Act 1984).

Chapter 11

Legacies

There are three types of legacy that may be made in a will, namely:
- (a) a specific legacy;
- (b) a general legacy; or
- (c) a demonstrative legacy.

The category into which any particular gift falls is a question of construction.

1. Specific legacies

A specific legacy is a gift by will of some specified and distinguishable property forming part of the testator's estate at death, for example, "I give my grandfather clock to X." Any word of possession or reference to the acquisition of the specified property by the testator indicates that the testator intended to give that property, and not some property of the same kind to be purchased by the executors.

(a) Gifts of personal chattels

Where the testator wishes to make a gift of all his personal chattels, the phrase should be defined, usually by reference to s 55(1)(x) of the Administration of Estates Act 1925, in order to avoid any confusion (see Chapter 22 for a full discussion of the meaning of the term personal chattels). Individual items can be listed, although this makes no allowance for future additions to the property and can be cumbersome. It may be useful to incorporate Form 2 of the Statutory Will Forms 1925 (Appendix B), as this enables the will to be simplified and shortened.

C.11.1 Gift of personal chattels by incorporation of Statutory Will Forms 1925, Form 2

I GIVE to my wife [name] absolutely all my personal chattels and Form 2 of the Statutory Will Forms, 1925 is incorporated in this my will for that purpose.

C.11.2 Gift of personal chattels by incorporation of definition in the Administration of Estates Act 1925

I GIVE all my personal chattels as defined in Section 55(1)(x) of the Administration of Estates Act 1925 to my wife [name] absolutely PROVIDED THAT this disposition shall take effect subject to such specific gifts as are contained herein or in any codicil hereto.

C.11.3 Gift of personal chattels to wife

I GIVE to my wife [name] absolutely all my horses stable furniture and effects (not used for business purposes) garden effects domestic animals plate plated articles linen glass china books pictures prints furniture jewellery articles for household or personal use or ornament (including wearing apparel) also musical and scientific instruments and apparatus wines liquors and consumable stores but there is not included herein any chattels used at my death for business purposes nor money nor securities for money and this gift shall take effect subject to any specific disposition.

Note: This clause is akin to Form 2 of the Statutory Will Forms, 1925.

C.11.4 Gift of personal chattels – short form

I GIVE to my wife [name] absolutely all articles of personal domestic household or garden use or ornament not otherwise specifically disposed of by the provisions of this my will or by any codicil hereto.

C.11.5 Gift to wife of such articles as she may select

I GIVE to my wife [name] absolutely such of my personal chattels as defined in Section 55(1)(x) of the Administration of Estates Act

1925 other than those specifically disposed of by the provisions of
this my will or by any codicil hereto as she may select within [six]
months after my death (the selection period) and any such articles
not selected by her within the said time shall fall into my residuary
estate [PROVIDED THAT during the said selection period no beneficiary under the provisions hereof or of any codicil hereto shall be
entitled to the use or enjoyment of any articles which are subject to
this clause and which have not been so selected by my wife] [and
any income thereof shall be accumulated as an accretion to my
residuary estate].

Note: The wife may select the whole of such articles not specifically
bequeathed. If she should die within the selection period then her
right of selection would cease and could not be exercised by her personal representatives.

C.11.6 Gift to wife of part only of personal chattels to be selected by her up to a given value, the remainder to be given to two sons

I GIVE to my wife [name] absolutely such of my personal chattels
as defined in Section 55(1)(x) of the Administration of Estates Act
1925 save those otherwise specifically disposed of as she may within [six] months of my death (the selection period) select up to the
value of [£1000] such value to be determined by my personal representatives in such manner as they think fit and I GIVE the remainder
of my personal chattels as aforesaid not so selected by my said wife
or the whole of them if my wife shall for any reason not make any
selection within the said selection period to my two sons [name] and
[name] in equal shares [and I DIRECT that if there be any dispute as
between my sons aforesaid in respect of any articles then my personal representatives shall sell the same and divide the net proceeds of
such sale between my two sons aforesaid equally].

Note: If only the residue after the wife's selection were given to the sons,
then the latter gift would fail in the event of the wife's predeceasing
the testator – *Boyce* v *Boyce* (1849) 16 Sim 476.

C.11.7 Power to trustees to dispose of articles of little value

My trustees shall have power to dispose by way of gift to whosoever
they think fit such articles of household or personal use or ornament
as in their opinion are of trivial value or for any reason impractical
to sell.

C.11.8 Gift to be distributed in accordance with list left by testator – no trust

I GIVE to [name] absolutely all the contents of my house at [place] and I request that he should distribute the same in accordance with a list to be placed with this will ALWAYS PROVIDED THAT nothing in this gift shall impose any trust or binding obligation on [name] or confer any interest upon any other person and in default of such a list as aforesaid I request [name] to divide the said property between each of my children living at my death as he thinks fit.

Note: For details regarding incorporation see Chapter 3.

This is an absolute gift and the testator should be made aware that the named beneficiary may take the property without carrying out the testator's wishes. This form of gift may be useful if the testator wishes to maintain flexibility without constantly changing or replacing the will, provided the testator can trust the named beneficiary.

Under s 143 of the Inheritance Tax Act 1984 a distribution of personal property made by the legatee in accordance with the will and within two years of the testator's death will be treated as a distribution by the testator for inheritance tax purposes.

(b) Gifts of furniture

The term "furniture" generally means only ordinary household and movable furniture; valuable articles such as fixtures, pictures, books or similar articles should be specifically dealt with.

C.11.9 Gift of furniture to wife

I GIVE to my wife [name] absolutely all my furniture except such as is fixed to the premises whether or not the same is in law a fixture.

C.11.10 Gift to daughter of furniture and effects in her bedroom

I GIVE to my daughter [name] all articles of household or domestic furniture pictures and other effects whatsoever ordinarily used by her in her bedroom in such house as I may reside in at my death.

Note: See Chapter 22 for the meaning of the phrase "as I may reside in at my death".

C.11.11 Gift of furniture and household effects to wife during widow-hood (or for life); no obligation to sign inventory

(1) I GIVE all my household furniture to my wife [name] during her widowhood [life] and upon her remarriage or death whichever shall first happen I DIRECT that the said furniture shall fall into and become part of my residuary estate.

(2) I DECLARE that it shall be a condition of this gift that my wife shall keep the said furniture in good repair and insured in the names of my trustees against all risks so far as is practicable ALWAYS PROVIDED THAT all moneys received in respect of any insurance of the said furniture shall be applied in the replacement and rein-statement thereof.

(3) I DECLARE that my trustees shall not be bound to prepare an inventory of the said furniture nor shall my wife be obliged to sign such an inventory and I FURTHER DECLARE that my trustees shall not be personally liable for any loss resulting to my estate aris-ing from the failure of my wife to repair insure or adequately insure the said furniture but that my trustees may take such steps as they consider fit for the protection and preservation of such furniture.

Note: (i) Paragraph 3 releases the tenant for life from signing an inventory and a special direction to this effect is required to remove that obli-gation.

(ii) Where property is given directly to a tenant for life, rather than to trustees, the property is held by the tenant for life as a trustee for himself and the remainderman – *Re Swan* [1915] 1 Ch 829.

(iii) The widow will have an interest in possession for inheritance tax purposes which will terminate on her remarriage, giving rise to a charge to tax under s 52(1) of the Inheritance Tax Act 1984.

(iv) It is not possible to use this form where the subject matter is consumed when used, such as the contents of a wine cellar.

C.11.12 Gift of furniture and effects to wife during widowhood; widow to repair and insure and to sign inventory

(1) I GIVE my furniture books paintings and other household and domestic effects to my trustees UPON TRUST to permit my wife [name] to use the same during her widowhood provided she shall keep the same in good repair and condition and insured in the names of my trustees but at the expense of my said wife for such value and against such risks as my trustees shall consider appropriate and upon the death or remarriage of my said wife whichever shall happen first the said furniture shall fall into and become part of my residuary

estate.

(2) I DIRECT that my trustees shall as soon as practicable after my death make or cause to be made an inventory of all such furniture books paintings and other effects as hereinbefore mentioned and that they shall procure the signature of my said wife upon the said inventory and shall thereafter retain the same in their safekeeping ALWAYS PROVIDED THAT my trustees shall not be held responsible or liable in any way for any loss caused to my residuary estate arising from the failure of my said wife to repair or adequately insure the said furniture and effects [but any moneys received under any insurance policy in respect of the same shall be applied in the replacement and reinstatement of any article lost or damaged].

C.11.13 Gift of furniture to widow for life and then to son, incorporating Statutory Will Form as to inventory

(1) I GIVE all my furniture to my trustees UPON TRUST to permit and suffer my wife [name] to use and enjoy the same during her lifetime and upon her death to hold the same for my son [name] absolutely.

(2) Form No. 3 of the Statutory Will Forms, 1925 is hereby incorporated in this my will.

(3) [Power of reinstatement clause; Form C.11.11 sub-clause (2) – above].

(c) Gifts of copyright, unpublished works and patents

C.11.14 Gift of copyrights and unpublished works to literary executor

I GIVE to my literary executor absolutely all my works manuscripts letters and writings whether published or unpublished together with the copyright and all other rights and privileges in respect thereof for his own absolute use hereof.

C.11.15 Gift of copyrights and unpublished works to literary executors to administer same and transfer net proceeds to general executors and trustees

I GIVE to my literary executors all my works manuscripts letters and writings whether published or unpublished (except those required for the administration of my general estate) together with the copyrights and all other rights and privileges in respect thereof with full liberty to publish any unpublished works and to complete and publish any unfinished work SUBJECT to such terms and conditions as my literary executors may in their absolute discretion think fit PROVIDED THAT my literary executors shall not be liable for any loss sustained in the exercise of such discretion which shall primarily be borne by the literary assets hereby bequeathed and thereafter by my general estate AND I DECLARE THAT my literary executors shall collect all payments of every kind made in respect of my works as aforesaid and after defraying thereout all administrative and other expenses necessary to carry out the terms of this bequest shall transfer the net proceeds to my trustees to hold upon the same trusts as are herein declared in respect of my residuary estate.

C.11.16   Gift of patents

1. I GIVE all patents and interests in patents to which I am entitled to my trustees with full power to deal with the same as if absolute beneficial owners thereof.

2. My trustees shall hold the said patents [upon the trusts herein declared in respect of my residuary estate] [upon the following trusts].

(d) Gifts of stocks and shares

A gift of stocks and shares may be either specific or general. It is specific if it is, for example, a gift of "my shares" or "such shares in X company as I own at date of my death", and the testator dies owning shares, or such shares.

Alternatively, the gift of shares may be a general legacy if worded in the following manner "Y [number] of shares in Z company Plc". In this case the executor will be obliged to purchase that number of shares in the specified company if the testator does not own such shares at the date of his death. In the former case, if there were no shares, or no shares in the specified company, in the estate, the gift would lapse.

Whether a gift is specific or general in nature is a question of construction which depends on the wording of the will.

C.11.17   Gift of stock – general legacy

I GIVE to [name] absolutely £500 worth of 2% consolidated stock and I DECLARE this gift to be a general legacy and not a specific legacy.

Note: See *Re Compton* [1914] 2 Ch 119.

C.11.18 Gift of stock – specific legacy

I GIVE to [name] absolutely all the 2% consolidated stock standing in my name at the date of my death as a specific legacy.

C.11.19 Gift of shares in public or private company – provision for lesser number of shares only being available

I GIVE to [name] absolutely [1,000] of my shares in X company [Limited] [plc] ALWAYS PROVIDED THAT if the number of shares in the said X company [Limited] [plc] held by me at the time of my death be insufficient to satisfy the provisions of this legacy then I GIVE to the said [name] in lieu of each share by which my holding in the said company falls short a sum equal to the mean market value of such shares at the date of my death [such value to be ascertained by my trustees by such means as they in their absolute discretion think fit] AND I DIRECT that any charge affecting any shares given hereunder shall be discharged primarily from my residuary estate.

Note: A provision regarding valuation is generally required only where the relevant shares are not officially quoted.

C.11.20 Specific legacy of shares with words added negativing apportionment

I GIVE to [name] all my [500] £1 ordinary shares in ...... [plc] [Limited] now standing in my name together with all dividends already accrued due or accruing thereon at my death.

Note: Under the Apportionment Act 1870, dividends due before the death of the testator would form part of his residuary estate unless the will provided otherwise. The specific legatee is entitled to dividends accruing after death. The dividend moneys paid after death would have to be apportioned. The rules of apportionment apply generally to securities of both public and private companies. If the gift were of loan securities, such as debentures, a similar provision regarding accrued interest should be included. Arrears of dividends on cumulative preference shares are not apportioned; see *Re Wakley* [1920] 2 Ch 205. The apportionment rules do not apply to general legacies, as the legatee is entitled only to dividends accruing after the transfer of shares to him. If the transfer of shares is delayed for longer than one year from the testator's death then the legatee is entitled to interest on the value of the legacy until such time as the shares are transferred to him: *Re Hall* [1951] 1 All ER 1073. As to a gift of shares with "current" dividends, see *Re Raven* (1915) 111 LTR 938, and compare *Re Joel* [1936] 2 All ER 962. See also Chapter 20 for further details of apportionment.

(e)   Miscellaneous specific legacies

C.11.21   Gift of a library

I GIVE to [name] absolutely all my bookcases and library books save those otherwise specifically disposed of hereby or by any codicil hereto.

C.11.22   Gift of a stamp collection

I GIVE to [name] absolutely my collection of stamps together with all albums catalogues accessories loose stamps covers and other materials appertaining thereto [to a value not exceeding £......] [AND I DIRECT that if there be a disagreement such value shall be ascertained in such manner as my personal representatives shall determine] [AND I DIRECT that the value to be taken shall be the value agreed with the Capital Taxes Office for probate purposes].

Note: The phrase "taken at probate valuation" is the valuation put on the gift in the Inland Revenue affidavit for probate purposes: *Re Eumorfopoulos* [1944] Ch 133. However, the phrase "at the valuation agreed for probate" is said to be "the valuation ultimately agreed with the Stamp Duty Officer": *Re De Lisle's Will Trusts* [1968] 1 All ER 492.

C.11.23 Gift of entailed personalty

I GIVE all my personal property of which I am a tenant in tail in possession under [particulars of will or settlement] to [name] absolutely.

C.11.24   Gift of money secured by an assurance policy on testator's life

I GIVE to [name] absolutely all moneys due under the policy of assurance on my life with policy number ...... effected with the ...... Life Assurance Society including all bonuses and other sums payable in respect thereof [SUBJECT to any charge on the said policy as there may be at the date of my death].

Note: The words in brackets are not strictly necessary since s 35 of the Administration of Estates Act 1925 states that, in the absence of any indication or provision to the contrary, property or an interest in property charged with the payment of money has to bear that charge. An expression of contrary intention may be inserted but it must state from what property the charge is to be paid, and must show how the charge is to be met between the specific donee and the residuary estate. A direction may be included to pay any charge out of residue. It will be noted that life policies and shares are frequently used as security for loans and may be subject to such charges; see *Re Turner* [1938] 1 Ch 593. Furthermore a charge may arise where a testator makes a gift of land contracted to be purchased but dies before completion. In such a case there is a charge on the property in respect of any unpaid purchase moneys.

C.11.25 Clause exonerating specific bequests from charges

I DIRECT that if any property being the subject matter of any specific gift under this my will or any codicil hereto is subject at the date of my death to any charge for the payment of money then such charge shall be discharged primarily out of my residuary estate in exoneration of the property so charged.

C.11.26 Gift of ready money

I GIVE to my wife absolutely all ready money that is to say any cash in notes and coins and also all money standing to my credit on any current account in my name at the ...... Bank.

Note: The term "money" can lead to difficulties; see Chapter 22.

C.11.27 Gift of proceeds of premium savings bonds and prizes awarded since the testator's death

I DIRECT my trustees to cash all premium savings bonds in my name at the time of my death and I GIVE the net proceeds thereof together with any prize moneys arising therefrom since the date of my death to [beneficiary].

Note: Premium bonds are not transferable.

2. General legacies

A general legacy is a gift of money or property to be provided out of the testator's general estate whether or not the subject matter forms part of that estate at the testator's death. A general legacy is not made specific merely by the fact that the property referred to actually forms part of the testator's estate at death. The executors may, but need not, use the existing property to satisfy the legacy, or they may prefer to purchase other property in the same form out of the residue. A legacy is general unless the subject matter is referred to as belonging to the testator or otherwise defined to exclude the possibility of a replacement fitting the same description.

C.11.28 Immediate legacy to wife

I GIVE to my wife [name] the sum of £...... AND I DIRECT that the said sum shall be paid to her as soon as is practicable after my death in priority to all other legacies herein or in any codicil hereto.

C.11.29 Legacy to individual

I GIVE to [name] of [address] the sum of £...... [free of inheritance tax] [to be paid ...... months after my death].

Note: The time for payment does not place any obligation on the executors to pay the legacy within the executor's year, but interest on the legacy will run from the date on which the legacy is due to be paid (see Chapter 18).

C.11.30 Legacies given by reference to a schedule

I GIVE to each person or institution in the schedule following this clause such sum as appears opposite each name in the second column thereof AND I DECLARE that the receipt of the treasurer or other proper officer for the time being of any institution named in the said schedule shall be a sufficient discharge to my trustees in respect of the legacy herein bequeathed to it.

SCHEDULE

Name of Legatee	Amount of Legacy

C.11.31 Power to trustees to postpone payment of legacies

I DECLARE THAT my trustees shall have full power to postpone the payment of any legacy made in this my will or in any codicil hereto for so long as they shall in their absolute discretion think fit but not exceeding [three] years from the date of my death ALWAYS PROVIDED THAT any such postponed legacy shall carry interest from the date of my death until payment at the rate of [4] per cent per annum.

C.11.32 Legacy with a clause of substitution in the case of an individual legatee

I GIVE £1000 [free of inheritance tax] to A PROVIDED THAT if the said A shall die before me then I GIVE the said sum of £1000 to B.

C.11.33 Legacy to a creditor

I GIVE to [creditor] [free of inheritance tax] the sum of £500 and I declare that this gift is not made to discharge the debt due from me to him but is to be paid in addition thereto as an absolute gift.

C.11.34 Legacy to a debtor subject to deduction of sums owing

I GIVE to [debtor] the sum of [£5000] less any sums owed by him to me at my death AND I DIRECT my personal representative to release all documents and securities as may be held by me as security in respect of such sums and to execute at the expense of my residuary estate all proper releases surrenders or other documents required for the release of the said securities as aforesaid.

C.11.35 Legacy to minor

I GIVE to [minor] the sum of £1000 [free of inheritance tax] PROVIDED THAT:

(i) If the said [minor] shall at the time when the above legacy is payable have attained the age of sixteen years then the receipt of the said [minor] shall be a full and proper discharge to my trustees for the payment of the same.

(ii) If at the time when the above legacy is paid the said [minor] shall not have attained the age of sixteen years then the receipt of his parent or guardian shall be a full and proper discharge to my trustees for the payment of the same.

Note: Whenever property is given to a minor outside a trust, proper directions should be given for the discharge of the testator's personal representatives.

Where the legacy is small it is easier to allow the minor to sign a receipt for the moneys, provided he is of reasonable age. If the minor is too young or the legacy is large, the receipt of the minor's parent may be sought. As an alternative the personal representative may be directed to open a National Savings Bank Account in the name of the minor and to give the pass book to him.

For substantial sums, where no directions are given, the personal representatives of the testator may do any of the following:

(a) if they are the trustees of the will, retain the legacy together with accrued interest upon trust until the minor attains his majority; or

(b) pay the money into court under the Trustee Act 1925, s 63; or

(c) appoint trustees to hold the money until the minor's majority under the Administration of Estates Act 1925, s 42.

Where trustees retain the sums due to the minor they would be well advised to invest them in government stocks redeemable at the time of the minor's coming of age.

C.11.36 Legacy to minor with provision for advancing capital for maintenance, education, advancement or other benefit

I GIVE to [name] the sum of [£5000] [free of inheritance tax] and I DECLARE that if the said [name] shall not have attained the age of eighteen years at the time of my death my trustees may invest the same as they in their absolute discretion think fit as if beneficially entitled thereto and I DECLARE that my trustees may advance the whole or any part of the said sum and the whole or any part of the income therefrom in such manner as they shall in their absolute discretion think proper for the maintenance education advancement or benefit of the said [name] including the provision of an allowance for him during his minority and I FURTHER DECLARE that if all or any part of the said sum together with the income therefrom shall not be applied during the minority of the said [name] as aforesaid then the said sum or so much thereof as shall not have been so applied shall be paid to the said [name] upon his attaining the age of eighteen years ALWAYS PROVIDED THAT if the said [name] shall die before attaining the age of eighteen years the money held by my trustees under the provision shall be paid to the personal representatives of the said [name].

C.11.37 Legacy of a capital sum for the education of children

I GIVE the sum of [£1000] (the fund) [free of inheritance tax] to my trustees to invest the same in any investments hereby or by statute authorised with full power to vary and transpose the same and to hold such investments and the income thereof upon the following trusts:

(a) UPON TRUST to apply the income thereof at the sole discretion of my trustees for the education of my children who shall be under the age of [twenty-five] years or any one or more of them to the exclusion of the other or others in such manner and in such amounts as my trustees shall in their absolute discretion think fit.

(b) UPON TRUST in so far as the income of the fund proves to be insufficient for the purposes of the education of my said children to apply so much of the capital thereof as my trustees in their absolute discretion think necessary for the education of my children.

(c) For a period of twenty-one years from the date of my death my trustees shall invest any surplus income from the fund in any authorised investments to be held as augmentations to the said fund and after the expiration of the said twenty-one years all surplus income shall be deemed to be and distributed as part of my residuary estate.

(d) I DECLARE that my trustees may provide out of the said fund such books of reference or of any educational nature and all such instruments and other things as may be reasonably required by my said children in relation to such education and as my trustees in their absolute discretion think fit AND I FURTHER DIRECT that the term education shall be interpreted for the purposes of the trusts hereunder to include training articles pupillage or apprenticeship in relation to any trade or profession.

(e) When all my children shall have attained the age of [twenty-five] years or have died under that age the said fund or as much thereof as has not been expended in the execution of the foregoing trusts shall fall into and form part of my residuary estate.

C.11.38 Legacy to children including an illegitimate child

I GIVE to each of my children (including my child [name]) the sum of £400 [free of inheritance tax].

Note: The expressions "child", "son", "daughter" and "issue" now *prima facie* include illegitimate children, sons, daughters or issue. However, an express provision is advisable, especially where there could be a doubt as to paternity.

C.11.39 Legacy contingent on attaining eighteen or twenty-one or earlier marriage

I GIVE the sum of £1000 [free of inheritance tax] to [name] if he shall attain the age of [eighteen] [twenty-one] years [or marry under the age and in the latter event the receipt of the said [name] shall be sufficient discharge to my trustees] [and I DIRECT that such sum shall carry interest at the rate of [5] per cent per annum from my death until the said [name] attains the age of [eighteen] [twenty-one] years [or marries under that age]].

C.11.40 Legacies to two persons contingently on their attaining eighteen or twenty-one years of age with survivorship provision

I GIVE to each of [name] and [name] the sum of [£500] [free of inheritance tax] contingently on each attaining the age of [eighteen] [twenty-one] years and in the event of either of them dying under the said age the legacy hereby given to the one so dying with all interest accruing thereon shall be paid to the survivor of them on his or her attaining the said age PROVIDED THAT if both of them shall die before attaining the said age then the legacies herein and all interest thereon shall fall into and be distributed as part of my residuary estate.

C.11.41 Legacies with provision where some of the legatees cannot be found

I GIVE the sum of £1000 [free of inheritance tax] to each of my nephews [names] PROVIDED THAT if the whereabouts of any such nephew cannot be ascertained by my trustees by such means as they in their absolute discretion feel appropriate and such nephew does not claim the said legacy within two years of my death then the sum or sums bequeathed to that nephew or those nephews shall fall into and form part of my residuary estate and I DECLARE that the extent and nature of the enquiries made or to be made by my trustees shall not be open to challenge by any beneficiary or potential beneficiary hereunder or by any person or body.

Note: See *Hawkes* v *Baldwin* (1838) 9 Sim 355.

C.11.42 Reduction and abatement where estate insufficient

I DECLARE that in the event that my estate after deduction of any tax due thereon and after the payment of my debts funeral and testamentary expenses shall be insufficient to pay all legacies given by me hereunder and in any codicil hereto then the amount of each and every legacy as aforesaid shall abate and diminish so that the proportion of each legacy to be paid by my trustees to such legatees in satisfaction of the said legacies shall be in the same proportion as against every other such legacy hereunder and so that the total of my estate available to my trustees for the distribution after payment of my debts funeral and testamentary expenses and any taxes from my estate as aforesaid is used in the satisfaction of such legacies.

C.11.43 Declaration as to currency in which legacies payable

I DECLARE that all sums of money payable under this my will

shall be paid in pounds sterling.

3. Demonstrative legacies

A demonstrative legacy is, in essence, similar to a general legacy but in addition it contains a direction as to which property or fund is to be used first to satisfy the legacy.

The gift does not adeem merely because the fund or property specified is insufficient to meet the legacy. If there is a shortfall in the specified property then the remainder of the legacy will be payable out of the testator's general personal estate and that remainder will have the same priority as other general legacies.

C.11.44 Demonstrative legacy

I GIVE to [name] the sum of £1,000 to be paid primarily out of my deposit account with the ...... Bank plc PROVIDED THAT if there are insufficient funds in the said account to pay the whole of the legacy herein then any shortfall shall be payable out of my residuary estate.

4. Gifts to a debtor

Where a testator leaves money to a person who owes a debt to him, the amount of the debt will be set off against the legacy and the amount of the legacy actually paid reduced accordingly, but this does *not* apply where the bequest is a specific legacy unless it is of a sum of money.

Any of the following gifts may be subject to set-off:

(a) a pecuniary legacy;
(b) a gift of all or part of the residuary personal estate;
(c) a gift of part or all of the residuary estate where it includes either personalty or the proceeds of sale of realty or both;
(d) a specific legacy if (and only if) of money;
(e) a gift of personalty subject to a partial intestacy;
(f) the proceeds of sale under a trust for sale (although the proceeds of sale of personalty are applied to discharge debts prior

to the application of the proceeds of sale of realty).

The debt must be brought into account against all such interests under a will, regardless of how they are acquired. Thus, interests purchased from other beneficiaries and reversionary interests are also subject to the rule of set-off.

Only debts which are due to the testator personally and payable at the time the legacy is payable may be deducted. Debts due from a partnership in which the legatee is a partner are not deductible from the legacy.

Included in the debts which must be brought into account are the following:

(a) debts which are statute-barred when the testator dies;

(b) debts of which the testator was only an equitable owner;

(c) debts due from an estate of which the legatee is an executor.

C.11.45 Gift of a debt

I GIVE to [name] absolutely all moneys owing to me from [debtor] and all interest due and to become due in respect thereof together with all mortgages or other securities that I may hold in respect of the same at my death [and I appoint him executor of this my will so far as regards the said sums of money interest mortgages and securities].

Note: The words in square brackets give the legatee the ability to sue for the debt in his own name if he proves the will.

C.11.46 Release to a debtor of a debt

I forgive and release to [debtor] all moneys now owing by him to me.

C.11.47 Release of debts – including future debts

I RELEASE [debtor] from all debts owed by him to me at the date of my death whether of principal or interest and I DIRECT that any mortgages bonds or other securities in respect of any such debt shall be cancelled and released to [debtor] as soon as practicable after my death and my personal representative shall execute and deliver to [debtor] all necessary receipts reconveyances or reassignments AND I DECLARE that if the said [debtor] shall fail to survive me then this provision shall take effect as if the said [debtor] died immediately after my death and the benefit of the same shall pass to [debtor's] personal representatives accordingly.

Note: A provision forgiving or releasing all debts due to the testator may give rise to problems in respect of debentures held by the testator, balance at the testator's bank and the effect on secured and unsecured debts.

C.11.48 Release of mortgage debt to the mortgagor

I forgive and release to [mortgagor] absolutely all sums of principal and interest both due or accruing due at the date of my death and secured on [property] by a mortgage dated ...... and made between [parties] and I DIRECT my trustees at the cost to my residuary estate as soon as practicable after my death to execute in favour of the said [mortgagor] a full discharge of the said mortgage and of all claims thereunder and to deliver up to him all title deeds and other documents held by me in respect thereof.

C.11.49 Provision for hotchpot in respect of release of debt

I DIRECT that where any debts or other sums of money due or accruing due to my estate from the said [debtor] have been released by the provisions of this my will or any codicil hereto the said sums together with interest thereon from the date of my death [to the date of final distribution of my residuary estate] at the rate of [8] per cent per annum shall be brought into hotchpot as against the share of my residuary estate (hereby given to [debtor]) [in which the said [debtor] takes a life interest hereunder].

C.11.50 Declaration that gifts should not be brought into hotchpot

I DECLARE that [name] shall not be liable to repay or bring into account any sums given to him during my lifetime and my personal representatives shall make no claim against the said [name] or his estate.

5. Gifts to an executor

There is a presumption that any gift made by will to a person appointed as an executor is given to that person by reason of that office. The presumption may be rebutted, for example, by a statement in the gift that it is given to the executor as a relative or friend. The type of gift, for example, a gift of residue or a gift over after the death of a tenant for life, may also be sufficient to rebut the presumption.

Where a legacy is given to a person as executor he will not be entitled to the benefit of the gift if, for any reason, he fails to take up the office.

Legacies attached to the office of executor rank equally with other ordinary legacies and are therefore subject to abatement and tax.

Gifts to solicitors made in addition to a charging clause and conditional upon the proving of the will have been interpreted as reward for non-professional work as executor (*Re Parry* [1969] 2 All ER 512).

Where a testator has sought to make an *inter vivos* gift to a person and the gift has failed for technical reasons the appointment of that person as executor or trustee of the will may perfect the gift, provided it can be shown that the testator had a continuing intention to make the gift *(Strong* v *Bird* (1874) LR 18 Eq 315 and *Re Ralli's Marriage Settlement* [1964] Ch 288).

C.11.51 Legacy to executor and trustee

I GIVE to each of my trustees [names] [free of inheritance tax] the sum of [£1000] provided that he prove my will and act in the trusts thereof.

C.11.52 Annuity to trustee

(1) I GIVE to each of the trustees for the time being of this my will an annuity of [£500] per annum to be paid in equal half-yearly payments and to be clear of all deductions including income tax deductible at source.

(2) Any annuities payable hereunder shall commence from the expiration of one year from the date on which the said trustee takes office and continue so long as the trustee acts in the trusts hereof and shall accrue from day to day and be apportionable accordingly.

6. Gifts to employees

Where the legatees are described in the will by means of their employment then *prima facie* those fitting the description at the date of the will, and not the date of the testator's death, will take the gift.

Where a testator makes a gift to his employees as a class, rather than as named individuals, the members of that class will be ascertained as at the time of the will, rather than at the testator's death, unless the gift provides otherwise.

C.11.53 Legacy to housekeeper

I GIVE to my housekeeper [name] if in my service at the time of my death the sum of [£1000] [free of inheritance tax] in addition to any sums then owing to her for wages or otherwise and if she shall have left my service I GIVE her the sum of [£500] [free of inheritance tax].

Note: The words "at the time of my death" exclude a person who leaves the testator's service between the making of the will and the testator's death.

7. Gifts of undivided shares of personalty

The rules relating to the co-ownership of personalty differ significantly from those governing realty. Sections 34 to 36 of the Law of Property Act 1925 and s 36 of the Settled Land Act 1925 have no application to personalty. The result is legal joint tenancies and tenancies in common can co-exist, although a chose in action is an exception to the general rule and cannot be held under a legal tenancy in common.

C.11.54 Bequest of undivided share in personal property

I GIVE to [name] all my share and interest in any [car] owned by me at the date of my death as tenant in common with [co-owner] [or with any other person].

8. Gifts of settled legacies

C.11.55 Settled legacy – concise form

I GIVE to my trustees the sum of [£1000] [free of tax] upon trust to invest the same in any investments authorised by law for the investment of trust funds with power to vary the same as they shall in their absolute discretion think fit and to hold the same in trust to pay the income therefrom to [name] during his life and from and after his death as to both capital and income for all or any of the children or child of [name] who attain the age of [eighteen] years or marry under that age and if more than one in equal shares.

C.11.56 Settled legacy incorporating the Statutory Will Forms 1925, Form 7

I GIVE to [legatee] the sum of £...... [free of any inheritance tax and foreign death duties] and I declare Form 7 of the Statutory Will Forms, 1925 is incorporated in this my will and shall apply to this legacy [subject to the following modifications].

Chapter 12

Gifts of businesses

Where the testator is a partner in a business, any partnership deed or agreement must be consulted before drafting a gift concerning the business. Such a document may provide that on the death of any partner, the surviving partners may buy the testator's interest in the partnership from his estate.

Where there is no deed or agreement, or where there is such a document but it contains no provisions for the death of a partner, then the death of any partner will cause the dissolution of the partnership and the amount due to the deceased partner for his interest must be paid to his personal representatives.

If the business in question is incorporated, the testator can deal with his shares in accordance with the Articles of Association of the company. It may be that the Articles provide for the appointment by will of a permanent director to succeed the testator if he himself was a permanent director.

C.12.1 Gift of a small business

(1) I GIVE to [name] all my business of ...... trading as [name of business] from the premises of [address[es]] to include [the said premises and] all plant machinery stocks vehicles tools and all other things employed or used in carrying on the said business together with the goodwill of the same and the benefits of all contracts entered into and all book debts due to the said business and together

also with any cash at bank and cash in hand but subject in all respects to the liabilities of the said business.

(2) In the event of any premises from which my business trades being held under a lease or tenancy agreement at the time of my death then the said [name] shall pay the rent due from time to time in respect of those premises and shall observe and perform the lessee's covenants under the said lease or tenancy agreement and shall keep my estate indemnified against all liability under the said lease or tenancy including any liability that may have arisen in my lifetime or from acts or omissions done or arising in my lifetime.

(3) I appoint the said [name] as special executor of this my will to act only in respect of the business and other property bequeathed to him and I direct that the inheritance tax attributed to the above gift (allowing for any reduction in value for inheritance tax purposes) and the expenses of obtaining a grant limited to such property shall be paid by the said [name].

Note: Where a gift is of a "business", this will normally be taken to include all the testator's interest in all the assets of the business, including business premises – *Re Rhagg* [1938] Ch 828.

See Appendix A for a complete will disposing of a business.

C.12.2 Gift to trustees of a business upon trust to carry on for a limited period

I GIVE to my trustees all my business of ...... trading as [name of business] from the premises of [address[es]] to include [the said premises and] all plant machinery stocks vehicles tools and all other things employed or used in carrying on the said business together with the goodwill of the same and the benefits of all contracts entered into and all book debts due to the said business and together also with any cash at bank and cash in hand but subject in all respects to the liabilities of the said business UPON the following trusts:-

(1) To carry on the said business and/or any other business on the said premises or any other suitable premises for so long and in such manner and on such terms as they in their sole discretion may think fit and subject thereto without being liable to my estate for any loss arising therefrom.

(2) Upon trust to sell the said business including any premises used in connection with the said business as a going concern together with the goodwill thereof and all the then existing assets thereof or such of them as my trustees think fit but subject to the liabilities

thereof or such of them as my trustees think fit upon such terms as they may in their sole discretion think proper [and thereafter the proceeds of sale of the said business shall fall into and become part of my residuary estate].

C.12.3 Trusts of net profits until sale of business and proceeds of sale

I DECLARE that my trustees shall stand possessed of the said business and the net annual profits thereof after payment of all the expenses and liabilities of the same until sale of the said business as aforesaid and after the said sale shall also stand possessed of the net proceeds of sale thereof and of any other moneys arising therefrom or in connection therewith and of the income of such proceeds of sale and other moneys UPON TRUST to pay such annual profits or income as the case may be to my wife [name] during her life and after her death as to the said business and the said annual profits or (as the case may be) the said proceeds of sale and other moneys and the income thereof respectively UPON TRUST etc.

C.12.4 Provision for child of testator to take on business on payment to trustees

(1) I DECLARE that if any child of mine shall give notice to my trustees within [three] months of my death of his or her wish to carry on my said business and shall pay to my trustees the sum of £...... such sum if not paid at once to be paid within a period not exceeding [two] years from the date of my death and to bear interest at the rate of [five] per cent per annum then my trustees shall transfer the business as aforesaid including any premises but subject to all liabilities of the business to my said child and my trustees shall stand possessed of the said sum of £ ...... and any interest thereon as and when the same shall be received upon the following trusts ....
(2) I FURTHER DECLARE that where more than one of my children wish to carry on my business and give notice to my trustees as hereinbefore prescribed then the eldest of such children shall be entitled to the transfer of the business to his or her name on the making of the payments as aforesaid and in priority to and to the exclusion of my other children.

C.12.5 Power to trustees to carry on business where there is a trust for sale

I DECLARE that my trustees shall have full power to carry on my business of ...... at ...... and to postpone the sale and conversion thereof into money for so long as they shall think fit until such time as the same may be sold either as a going concern or otherwise and that during any period when the business is being carried on by my trustees they shall be free from control or interference from any person or persons beneficially entitled to the said business or the proceeds of sale thereof under this my will.

C.12.6 Power for willing trustees to carry on testator's business where other trustees refuse

I DECLARE that should any one or more of my trustees be unwilling to carry on my business then the other or others of my trustees may carry on such business and may exercise alone all powers authorities and discretions hereby conferred on my trustees in relation to carrying on the said business or the winding up or sale of the said business.

C.12.7 Provision of salary for trustees managing business

I DECLARE that any one or more or my trustees who act as manager or manageress of my business aforesaid shall be entitled to [a salary of £ ...... per annum] [such salary as may be agreed upon by my trustees for the time being] throughout the period during which he she or they shall so act without being liable to account to my estate in respect thereof.

C.12.8 Provision for exercise of powers though trustees interested in business

All or any of the above powers hereinbefore granted to my trustees shall be exercisable and may be exercised by any of my trustees notwithstanding that he or she may be interested as a partner in the said business or as a beneficiary under this my will.

C.12.9 Indemnity to trustees carrying on business

I DIRECT that each and every one of my trustees concerned in the running of my business shall be fully and effectively indemnified from my estate in respect of any personal loss or liability arising from the carrying on of the said business and I DECLARE that none of my trustees shall be liable to my estate or any part thereof for any loss arising from the carrying on of the said business.

Chapter 13

Gifts of land

1. General

Before drafting any provision dealing with land the draftsman should check the nature of the testator's interest in the property with the title deeds or office copy entries to ensure that the descriptions in both correspond with each other.

C.13.1 Absolute general gift of all freehold property

I DEVISE all my estate or interest in all my freehold property whatsoever and wheresoever situate including any property over which I may have any general power of disposition by will [and including all freehold land of which I am tenant in tail in possession under (describe the will and settlement)] to [name] absolutely.

Note: As to a devise of property of which the testator is tenant in tail in possession see Law of Property Act 1925, s 176.

Where the subject matter of the gift is referred to as "my land" or by some other generic term the gift is construed to include leasehold estates, unless a contrary intention appears. (See Chapter 22.)

C.13.2 Specific gift of freeholds

I DEVISE to [name] in fee simple my freehold property situate and known as ...... in the county of ...... [together with and subject to all easements appurtenances and other rights affecting the said property

124

or appertaining or reputed to appertain thereto or to any part thereof].

Note: The words in square brackets are required only if the testator owns land adjoining the property.

C.13.3 Specific gift of freehold land (free from inheritance tax)

I GIVE to [name] in fee simple absolutely my freehold property situate at and known as ...... in the county of ...... and I DIRECT that any inheritance tax payable on my death in respect of the property shall be payable out of my residuary estate in exoneration of the said property [and in priority to the pecuniary legacies given by this my said will or any codicil hereto].

Note: The payment of inheritance tax from the estate is treated as an additional pecuniary legacy for the purposes of abatement – see Administration of Justice Act 1925, s 55(1)(ix). The words in square brackets may be required if the gift is to have priority over other pecuniary legacies.

If there is no direction as to the payment of tax then inheritance tax on the land will be borne by the beneficiary to whom it is given.

C.13.4 Specific gift of registered land

I GIVE to [name] [in fee simple] my freehold property registered at the ...... District Land Registry under Title No ...... and known as ...... [and I DECLARE that all costs of the registration of the said [devisee] with absolute title thereto shall be payable out of my residuary estate].

Note: The cost of vesting a specific gift in the beneficiary is payable by the beneficiary unless there is a direction to the contrary.

C.13.5 Gift to joint tenants or tenants in common

I GIVE my freehold house and premises situate at and known as ...... [and now in the occupation of [tenant]] to my children [names] as joint tenants [or as tenants in common in equal shares].

C.13.6 Specific gift of property with provision against apportionment

I GIVE to [name] in fee simple my freehold property situate at and known as ...... in the county of ...... together with all the rents and profits due or accruing in respect thereof whether before or after my death but subject to the payment by the said [name] of all outgoings and expenses usually chargeable against the income of such property.

Note: As to outgoings usually chargeable against income see *Eccles* v *Mills* [1898] AC 360; *Re Hughes* [1913] 2 Ch 491.

C.13.7 Gift subject to a mortgage

I DEVISE my freehold land situate at and known as ...... subject to and charged with the payment of all principal sums and interest secured thereon by way of mortgage or otherwise at my death to [name] absolutely.

Note: In the absence of an express contrary intention a beneficiary of any property or interest in property will be primarily liable for the payment of any money charged on that property at the time of the deceased's death – see the Administration of Estates Act 1925, s 35, and the definition of property in s 55(1)(xvii). The fact that the mortgage debt attributable to the property exceeds the value of the property itself does not amount to a contrary intention for these purposes. However, if it is intended that the gift be subject to outstanding charges it is better in the interests of certainty expressly to state that fact.

Where other property forming part of the residuary estate is also subject to the mortgage or charge affecting the specific gift, then the debt is apportioned between the different properties according to value – *Re Neeld* [1962] Ch 643.

C.13.8 Gift of land free from a mortgage debt

I DEVISE my freehold lands situate [etc] to [name] absolutely free and discharged from all sums secured thereon by way of mortgage or otherwise at my death and I DIRECT that such sums including all interest in respect thereof and also the costs and expenses relating to the discharge of the said mortgage or charge [and of the registration of the absolute title of [name]] shall be paid out of my residuary estate.

C.13.9 Gift of freeholds subject to the payment of a legacy

I DEVISE my lands situate [etc] to [devisee] subject to and charged with the payment of [the clear sum of] £...... to [legatee] and the said [devisee] accepting this devise shall [not] be personally liable for such payment.

[Or I CHARGE my lands situate [etc] with the payment of [the clear sum of] £...... to [legatee] and subject to such charge devise the same to [devisee].]

Note: Where a gift of land is made upon the condition of certain payments by the devisee to another, those payments are usually construed as being a charge upon the land.

C.13.10 Gift subject to the payment of debts, funeral and testamentary expenses

I GIVE my freehold lands situate [etc] but subject to and charged [in exoneration of my personal estate] with the payment of my debts funeral and testamentary expenses and the legacies and annuities given by this my will and any codicil hereto and the inheritance tax on any legacy or annuity bequeathed free of inheritance tax to [devisee] absolutely.

C.13.11 Devise in exercise of a special power of appointment

In accordance with the will of [name] deceased dated ...... which will was proved in the [Principal] [......District Probate] Registry of the Family Division on...... [and in exercise of the power therein contained] and of every or any other power enabling me in this behalf I DEVISE and appoint such freehold property and such capital moneys and investments which may at my death be subject to such power of appointment to [names] [in equal shares as tenants in common absolutely].

C.13.12 Gift by reference to a settlement on trust for sale

I GIVE all my [freehold land] unto my trustees upon trust to vest the same in the trustees for the time being of a conveyance dated ...... and made between [parties] upon trust for sale and to hold the rents profits and other income thereof until sale and net proceeds of sale and the income thereof upon the trusts declared by the trust instrument referred to in the said conveyance in so far as the same are for the time being subsisting and capable of taking effect and so that the property hereby devised shall be dealt with and treated as if the same had formed part of the property conveyed in the said conveyance.

Note: Adding property to an existing settlement should be avoided if possible since it may be unclear how the original trusts and powers apply to the new property, and because it can be disadvantageous for inheritance tax purposes if the testator is the settlor of the settlement, especially if the original settlement is a discretionary settlement created before 27 March 1974.

C.13.13 Gift of real estate to testator's eldest son or his issue with successive gifts over to younger sons and issue

I GIVE all [my real estate] to my eldest son [name] in fee simple but if he shall die in my lifetime leaving [male] issue living at my death or then en ventre but born thereafter then to his personal representatives as part of his estate and in default of my said son or his personal representatives becoming entitled thereto hereunder I DEVISE the same to my second son [name] in fee simple but if my said son dies in my lifetime leaving [male] issue living at my death or then en ventre but born thereafter then to his personal representatives as part of his estate and in default of my said son or his personal representatives becoming entitled thereto hereunder I DECLARE that all my said real property shall fall into and form part of my residuary estate.

Note: But for the words vesting the property in the son's personal representatives, s 33 of the Wills Act 1837, as substituted by s 19 of the Administration of Justice Act 1982, would come into operation and confer an interest on the issue by substitution in the event of the son's predeceasing the testator. No inheritance tax will be payable on the estate of the son if he predeceases the testator, since the son will not at his death be beneficially entitled to anything under the testator's will.

C.13.14 Gift with provisions against lapse

I DEVISE all my freehold lands to [name] absolutely and if my said [nephew] shall fail to survive me then to his personal representatives as part of his estate as if the said [name] had died immediately following my death.

2. Gifts to minors

A minor cannot hold a legal estate in land, but if land is devised to a minor it will be held in trust for him during his minority – Law of Property Act 1925, s 1(6); Settled Land Act 1925, s 1(1)(ii)(d).

C.13.15 Gift to minor without trust for sale

1. I DEVISE all my freehold property situate at and known as ...... to [minor] absolutely.

2. If the said [minor] shall fail to survive me or shall die under the

age of [eighteen] years without leaving children living at his death
then I DEVISE the said land unto ...... PROVIDED that if the said
[minor] shall either predecease me or shall die under the age of
eighteen years and in either case leave issue living at the date of my
death or thereafter then I DEVISE the said land to such issue and if
more than one as tenants in common in equal shares per stirpes but
so that no issue shall take whose parent is living at my death and so
capable of taking.

3. Directions as to Inheritance Tax

Inheritance tax on a specific devise of land is a testamentary expense
payable out of the residue provided there is no contrary intention
expressed in the will – IHTA 1984, s 211. This section does not, however, treat the IHT attributable to property comprised in a settlement
immediately before the testator's death as a testamentary expense. A
settlement for IHT purposes includes entailed property (s 43(2) IHTA
1984) and therefore any property disposed of by means of a special or
general power of appointment of settled property, or by means of s
176 of the Law of Property Act 1925, bears its own IHT unless the
will demonstrates a contrary intention.

C.13.16 Declaration as to payment of inheritance tax on specific devises
I DECLARE that any inheritance tax payable on my death in respect
of [property] hereinbefore devised to [name] [and any inheritance
tax payable on my death in respect of [property] devised to my
trustees in trust for [name]] shall be a charge on such specifically
devised property in exoneration of my residuary [personal] estate.

C.13.17 Specific devise subject to inheritance tax
I GIVE to [name] in fee simple my freehold property situate at ......
subject to all inheritance tax (if any) attributable thereto and payable
on my death.

4. Gifts of undivided shares and clauses dealing with joint property

Where property is given to several persons concurrently, the question is whether the gift is one of a joint tenancy or a tenancy in common. *Prima facie* the persons take under a joint tenancy but anything indicating an intention to divide the property negatives the presumption.

Any words indicating an intention to divide property creates a tenancy in common and the following words have been held to be sufficient: "between", "divided", "equally", "equal proportions", "equal shares", "equally to be divided", "share and share alike" and "among".

C.13.18 Gift of undivided share in equity of real property

I HEREBY GIVE to [name] all my share of and interest in [property] and all my share and interest in the proceeds of sale thereof and any income arising from the property whether before or after the sale absolutely.

C.13.19 Clause dealing with property held in joint tenancy

WHEREAS I am beneficial joint tenant of [property] together with [name A] in fee simple in possession be it provided that:

1. Should the said joint tenancy be severed in my lifetime then I BEQUEATH all my interest in the said property and the proceeds of sale thereof to [name B].

2. Should there be no such severance and if the said [name A] shall die in my lifetime then I DEVISE the said property to [name B].

Note: A testator cannot sever an equitable joint tenancy by will. By dealing with these matters contingently in the will the need for a later codicil may be obviated on severance or death of a joint tenant. However, the testator may wish to sever the joint tenancy (by notice as provided by the Law of Property Act 1925, s 36 (2)), and dispose of the severed share by will.

5. Gifts of personal residence

The most common ways of providing for a gift of residence are as follows:

(a) By means of a grant of a lease by the trustees to the beneficiary. Such a gift may however be caught by ss 43(3) and 48(1)(c) of IHTA 1984 if the gift of the lease is terminable on or by reference to death, since it is treated as equivalent to a life interest (for inheritance tax purposes only).

(b) By means of a trust for sale with a power for the trustees to postpone sale. This is the most suitable method in most cases. Careful wording should be used, since the courts are more ready to infer a strict settlement than a trust for sale where it is not envisaged that sale will take place at any moment, and the property will instead be used to give the beneficiary a right to reside in the property – *Re Hanson* [1928] Ch 96; *Dodsworth* v *Dodsworth* (1973) 228 Est Gaz 1115.

(c) By means of a settlement taking effect under the Settled Land Act 1925. The advantage of this is that the beneficiary has a right to occupy the property and to control when and if the property is sold and how the proceeds are to be re-invested.

(d) By means of a power given to the trustees to purchase property as a residence for the beneficiary (see Chapter 20).

C.13.20 Gift to wife for life or until remarriage with remainder to son on trust for sale

I GIVE my freehold property situate at ...... [free of all moneys charged or otherwise secured thereon at my death [such moneys to be paid out of my residuary estate]] to my trustees upon trust PROVIDED THAT during the life [widowhood] of my wife [name] no sale shall take place without her consent thereto and my trustees shall hold the net rents and profits until sale and the net income from the proceeds of sale in trust for my wife during her life [so long as she shall remain my widow] and after her death [or remarriage] my trustees shall hold the said property if unsold or the net proceeds of sale or the investments representing the same together with any income therefrom for my son [name] absolutely AND I DECLARE that my trustees may allow my said wife to occupy the said property during her lifetime [widowhood] PROVIDED THAT she shall pay and discharge all taxes and other outgoings payable in respect of the property throughout her occupation of the same and keep the said property in good repair and condition and shall pay to my trustees such sum as is required to keep the same insured to the full value thereof against such risks as my trustees shall in their absolute discretion from time to time think fit.

C.13.21 Settled bequest of leasehold on trust for sale with power to permit widow to reside

(1) I GIVE my leasehold property [description] to my trustees upon trust to sell the same with power to postpone such sale so long as they shall think fit PROVIDED THAT they shall not sell the same during the lifetime [widowhood] of my wife [name] without her consent in writing.

(2) My trustees shall pay all the costs and expenses connected with the sale of the said property and any other administrative or other costs or expenses connected with the trusts hereunder and any other expenses which my trustees in their absolute discretion shall consider to be payable out of the proceeds of sale of the said property and shall hold the residue of such money upon trust to invest the same as hereinafter authorised.

(3) My trustees shall hold the net rents and profits until sale and the net income from any net proceeds of sale in trust for my said wife during her life [widowhood] and upon her death [or remarriage] my trustees shall hold the said leasehold property (if unsold) or the said net proceeds of sale or the investments representing the same in trust for my son [name] absolutely.

(4) My trustees may in their absolute discretion allow my said wife to occupy the said leasehold property during her lifetime [widowhood] PROVIDED THAT she shall pay any rent due in respect of the same and shall observe and perform the lessee's covenants and conditions reserved by and contained in the lease of the said property throughout her period of occupation [AND I DIRECT THAT any inheritance tax payable at any time in respect of the said property shall be paid by my trustees out of the said property or the proceeds of sale thereof in exoneration of my residuary estate].

C.13.22 Strict settlement of house and contents to wife for life and then to son with direction as to repairs and insurance

I DEVISE and bequeath my freehold property situate at [etc] together with my furniture and effects of household use and ornament therein or belonging thereto (save such of the same as may be otherwise specifically disposed of by this my will or any codicil hereto) to my trustees upon trust for my wife [name] during her life [so long as she remains my widow] and after her death [or remarriage] upon trust for my son [name] absolutely AND I DIRECT that my wife shall during her life [widowhood] at her own expense keep the said property and its contents in good repair and condition and insured so far as is practicable against fire [and theft] to the full value thereof [to the satisfaction of my trustees in all respects] [PROVIDED THAT my trustees shall not be bound to enquire as to the insurance of the said property and its contents and shall not be liable in the event of the same being uninsured or under-insured at any time].

C.13.23 Gift to trustees in strict settlement upon trust to permit the testator's unmarried daughters to reside

I GIVE my freehold residence situate at [etc] [free of inheritance tax] [and free of all moneys secured thereon at my death (which moneys shall be paid out of my residuary estate)] to my trustees in fee simple upon trust AND I DIRECT that my trustees shall permit such one or more of my daughters [names] as shall be unmarried at my death to reside there rent free for so long as each of them shall remain unmarried [PROVIDED such period shall not exceed ...... years after my death] she or they keeping the same in good repair and insured to the satisfaction of my trustees throughout the period of their residence and I DECLARE that upon the death or marriage of the last of my unmarried daughters for the time being [or after the expiration of the said period whichever be the sooner] or if none of my unmarried daughters for the time being after my death shall be willing to reside therein my trustees shall stand possessed of the said premises upon the following trusts ......

C.13.24 Gift of testator's interest as tenant in common in a house, postponed to allow other tenants in common to reside there

I GIVE free of inheritance tax all my share and interest as beneficial tenant in common in the proceeds of sale and in the net rents and profits until sale of the freehold property known as [etc] to my trustees to hold the same upon the following trusts:

(a) While any one or more of the following persons namely [names of the other tenants in common] remain alive and desire to reside in the property and PROVIDED THAT my trustees are kept indemnified from and against all taxes and other outgoings in respect of the property my trustees shall not make any objection to such residence and shall not interfere with the same nor take any steps to enforce the trust for sale on which the property is held or to realise my share therein and my trustees shall make no claim in respect of any rent or profits from the property.

(b) Subject as aforesaid my trustees shall hold the same as to both capital and income upon trust absolutely for ......

6. Gifts of testamentary options

An option to purchase may be personal to the holder of the option and exercisable only by him, or it may be transferable to his personal representatives in which case it may be exercised after his death. This is a matter of construction.

The option may be given for no consideration or for full value. The latter may be at a price fixed by the testator in his will or subject to a valuation after his death in which case the method of valuation should be stated. Any time limit in the will for the exercise of the option must be strictly observed. If the will does not provide a specific time limit then the option must be exercised within a reasonable time. If the price has to be fixed, the time cannot run until the price has been communicated to the grantee. The date for the exercise of the option must be within the period allowed by the perpetuity rule (see s 9(2) Perpetuities and Accumulations Act 1964). It is generally advisable expressly to limit the period during which the option remains exercisable.

Where an option to purchase given to a grantee is to be exercised after the death of a tenant for life then, if the property has been sold during the life of the life tenant, the grantee will be entitled to the proceeds of sale after the life tenant's death if he exercises his option and pays any price fixed in relation to the property. For this situation to arise there must be an actual option to purchase granted to the grantee, and not merely a power granted to the trustees to sell the property at a fixed price to a particular person. In the latter case, the trustees are not under an obligation to sell the property to any particular person or for less than market value.

In all cases where it is intended to grant an option to purchase to a beneficiary it is useful to provide expressly for the trustees to give notice of the option to the beneficiary; this will avoid the possibility of the intended grantee's failing to exercise the option through ignorance of its existence.

C.13.25 Clause granting option to purchase land

(1) I DIRECT my trustees to offer my freehold property situate at [etc] to [name] at the purchase price of £...... such offer to be made within six months of the date of the grant of probate or administra-

tion to my estate and to be accepted by [name] within one year from the date on which such offer is made by my trustees whereupon the right of the said [name] to exercise the option by accepting such offer shall absolutely cease and I DIRECT that my trustees shall take such steps as may reasonably be required to bring the said offer to the attention of the said [name] as soon as may be practicable.

(2) I FURTHER DIRECT that

(i) the option is personal to [name] and may not be exercised by any person save for himself and is not transmissible to his personal representative or otherwise;

(ii) following the payment of the price as aforesaid the said [name] shall be indemnified out of my residuary estate from and against any inheritance tax and any foreign death duties payable in respect of the said property on or by reason of my death or in the administration of my estate;

(iii) my trustees may in their absolute and uncontrolled discretion accept payment of the said purchase price in instalments or otherwise and may accept such security as they in their absolute discretion think fit in respect of any sum remaining unpaid and may charge interest on any outstanding sum at such rate as they shall in their absolute discretion determine;

(iv) upon the said [name] exercising the said option my trustees shall forthwith convey to him the fee simple of the said property free from incumbrances save any mortgage or other security in respect of part or all of the said purchase price for the time being remaining outstanding and any interest due in respect of the same;

(v) I DECLARE that if the said option is not exercised within the said period then at any time after the expiration of the said period my trustees shall deal with the property in accordance with the trusts hereof and in any deed relating to the said property executed by my trustees any recital or other statement in writing to the effect that the offer to sell the property to [name] hereunder has not been accepted shall be conclusive evidence of the same to anyone dealing with my trustees for money or money's worth; and

(vi) my trustees shall accumulate the income of the said property until the exercise of the said option or the expiry of the time for its exercise whichever is the sooner and hold such accumulations as part of my residuary estate.

C.13.26 Clause granting option to take shares in family company

I DIRECT my trustees as soon as conveniently may be after my death to give in writing to my son [name] if living at my death the option to purchase ...... shares in ...... Company Limited at a price to be determined by an accountant chosen by my trustees and I DECLARE that my son shall have [six] months from the date of the receipt of such notice in which to exercise the same ALWAYS PROVIDED THAT this option shall absolutely cease to be exercisable on the expiry of one year from the date of my death and no purchaser of the said shares shall be in any way affected by the terms of this clause whether or not the same have purchased prior to the expiry of the said period of one year.

7. Gifts of leaseholds

Although leaseholds are personalty they nevertheless relate to land and any gift of "land" should distinguish between freehold and leasehold land if the two are to be dealt with separately by the testator. A beneficiary will take any leasehold property subject to the rent payable and any other covenants under the lease.

C.13.27 Gift of leaseholds

I GIVE to [name] my leasehold property situate at [etc] for all the residue [that shall at my death be unexpired of the term or terms upon which the same is held] [of the term created by the lease dated ...... and made between [parties]] and subject to the rent and covenants and conditions therein reserved and contained.

C.13.28 Gift of leasehold house free from mortgage

I GIVE my leasehold residence and premises situate at [etc] to my wife absolutely free from any incumbrances and I DIRECT that my said wife shall be kept indemnified in respect of any mortgage debt or other charge in relation to the property which shall be paid out of my residuary personal estate but provided that my said wife shall take the said residue and premises subject to any rent from time to time payable and subject to the covenants and conditions contained in the lease under which the said property is or may be held.

C.13.29 Gift of leaseholds: legatee to pay all arrears of rent and cost of dilapidations

I GIVE my leasehold residence and premises at .... to [name] absolutely PROVIDED THAT he shall pay any rent payable in respect thereof and perform and observe the covenants and conditions contained in the lease under which the same is held and on the lessee's part to be performed and observed and I DECLARE that the rent in respect thereof owing or accruing at my death and the costs and expenses of putting the said premises into repair in compliance with the provisions of the said lease shall be borne and paid by the said [name] in exoneration of my residuary estate.

8. Disposition of an entailed interest

Section 176 of the Law of Property Act 1925 provides that a tenant in tail of full age may dispose by will of property of which he is a tenant in tail in possession at his death. The term "in possession" includes the receipt of rents and profits or the right to receive rents and profits. To exercise this power of disposition any devise or bequest must specifically refer to:
  (a) the property; or
  (b) the instrument under which it was acquired; or
  (c) the entailed property generally.
The accuracy of such a reference is not vital, but the will should operate to disentail the property which the testator wishes to be disentailed – *Acheson v Russell* [1951] Ch 67.

C.13.30 Gift of land of which the testator is tenant in tail
I GIVE all the land of which I am tenant in tail in possession under [particulars of will or settlement] to [name] in fee simple absolutely.

Note: A tenant in tail under s 176 includes the owner of a base fee in possession. This gift will bear its own inheritance tax unless there is some provision to the contrary in the will (ante).

C.13.31 Gift of entailed property generally
I GIVE and bequeath all entailed property whatsoever and wheresoever of which by virtue of s 176 of the Law of Property Act 1925 I have the power to dispose by will to [name] absolutely [or in fee simple or for all the residue of the several terms of which the same are held or absolutely according to the nature of the property].

Note: The LPA 1925, s 176 gives the testator power to dispose not only of property of which he is tenant in tail in possession, but also of money to be invested in the purchase of property, of which, if it had been so invested, he would have been the tenant in tail in possession at his death.

Chapter 14

Conditions attached to gifts

1. Conditions precedent and subsequent

A condition can be of two kinds:
- (a) a condition precedent;
- (b) a condition subsequent.

The nature of the condition depends on the wording of the will and the construction of such wording.

If a gift is not intended to take effect until the condition has been fulfilled the condition is a condition precedent. Conditions precedent are valid if expressed to allow a particular individual to come with evidence to the court and show that he does or does not satisfy that condition – *Re Tepper's Will Trusts* [1987] Ch 358. A condition is a condition subsequent if the gift is already vested and the object of the condition is to put an end to the gift if such a condition occurs.

In the case of a condition precedent, if the condition is void the whole gift fails, whereas in the case of a condition subsequent the gift takes effect free from a void condition (see below).

2. General

A testator may attach any condition he wishes to the gifts he makes in

his will, but such conditions may be void if they are:
- (a) against public policy or illegal;
- (b) either repugnant to the interest given to the beneficiary or other gifts or provisions in the will;
- (c) too uncertain to be enforced;
- (d) impossible to perform;
- (e) made against the beneficiary "in terrorem".

(a) Public policy

A condition is void as being against public policy if it is in the interest of the state that it should not be performed. What has been held to amount to be void under this category has varied from time to time but has included the following:
- (i) a condition inciting a beneficiary to commit a crime;
- (ii) a condition requiring a beneficiary to exert his influence in a political manner;
- (iii) a condition tending to induce the future separation of a husband and wife;
- (iv) a condition in total or virtual restraint of marriage. Partial restraints, for example a condition prohibiting a person's marriage with a Papist or a Scotsman, have been allowed. If the intention of the condition is not to restrain marriage but to provide for the donee until marriage then such a condition will be allowed.

(b) Repugnant conditions

These are conditions which attempt to make a beneficiary's enjoyment of a vested interest contrary to the basic principles of the law affecting such gifts. An example is a gift of capital to an adult subject to a condition that it is not to be paid to him until he reaches an age which is greater than eighteen. Such an object cannot be achieved unless the income is given to another person until the primary beneficiary attains that age. A further way of achieving this is to make a gift by means of a discretionary trust. If the gift is worded in such a way as clearly to take the income from the legatee, the court will declare there to be an intestacy of that income.

A further example of a condition which is void for repugnancy is a condition limiting the power of absolute alienation of property, since one of the primary rights of ownership of property is the right to sell, give or otherwise dispose of it. Once again partial restraints are valid so that a devise to a beneficiary on condition that he never sells the property to a person who is not a member of the family is not void.

A condition may also be repugnant where it is impossible to perform.

(c) Uncertainty

The test whether a condition is void for uncertainty differs depending on whether the condition is a condition precedent or a condition subsequent. Where there is a condition subsequent it must be drafted so that the court or persons affected by it can see from the outset exactly upon what event the preceding vested interest is to determine. In the case of a condition precedent no such test is needed – see *Tuck's Settlement Trusts* [1978] 1 All ER 1047 and *Re Barlow's Will Trusts* [1979] 1 All ER 296. In *Re Tepper's Will Trusts* [1987] (above) a condition subsequent forfeiting the interests of beneficiaries who remained outside the Jewish faith was held to be void for uncertainty in the absence of admissible evidence as to the nature of the Jewish faith practised by the testator and family.

(d) Impossibility

This consists of a state of affairs which does not or cannot exist – see *Re Jones* [1948] Ch 67. If the performance of a condition is highly improbable or is out of the power of the donee, this does not mean that the condition is impossible.

Where a condition is a condition precedent and is either impossible or becomes impossible by operation of law before the date of the will the gift remains intact and the condition is void. Where the condition is intended to be operative in any event, and performance is possible at the date of the will, but afterwards becomes impossible by an act of God or circumstances over which neither the legatee nor the testator had any control, the gift does not vest. Where a condition subsequent is impossible, the gift always takes effect free from the condition.

(e) Conditions "in terrorem"

Certain conditions may be void against the legatee if made as a "threat" to induce him to comply with the condition. Such conditions include those in partial restraint of marriage or forbidding the legatee to dispute the will.

This rule does not apply to freeholds, or to legacies charged on freeholds or to personalty directed to be paid out in the purchase of land.

The court may, however, avoid the question of the validity of such words by construing them not as a condition but as a limitation or a trust – *Page* v *Hayward* (1705) 11 Mod Rep 61.

Examples of such a construction include:

(i)   a gift to a person so long as that person remains unmarried – *Webb* v *Grace* (1848) 2 Ph 701;

(ii)   a gift subject to marriage with consent – *Fry* v *Porter* (1670) 1 Mod Rep 300;

(iii)   a reduction of an annuity on marriage – *Brown* v *Cutter* (1683) 2 Show 152;

(iv)   a proviso against alienation – *Newis* v *Lark* (1571) 2 Plowd 408.

C.14.1   Interest to wife for life or during widowhood

My trustees shall pay any and all income arising from my residuary estate or any part thereof to my wife so long as she shall live [or until her remarriage whichever shall be the shorter period].

C.14.2   Interest to wife for life to be reduced on remarriage

My trustees shall pay the income of my residuary estate to my wife so long as she shall live and remain my widow PROVIDED THAT if she shall remarry then my trustees shall pay her [one half only] of the income of my residuary estate and the remainder of the income therefrom shall be paid to [name] [accrue to and form part of my residuary estate].

C.14.3   Trust for wife during widowhood subject to an obligation to maintain children

My trustees shall pay the income of my residuary estate to my wife during her widowhood PROVIDED THAT she shall maintain and educate our children while under the age of twenty-five years to the satisfaction of my trustees.

C.14.4 Trust for wife during widowhood with request to maintain children; no binding legal obligation

My trustees shall pay the income of my residuary estate to my wife during her widowhood and I request that she shall maintain and educate our children ALWAYS PROVIDED THAT nothing in this provision shall be construed as to impose any condition or legal obligation whatsoever upon my said wife.

C.14.5 Trust for wife for life or widowhood with gift over to children in equal shares

(1) My trustees shall pay the income from my residuary estate to my said wife until her death [or remarriage].

(2) Upon the death [or remarriage] of my said wife my trustees shall hold my residuary estate together with any interest accruing thereon after her death [or remarriage] for all my children who attain the age of [eighteen] years or marry under that age in equal shares if more than one PROVIDED THAT if any child of mine shall fail to survive me and dies leaving issue alive at the date of my death such issue if and when they attain the age of [eighteen] years or marry under that age shall take by substitution and if more than one in equal shares per stirpes the same share of my residuary estate that such deceased child of mine would have taken had he or she survived me but so that no issue shall take whose parent is alive at my death and so capable of taking.

3. Effect of invalidity

In a condition precedent, if the condition is void the gift fails, whereas if a condition subsequent is void, the gift takes effect free from the condition. In the case of voidable conditions avoided by the donee, or a condition repugnant to the gift to which it is attached, then the gift takes effect free from the condition irrespective of whether the condition is precedent or subsequent.

Where a condition precedent is invalid as being *"malum in se"* (wrong in itself) both the gift and the condition are void and the gift fails, but where such a condition is invalid as being *"malum prohibitum"* (prohibited by law) the condition only is void and the gift becomes absolute.

C.14.6 Forfeiture of gift: condition subsequent: marriage to a person of a specified religion

I DIRECT that if any child or children of mine has or have married or shall have married at the date of my death or shall marry at any time any person who did not at the time of such marriage profess the ...... religion such child or children shall from the date of that marriage absolutely forfeit and lose all his her or their interest in and right to the capital or income given to him her or them under the provisions hereof [and the gift so forfeited shall fall into and form part of my residuary estate] PROVIDED ALWAYS THAT this provision shall not operate in respect of any marriage for which I have given my approval or forgiveness AND I DIRECT that the decision of my trustees both as to whether or not I have given my approval or forgiveness as aforesaid and as to whether or not any person professed the ...... religion at the time of any marriage shall be absolute and binding upon all beneficiaries claiming under this will.

C.14.7 Forfeiture of gift: condition precedent: marriage to a person not professing a specified religion

I DECLARE that the share of any child of mine in my residuary estate shall not be paid or transferred to that child immediately upon my death but shall be retained by my trustees and held by them upon the following trusts:

(a)(i) In the case of any child married at the time of my death to a person of the ...... religion then UPON TRUST as to both capital and income for that child absolutely.

(ii) In the case of any child of mine married at the date of my death to a person not of the ...... religion the share given to that child shall be forfeit and shall be applied as if my said child had predeceased me without issue UNLESS my trustees are of the opinion that at the date of my death I had approved or forgiven the said marriage and if so my trustees shall hold the said share UPON TRUST as to both capital and income for that child absolutely.

(b) In the case of any child of mine unmarried or divorced at the date of my death UPON TRUST to pay the income thereof to the said child during his or her lifetime or until the said child shall marry or marry again, and

(i) if the said marriage be to a person of the ...... religion then UPON TRUST as to both capital and income for such child absolutely, but

(ii) if the said marriage be to a person not of the ...... religion the share given to that child shall be forfeit and shall be applied as if my child had predeceased me without issue.

4. Determinable interests

A condition or proviso against alienation or forfeiture on bankruptcy is void, but a limitation until bankruptcy or until an attempted alienation is valid. In the former case the beneficiary is given, for example, a complete life interest, whereas in the latter case he is given a limited life interest, that is, a life interest until the attempted alienation. The limitation in the determinable interest marks the bounds of the interest, whereas the condition in the conditional interest attempts to defeat the interest before it attains its boundary.

C.14.8 Determinable life interest

(1) Until the death of my son [name] my trustees shall pay the income of [my residuary estate] to him PROVIDED THAT no act or thing shall have been done permitted or suffered by my said son or shall have been attempted to have been done and no event shall have happened (other than a consent to any advancement under any statutory or express power) whereby the income of [my residuary estate] or some part thereof would or might if belonging absolutely to my said son become vested in or charged in favour of some other persons or a corporation or my said son would or might be deprived of the right to receive the same or any part thereof and my trustees shall continue to pay the said income to my said son during his life until some such event as aforesaid shall happen.

(2) After the death or earlier failure or determination of the trust hereinbefore contained my trustees shall stand possessed of [my residuary estate] and the income thereof in trust etc.

Chapter 15

Annuities

1. General

An annuity is a periodic payment. Such a payment may be secured on land or on personalty. In the former case the charge is known as a rentcharge, in the latter case it is known as an annuity. An annuity may be payable out of income or capital depending upon the construction of the gift: the words will be given their ordinary grammatical meaning – *Re Coller's Deed Trusts* [1937] 3 All ER 292. An annuity is a form of pecuniary legacy since AEA 1925, s 55(1)(ix) defines a pecuniary legacy to include an annuity. Thus it abates and bears inheritance tax in the same manner as other pecuniary legacies and it is therefore important that it is drafted so as to be free of inheritance tax.

The problem with annuities is that their real value is subject to the ravages of inflation. If it is sought to avoid this by giving an "index-linked" annuity the result may be that all the income and capital are exhausted. Another difficulty is that by s 50(2) IHTA 1984 an annuitant is treated as having an interest in possession in the same proportion of the capital fund as the proportion the annuity bears to the income of the fund. As the extent of the interest in possession will vary with the yield of the property, the Inland Revenue has power to prescribe a maximum and minimum yield (see SI 1980 No 1000). This may give rise to a charge to inheritance tax of more than the value of the fund in some circumstances.

Thought should be given to other methods of providing maintenance, such as:

(a)   a life interest in all or part of a capital sum; or
(b)   a life interest in all or part of the income from a capital fund; or
(c)   a life interest in a settled legacy; or
(d)   a legacy of a capital sum with which the legatee may purchase
      an annuity.

2. Abatement

Where the estate is insufficient to meet immediate annuities in full
then, unless express provisions in the will give priority to one annuity
over another, all will abate proportionately, according to their value.
Where the estate is able to pay the annuities in full the rule of abatement does not apply – *Re Hill* [1944] Ch 270. Here the testator gave
annuities to A, B, C and D for life, payable out of both capital and
income. The ages of the annuitants varied from 59 to 64 years. The
estate was solvent, but there was insufficient income to pay the annuities from it. The annuities could have lasted theoretically for a period
of 54 years if they were paid out of capital and income, and as soon as
one of the annuities ceased to be payable the income alone would
have been sufficient to pay the rest. The court held that, as there was
no commercial risk involved in paying the annuities out of capital and
income, the abatement rule did not apply. Abatement will arise only
where there is more than one annuity, unless one annuity and one or
more legacies rank equally in priority for payment.

Valuations are normally taken as at the date of the testator's death.
However if at the time the court makes the order for valuation there
has been some material change in the position since the testator's
death, the valuation will be at that date. An actuarial valuation is
applied except that the health of the annuitant and the risks from his
employment are not taken into account.

3. Commencement

An annuity will usually commence from the date of death of the testator unless there is a contrary intention in the will. Weekly or monthly annuities are first payable one month after the testator's death. Quarterly annuities are first payable on the first quarter day following the testator's death, but reduced proportionately in respect of the portion of that quarter before the date of death. Where the annuity is to be paid within one month of the testator's death, a year's payment is made within one month, but the second payment does not fall due until two years after the testator's death. Arrears do not carry interest unless there are exceptional circumstances – see *Re Berkeley* [1968] Ch 744.

4. Duration

The duration of any annuity may be determined by the construction of the will, but if the will is silent the annuity will be presumed to be for life only – *Blight* v *Hartnoll* (1881) 19 Ch D 294. The onus is upon the annuitant to establish an exception to this general rule if he is claiming the annuity is for a longer period. The annuity may be expressed to be perpetual. Otherwise it will be construed to be perpetual, *inter alia*, where there is a power to leave the annuity by will or where there is provision for a gift over of the annuity if the original annuitant dies without issue. An annuity given to a corporation or an unincorporated body capable of existing for ever is *prima facie* perpetual. The duration of a particular annuity may be restricted by the purpose for which the annuity is given, if the purpose itself is satisfied or ceases.

Where a single annuity is given to two persons during their lives it will cease to be payable only on the death of the survivor, who will take the whole after the death of the first to die. A direction to purchase an annuity for the life of A and B will be construed as an annuity for their joint lives. Annuities may be made conditional and may be determinable upon a certain event.

5. Methods of providing annuities

There are several methods of providing for an annuity in a will:

(a) The trustees may be given a power to take sufficient capital from the deceased's estate to provide income for the payment of the annuities given in the will. There may also be a power to resort to the capital itself if necessary. Inheritance tax will be payable on the annuitant's death in respect of the capital sum, and if the trustees resort to any part of the capital of the fund to pay the annuity then that part of the capital paid to the annuitant will be taxable as income in his hands.

(b) The trustees may be directed to purchase an annuity. There is no gift of capital and therefore no charge to IHT. Also the purchase is "once and for all" in nature, and delay and difficulties involved in dealing with a capital fund are avoided. One disadvantage of such a direction, however, is that the intended annuitant may be able to demand the capital which has been directed to be spent on the purchase of the annuity, and use that money as he chooses. It should also be noted that annuities purchased in pursuance of a direction in a will, or payable by virtue of a will or settlement, are excluded from provisions applicable to other purchased annuities exempting the capital element in the periodical annuity payment – Income and Corporation Taxes Act (ICTA) 1970, s 230(7).

(c) A power may be given to the trustees to satisfy a gift of an annuity by the purchase of an annuity for the annuitant. Until the trustees decide to exercise that power the annuitant has no right to demand the capital in lieu. Until then the annuitant will be in the same position as in (b) above. Provided there is no agreement between the trustees and the annuitant to substitute a purchased annuity for one paid out of the income of the estate, then the Inland Revenue does not regard the substitution as an occasion of charge under s 52(4)(h) Income Taxes Act 1984 ("ITA 1984"). If an annuity fund were created in which no interest in possession occurred until the trustees decided how the annuities were to be met, then, provided the decision were made within two years of the death of the testator, the trustees' actions would be treated as those of the deceased under s 144 ITA 1984.

(d)　The annuitant may be given a lump sum. He would be in a position to use that lump sum as he liked but the testator could include in the gift a suggestion that he purchase an annuity. If the beneficiary indeed purchases an annuity with the gift the capital element of it is not taxable in the hands of the annuitant.

(e)　In order to avoid the tax disadvantages of annuities purchased in pursuance of a will (as in para (c) above) the trustees can be given a power to commute the annuity into a lump sum, allowing the annuitant to purchase an annuity for himself using that lump sum payment.

(f)　The testator may create a personal obligation for one of his beneficiaries (such as the residuary beneficiary) to pay an annuity to a third party as a condition of the gift to the first beneficiary.

C.15.1 Gift of simple annuity

I GIVE to [name] for his [her] life an annuity of [£1000] per annum free of all taxes and deductions and payable by equal quarterly payments the first payment to fall due three months after the date of my death.

C.15.2 Gift of annuity tax-free

I GIVE to [name] for his [her] life an annuity of [£1000] per annum free of all taxes and deductions whatsoever and payable by equal quarterly payments [the first payment to be made three months after the date of my death] [the first payment to be made on the first usual quarter day after the expiry of three months from the date of my death and such payment to include an apportioned payment in respect of that period from the date of my death to the first following quarter day if the same shall occur within three months of the date of my death.]

[AND I DECLARE and direct that any rebate allowance or repayment of income tax allowed or paid to the said [name] in respect of the annuity herein provided for [shall enure for his [her] benefit] [shall be accounted for by the said [name] to my trustees].]

C.15.3 Gift of annuity including/excluding rule in *Re Pettit*

I GIVE to [name] an annuity of such sum as after deduction of income tax [at the basic rate for the time being (but not at any higher rate)] [whether at the basic rate or any higher rate] amounts to the clear sum of [£2500] and I direct that any relief rebate allowance or repayment of income tax allowed or payable to [name] [shall enure for [his] own benefit] [shall be accounted for by [him] to my trustees].

Note: The general rule in *Re Pettit* [1922] 2 Ch 765 is that any allowance or repayment of income tax made or paid to the annuitant on an annuity that has been paid free of tax is returnable by the annuitant to the personal representatives.

C.15.4 Gift of annuity of such sum as after deduction of income tax will amount to a stated sum to be varied with reference to the Index of Retail Prices

I GIVE to my wife [name] an annuity of such sum as after deduction of [all] income tax [at the basic rate for the time being in force] will amount to the clear sum of £10,000 subject to such adjustments as are hereinafter provided payable in equal monthly payments and the first payment shall be made one month after the date of my death AND I HEREBY DIRECT THAT:

(i) The amount of the sum hereinbefore referred to shall be increased or decreased on the first day of January in each year by such percentage as the Retail Prices Index as hereinafter defined shall have risen or fallen above or below the figure at which the said Index stood on the first of January in the preceding year such increases or decreases to be calculated and applied as from the date of this my will and throughout the duration of the said annuity.

(ii) Any rebate allowance or repayment of income tax allowed or paid to my said wife in respect of the annuity hereinbefore given shall [enure for her benefit] [be accounted for by my said wife to my trustees].

(iii) My trustees [shall] [may] set aside from my estate such sum as they in their opinion think necessary to provide sufficient income therefrom to pay the aforesaid annuity (such sum being hereinafter referred to as the annuity fund) AND my trustees shall not be liable for any loss incurred by the annuitant should the annuity fund prove to be insufficient to provide for the annuity.

(iv) Having set aside the annuity fund as aforesaid the annuity shall be wholly charged thereon in exoneration of the remainder of my estate but my trustees may resort to the capital of the annuity fund if at any time the income thereof is insufficient to pay the annuity.

(v) If in any year the income from the annuity fund shall exceed the sum required to pay the annuity my trustees shall during the lifetime of my said wife or for 21 years from the date of my death whichever period shall be the shorter accumulate any amount of income not so required by investing the same in such investments as my trustees shall in their absolute discretion think fit PROVIDED THAT such accumulations and the interest or income thereof shall be applied by my trustees insofar as may be required to make up any deficiency of the annuity in any subsequent year and in so far as they are not so required they shall form an accretion to the annuity fund and on the determination of the said annuity shall with the annuity fund fall into and form part of my residuary estate.

(vi) For the purposes hereof the Retail Prices Index shall mean the Index of Retail Prices published by HM Stationery Office or any official publication substituted therefor.

C.15.5 Gift of several annuities

I GIVE the following annuities to the following persons for their respective lives to be paid free of all deductions by equal quarterly payments the first payment in each case to be made on the expiry of three months from the date of my death. [State amounts of annuities and names of annuitants in separate paragraphs.]

C.15.6 Gift of annuity charged on land

[Commence as in precedent C.15.1 (above)] And I hereby CHARGE my lands and premises situate at and known as ...... with the payment of the said annuities [in exoneration of the remainder of my estate] and I DIRECT that the said annuity shall be paid clear of all deductions by equal half-yearly payments the first payment to be made six months after the date of my death [AND I FURTHER DIRECT that any inheritance tax payable by reason of my death in respect of such lands and premises shall be borne and paid by the person or persons entitled (subject to the said annuity) to the said lands and premises in exoneration of the said annuity and annuitant].

Note: If it is intended to charge the land with the payment of the annuities in exoneration of the testator's personal estate, this must be expressly stated. Such a charge will create a strict settlement; see Settled Land Act 1925, s 1(1)(v).

C.15.7 Power to purchase annuities, the capital cost being recouped out of income

1. [Gift of annuities as in precedent C.15.1].

2. My trustees shall have the power if in their discretion they think fit to purchase out of my residuary [personal] estate the above annuities from an insurance office of repute.

3. After the exercise of the power hereinbefore contained my trustees shall each year thereafter out of the income of my residuary estate add to the capital thereof such sum as is necessary to recoup the whole of the purchase price of the said annuities divided into equal yearly payments the first payment being made on the anniversary of my death next following the exercise of the power as aforesaid and the last payment being made 21 years following the date of my death.

C.15.8 Power to trustees to set aside parts of the estate as separate annuity funds

My trustees shall have power to set aside from my residuary (personal) estate such part or parts thereof as they in their absolute discretion think necessary to provide sufficient income therefrom to pay any annuity hereby or by any codicil hereto bequeathed and keep a separate part in respect of each and every annuity AND I DECLARE that having appropriated such part or parts of my estate the annuity in respect of which the appropriation shall be made shall be wholly charged upon that part appropriated (hereinafter referred to as "the annuity fund") in exoneration of the remainder of my estate but my trustees may resort to the capital of the annuity fund if at any time the income thereof is insufficient to pay such annuity AND I FURTHER DECLARE that when any annuity ceases the annuity fund so set aside in each case shall revert to and form part of my residuary estate and that any surplus income arising from the annuity fund shall be applied as income of my residuary estate.

C.15.9 Gift of annuity with direction to purchase

I GIVE to [name] for his [her] life an annuity of [£1000] per annum free of all deductions and payable by equal quarterly payments the first payment to be made three months after the date of my death and I direct my [executors] [trustees] shall provide for the payment of the said annuity by purchasing the same from any public company.

Note: Where there is a direction to the trustees to purchase an annuity (but not a mere power allowing them to do so) the annuitant is entitled upon the death of the testator to elect to be paid a sum equal to that which would be required to purchase the annuity. If the annuitant dies after the testator but before the first payment of the annuity becomes payable his or her personal representatives are entitled to the sum necessary for such purchase: *Re Robbins* [1907] 2 Ch 8; *Re Brunning* [1909] 1 Ch 276.

C.15.10 Annuity provisions designed to mitigate inheritance tax and income tax

(a) Commence as in precedent C.15.2.

(b) My trustees may satisfy the said annuity by such one or more of the following methods as they in their absolute discretion consider fit:-

(i) By setting aside such part of my residuary (personal) estate as my trustees shall in their absolute discretion think necessary to provide sufficient income to pay the annuity and any administrative expenses in respect of the said annuity and if they exercise this power then the annuity shall be charged wholly on the part of my estate so set aside (hereinafter referred to as the annuity fund) in exoneration of the remainder of my estate but my trustees may resort to the capital of the annuity fund if at any time the income thereof is insufficient to pay the annuity and when the annuity ceases the annuity fund shall revert to and form part of my residuary estate and any surplus income arising from the annuity fund shall be applied as income of my residuary estate.

(ii) By purchasing in their names an annuity from any public company and paying it to the annuitant but if my trustees decide to exercise this power the annuitant shall not be entitled to the capital value of the annuity given to him and if either before or after the commencement of the annuity given the annuitant does or permits any act or event or process by which the annuity purchased hereunder would or might (but for this provision) become vested in or payable to any other person then his or her annuity shall immediately cease and the payments received by my trustees during the remainder of his or her life under the purchased annuity shall be applied as income of my residuary estate.

(iii) By commuting the annuity [with the annuitant's consent] and paying to the annuitant such capital sum as my trustees may in their absolute discretion think just having regard to all the circumstances and in particular to any inheritance tax that may be avoided and whether the administration of my estate may be simplified and to the position in relation to income tax ALWAYS PROVIDED THAT if my trustees exercise this power the annuitant shall have no further claim against my estate in respect of this annuity.

(iv) By accepting from [name of residuary legatee or other] a Deed of Covenant providing for the payment of the annuity by [name] and his [her] personal representatives to the annuitant for the remainder of the annuitant's lifetime and if such a Deed is approved by my trustees and made accordingly then the said annuitant shall have no further claim against my estate in respect of the annuity hereinbefore given.

C.15.11 General direction that annuities are to be paid clear of all deductions

I DECLARE that all the annuities given under this my will or any codicil hereto shall be paid clear of all deductions whatsoever [including [all] income tax [at the basic rate] deductible at source] and that the expenses of and incidental to the purchase or payment of any annuity under the provisions of this my will shall be borne by my residuary estate [AND I further declare that any rebate allowance or repayment of income tax which may be allowed or paid to any annuitant under this my will shall enure for the benefit of such annuitant].

C.15.12 Annuity to widow with substitution of lesser annuity on remarriage and provision for minor children residing with widow

I GIVE to my wife the following annuities [to have priority over all other pecuniary legacies and annuities hereby or by any codicil hereto given]

(1) as from the date of my death and for so long as she shall remain my widow an annuity of [£10,000] per annum

(2) as from the date of her remarriage and for so long as she shall live an annuity of [£2,000] per annum

(3) as from my death and for so long as any child of mine being a minor and unmarried resides with her an annuity of [£2,000] in respect of each such child

AND IN RESPECT of all the within mentioned annuities I DECLARE as follows:

(a) If and for as long as each annuity hereinbefore mentioned shall be payable the same shall be paid clear of all deductions and payable by equal quarterly payments the first payment to be made three months after the respective commencement of each such annuity and my trustees shall not be bound to enquire as to the application of any annuity payable to my said wife in respect of any child of mine.

(b) (Provisions as to the method of satisfying the annuities as in precedent C.15.10 (b) or otherwise as appropriate.)

Chapter 16

Gifts of residue

1. General

Every will should contain a residuary gift clause in order to ensure that the residue of the estate devolves to the beneficiaries chosen by the testator. After the payment of debts and testamentary expenses a residuary gift has the effect of passing the property not otherwise disposed of for whatever reason. The residuary gift may be one of the entire net estate (if no other dispositions have been made) or of whatever is left after the payment of specific and general gifts. It may be limited, but is generally not, or it can pass all property including property over which the testator had a general power of appointment at the time of his death. Thought should also be given as to whether substitutional gifts and survivorship clauses are to be included in the will. The will should be drafted so as to deal with the payment of debts and testamentary expenses in a manner which complies with the testator's wishes. Usually this means that the debts and expenses are payable out of the residuary estate, and this can be achieved in one of two ways:

    (a) by making the residuary gift subject to the payment of debts and expenses; or

    (b) by creating a trust for sale, the first object of which is the payment of the debts.

C.16.1 Residuary gift to one person without a trust for sale

Subject to the payment of my debts funeral and testamentary expenses legacies and all tax payable from my estate I GIVE all my real and personal property whatsoever and wheresoever situate not hereby or by any codicil hereto specifically disposed of (including any property over which I may have a general power of appointment or disposition by will) to [name] absolutely.

C.16.2 Residuary gift to a class without a trust for sale

I GIVE all my real and personal property whatsoever and wheresoever (including any property over which I may have a general power of appointment or disposition by will) to my trustees for the payment of my debts funeral and testamentary expenses legacies and all tax payable from my estate and subject thereto to be divided between all [my children] in equal shares absolutely.

Note: See Chapter 21 on class closing rules, the effect of which should be explained to the testator.

C.16.3 Gift of residuary personal estate only without a trust for sale

Subject to the payment of my debts funeral and testamentary expenses legacies and all inheritance tax on any legacy or annuity hereinbefore stated to be given free of duty I GIVE all my personal property whatsoever and wheresoever ([but not] including any leasehold property) not hereby or by any codicil hereto specifically disposed of (including such personal property over which I may have a general power of appointment or disposition by will) to [name] absolutely.

C.16.4 Gift of residuary real estate only without a trust for sale

Subject to the payment of my debts funeral and testamentary expenses and all inheritance tax on any legacy or annuity hereinbefore stated to be given free of tax (such tax to be paid primarily out of my personal estate) I GIVE all my real estate ([but not] including any leasehold property) not hereby or by any codicil hereto specifically disposed of (including such real property over which I may have a general power of appointment or disposition by will) to [name] absolutely.

C.16.5 Gift of residuary estate to named persons without a trust for sale

My trustees shall hold my residuary estate in trust for [names] as tenants in common in equal shares PROVIDED THAT if any one or more of them shall die in my lifetime leaving issue the share of each so dying shall be held in trust for his or her respective issue living at my death and attaining the age of [eighteen] years or marrying under that age in equal shares per stirpes but so that no issue shall take whose parent is alive at my death and so capable of taking and further provided that if any of the said [names] shall die in my lifetime and are not survived by issue who attain the age of [eighteen] or who marry under that age the share of anyone so dying shall be held for the other [persons] entitled to my residuary estate hereunder as if the one or more so dying had never been named or included in this gift.

2. Trust for sale

It is usual to impose a trust for sale and conversion on all the property not otherwise disposed of in the will, that is, on the property being disposed of in the residue clause. Where land is settled or subject to a contingency, then unless an express trust for sale is imposed, it is settled land under the Settled Land Act 1925, s 1. Therefore, unless the beneficial interests are absolute and immediate, an express trust for sale should always be imposed on the residue.

Additionally a power to postpone should expressly be inserted since the power implied by statute applies to land only – see Law of Property Act 1925, s 25(1). Under a power to postpone sale the trustees may postpone the conversion for an indefinite period without liability for any consequential loss, unless there is a direction to the contrary in the will – Law of Property Act 1925, s 25(2). The concurrence of all the trustees must be sought in order to exercise the power to postpone a sale – *Re Mayo* [1943] Ch 302.

Gifts to trustees upon trust for sale where the beneficial interests are immediate
C.16.6 General residuary gift to trustees
I GIVE to my trustees absolutely all my real and personal property whatsoever and wheresoever not hereby or by any codicil hereto specifically disposed of (including any property over which I may have a general power of appointment or disposition by will) TO

HOLD UPON the following trusts ......

C.16.7 General residuary gift to trustees upon trust for sale

I GIVE all my real and personal property whatsoever and wheresoever not hereby or by any codicil hereto specifically disposed of (including any property over which I may have a general power of appointment or disposition by will) to my trustees upon trust to sell call in and convert the same into money with power to postpone the sale calling in and conversion thereof so long as they shall in their absolute discretion think fit without being liable for loss.

C.16.8 Trust to pay debts and invest residue – directions as to interest and tax

My trustees shall pay or provide for my debts funeral and testamentary expenses including any taxes payable from my estate by reason of any declaration in this will or any codicil hereto or by reason or any statute or otherwise and the pecuniary legacies [and annuities] hereby or by any codicil hereto given and subject thereto my trustees shall invest all moneys arising from the said sale calling in and conversion in such manner as may be authorised by statute or by the provisions hereof with full power to vary and transpose such investments and stand possessed of them and of all parts of my estate for the time being unsold and any ready money (hereinafter called my residuary estate) upon the trusts hereinafter declared concerning the same.

C.16.9 Definition of residuary estate

My trustees shall stand possessed of such investments and of all parts of my estate for the time being remaining unsold and any ready money (hereinafter called my residuary estate) and of the annual income thereof upon the following trusts ......

C.16.10 Gift of residue to trustees who are different persons from the executors

After paying or providing for my debts funeral and testamentary expenses legacies and all inheritance tax on any legacy or annuity given free of duty my executors shall transfer all the residue of my estate (including any property over which I may have a general power of appointment or disposition by will) to [name] and [name] (hereinafter called my trustees) to hold the same upon trust [here add trusts for sale and other trust provisions].

C.16.11 Gift of a reversionary interest

I GIVE to [name] all or any share or interest to which I am at my death entitled or to which I may thereafter be or become entitled under the trusts of the will of ...... deceased dated ...... including any interest in reversion expectant on the death [or remarriage] of ...... and the investments and property representing the residuary estate of the said ...... deceased and all other interests under the said will.

3. Survivorship clauses

Survivorship clauses are most commonly used to ensure that property does not pass through two estates in close succession. This would occur when a beneficiary under a will dies shortly after the testator. Such a clause may also help to avoid a double charge to inheritance tax.

Where a survivorship clause is used the estate cannot be distributed until after the expiry of the survivorship period, unless the beneficiary to whom the clause relates dies before the period ends. A survivorship period should not exceed six months since, if it does, a settlement will be created for inheritance tax purposes. This may lead to a double charge to tax.

C.16.12 Survivorship clause

If my husband fails to survive me by [28 days] or if the gift to my husband fails for any other reason (but not otherwise) I GIVE my residuary estate unto my trustees to hold the same on trust to sell call in and convert the same into money with full power to postpone the said sale calling in and conversion thereof so long as they shall in their absolute discretion think fit without being liable for any loss UPON TRUST to hold the proceeds of the said sale calling in and conversion and any property for the time being remaining unsold and unconverted for such of my children as attain the age of [18] years and if more than one in equal shares absolutely.

Note:　The usual period for a survivorship clause is 28 days.

4. Substitutional gifts

In most cases a testator will wish to provide for his intended beneficiaries dying within his lifetime or before the expiry of any stated survivorship period. This is particularly important in the case of gifts of
residue as it is usually desirable to avoid a partial or total intestacy.

Frequently the substitutional gift is made to the children or issue of
the original beneficiary should that beneficiary fail to survive.

If no provision is made for the death of the beneficiary then s 33 of
the Wills Act 1837 provides a statutory substitutional gift in the case
of gifts to the testator's children. Where that child predeceases the testator, leaving issue, the issue of the child take the share of their parent.
An express provision is, however, preferable, to show the testator's
intention.

Where the primary beneficiary is the spouse of the testator the
effect of the Administration of Estates Act 1982, s 18A should be
borne in mind when drafting the will. Since that section came into
force a divorce now causes a gift made to a spouse to fail. If the will
gives the residue to the spouse, the residue will pass as undisposed of
property unless a substitutional gift can take effect. In order to take
account of this a draftsman can:

(a) include a separate clause in the will stating that in the event of
    divorce a spouse is to be treated as having predeceased the testa-
    tor; or

(b) state that the gift over is to take effect if the spouse predeceases
    the testator or fails to survive for a specified period following the
    testator's death or if the gift fails for "any other reason".

C.16.13 Substitution clause limited to children of deceased children

...... Provided that if any of my said children is already dead or shall
predecease me or shall die after my death without attaining the age
of [twenty-one] years leaving a child or children who shall attain the
age of [eighteen] years or marry under that age such surviving child
or children shall take by substitution and if more than one in equal
shares the share of [my residuary estate] which his her or their parent would have taken if he or she had survived me and attained a
vested interest.

C.16.14 Trust for testator's children at twenty-five with substitution of issue of a child who predeceases the testator and further substitution of children on death after the testator's death without attaining a vested interest

My trustees shall hold [my residuary estate] in trust for such of my children as shall be living at or after my death and attain the age of [25] years and if more than one in equal shares PROVIDED THAT if any of my children is already dead or dies during my lifetime the share of [my residuary estate] to which such child would be entitled if he or she survived me and attained a vested interest shall be held in trust for such of his or her children and remoter issue (if any) as shall be living at my death and attain the age of [25] years in equal shares per stirpes but so that no issue shall take whose parent is living at my death and capable of taking AND FURTHER PROVIDED THAT if any child of mine or any remoter issue of mine presumptively entitled under the foregoing proviso survives me but dies without attaining a vested interest under the foregoing trusts the share of [my residuary estate] to which such child or issue of mine would be entitled if he or she lived to attain such a vested interest shall be held in trust for such of his children (if any) as attain the age of [21] years or marry under that age if more than one in equal shares.

Chapter 17

Powers and discretionary trusts

1. Nature and classification of powers

Powers of appointment are classified as general, special or hybrid. A power is a discretion given to a person to deal with or dispose of property of which he is not the owner. Powers may be administrative (see page 191 *et seq*), for example, where a power is given to trustees to insure trust property; or may be powers of appointment, for example "I devise Blackacre to my wife Sarah [who is the donee and appointor of the power] for life and declare that at her death my said wife may appoint whichever one of our children as she wishes to be the fee simple owner of Blackacre".

The donor may specify that an appointment is to be made in a specified way, for example by will or by deed, and if the appointment is not made in such a manner it is void.

Powers of appointment can be distinguished from trusts because the donee of a power of appointment can choose whether or not to make the appointment. If he chooses not to make the appointment, any gift over will take effect. If there is not gift over, a resulting trust in favour of the testator's estate will arise in respect of the property.

(a) General powers
General powers are those where the donee of the power is free to

exercise it in favour of anyone he chooses including himself. Title is derived not from the appointment itself but from the instrument conferring the power. All property appointed by will under such a power passes to the appointor's personal representatives, and may be applied to the payment of the appointor's debts, although first recourse must always be made to the appointor's own property. Where an appointment is made but the funds appointed are subsequently transferred or bequeathed upon trust, the appointment will not take effect, unless express words are used to designate the funds an addition to the original trust funds. Interests given in default of appointment may be defeated by the execution of the power at any time and any assignments of such an interest before the exercise of the power will, in effect, pass nothing.

If, for any reason, an appointment is ineffectual, the property devolves as part of the testator's estate. Where no appointment is made the property will pass according to the intention of the donor as expressed in the deed of appointment. Any exercise of a power must be in accordance with any prescribed conditions.

(b) Special powers

A special power restricts the appointor as to the class of possible appointee, for example by reference to the relationship of the possible appointees to the donor. This does not, however, prevent the appointor from being appointed if he is a member of the restricted group.

(c) Hybrid powers

A "hybrid" or "intermediary" power does not fit into either of the two previous categories; it permits the donee to appoint anyone as appointee except a certain person or class of people. Intermediate powers are treated as special powers for the purpose of the Wills Act 1837, s 27 and for perpetuity purposes (see Chapter 21).

A power which is exercisable by will only, whether general or special, is known as a testamentary power.

2. Wills Act 1837, s 27

The Wills Act 1837, s 27 provides that, in the absence of an expressed contrary intention, a general devise or bequest shall operate as an execution of "a power to appoint in any manner [the appointor] may think proper", whether that power relates to real or personal property. For example, if A has a general power of appointment over Blackacre, but fails to mention the power over Blackacre in his will, a general gift of "all my realty" would successfully dispose of Blackacre. The provision does not apply to special or hybrid powers which in any way restrict the choice of appointee, but it does apply even if a will is executed before the power is created. To satisfy s 27, the general gift may be of the whole or any part of the testator's estate, provided any part is sufficiently well described to include the property to which the power relates.

Any power to which s 27 does not apply can be exercised by will only if the disposition is expressed to be in exercise of such a power.

3. Delegation of powers

The general rule is that a power involving the exercise of personal discretion by the donee cannot be delegated; any attempt to do so is a nullity although it in no way affects the validity of the interests limited in default of execution of the power. A special power can never be delegated since by the terms of its creation the obligation on the donee is to exercise personal discretion. Conversely, in a general power the obligation to exercise the donee's personal discretion is never an inherent part of the power.

The donee of any power may delegate the performance of any administrative act provided it involves no act of personal discretion (for example, the execution of a document already approved may be delegated).

4. Consent to exercise power

Where a power is exercisable only with the consent of some person, that consent must be given during the donee's lifetime. If the person whose consent is required dies the power cannot be exercised.

5. Release of powers

A power involving a duty or a power in the nature of a trust cannot be released but other powers may be released by deed. Powers must generally be exercised in good faith in order to carry out the intention of the donor of the power. However, this will not prevent the release of a special power or the release of a power of revocation contained in the instrument exercising the power. The donee may release the power either wholly or in part, and any dealing with the property which is inconsistent with the exercise of the power operates as a release. An absolute release of a power is irrevocable and any attempt to exercise the power after the release is void.

Where it is provided that in default of appointment a trust (either express or implied) arises in favour of the members of a class of objects, the donee of the power cannot defeat the interest of the members of the class of objects, either by attempting to release the power or failing to appoint. The donee is under a duty to exercise the power and it cannot, therefore, be released. However, the court cannot compel the appointor to exercise the power but can only execute the trust in default of the appointment.

A power conferred on trustees *virtute officii* in relation to their trust property cannot be released unless such release is authorised in the trust deed – see *Muir v IRC* [1966] 3 All ER 38. This is also the case where the power is conferred on named persons chosen by reason of their office as trustees of the settlement.

Provided the donee of a power is not a trustee of the property to which it relates or, if he is such a trustee, the power is not conferred on him in that capacity, then, in the absence of a trust in favour of the objects of the power in default of appointment, the donee of such a power can release it.

C.17.1 **Powers exercisable in favour of a beneficiary who is also a trustee**
I DECLARE that the powers and discretions hereinbefore contained or otherwise vested in my trustees may be exercised in favour of a beneficiary notwithstanding that he or she may be one of my trustees ALWAYS PROVIDED that such power or discretion shall not be so exercised unless my trustees for the time being include at

least one other person who is not such a beneficiary or the spouse or child of such a beneficiary.

C.17.2 Power to release powers

I HEREBY AUTHORISE my trustees at any time to release by deed or otherwise restrict in any manner the future exercise of any powers or discretions hereinbefore or otherwise conferred on them so as to bind their successors as trustees hereof whether or not such power or discretion shall be vested in them in a fiduciary capacity ALWAYS PROVIDED that no such release or restriction shall prejudice or affect the exercise of any such powers or discretions made before any such release or restriction.

C.17.3 Power to trustees to settle daughter's share in case of marriage before entitlement

I HEREBY DECLARE that if any one or more of my daughters shall marry before attaining the prescribed age to become entitled to any gift contained in this my will or any codicil hereto then my trustees shall hereby be empowered at any time before each such daughter has attained the prescribed age as aforesaid to appoint by deed or deeds to settle the whole or any part of the [share of residue] [property] hereinbefore bequeathed to such daughter or any specific property appropriated to the said share UPON SUCH TRUSTS for the benefit of such daughter and her husband and their children or issue or any of them and in such manner and form as my trustees shall in their absolute discretion think fit and this power shall extend to any appointment deed or settlement contingent or dependent upon the future marriage of any such daughter while under the prescribed age as aforesaid and my trustees shall have power to execute such a deed accordingly should they in their absolute discretion see fit to do so ALWAYS PROVIDED that the foregoing powers if exercised shall be exercised at all times to ensure that such daughter becomes entitled to the said share or to an interest in possession therein on or before attaining the age of 25 years and so as to ensure that the income of the said share insofar as the same shall not be applied for such daughter's maintenance education or benefit shall be accumulated until such daughter becomes entitled.

C.17.4 Clause conferring a power to raise and pay capital

I GIVE to my trustees [the residue of my property both real and personal whatsoever and wherever situated (hereinafter termed my residuary estate)] as to the income thereof upon protective trusts for the benefit of [name] during his life and I HEREBY DECLARE that my trustees shall have power at their absolute discretion and at any time or times before the failure or determination of the said trust of income and without being liable in any way to account for the exercise of such discretion to raise and pay to the said [name] for his own absolute use and benefit [the whole or any part or parts of] the capital of [my residuary estate] and my trustee shall hold any part of [residue] not so transferred to [name] during his lifetime as the said [name] shall by will or codicil appoint and in default of and subject to any such appointment upon the following trusts [......] AND I DIRECT that my trustees shall on no account be liable or responsible for making any such payments whether of income or capital to the said [name] after the failure or determination of his said determinable life interest unless or until they shall have received express notice of the act or event causing such failure or determination.

C.17.5 Trust for wife for life and then to such children as she shall appoint

[Commence with gift of property to trustees ......]

(i) Upon trust to pay the income thereof to my wife for her life and after her death

(ii) Upon trust as to both capital and income for all or any one or more of my children and remoter issue in such shares and subject to such powers provisions and generally in such manner as my said wife shall by deed or will appoint and subject to any such appointment or in default of the same upon trust for all my children living at my death if more than one in equal shares as tenants in common.

6. Discretionary trusts

Such a trust is one under which the trustees are given a discretion to pay or apply the income or capital, or both, for the benefit of all or any one or more of the beneficiaries. The beneficiary is given no right to any part of the income or capital of the trust property and there is no way of his knowing whether any discretion will be exercised in his favour. A discretionary trust can be either exhaustive or non-exhaustive. In the former case the trustees are under a duty to distribute the whole of the income but have a discretion as to whom to distribute it.

In the latter case the trustees are given a discretion to determine not only to whom the income should be distributed, but also whether and to what extent it should be distributed if at all. The trustees must exercise the discretion as and when necessary, but failure to do so does not extinguish the power.

C.17.6 Devise on discretionary trust

I DEVISE my freehold land situate at [......] to my trustees upon trust to sell the same and to hold all rents and profits until sale after payment thereout of all outgoings usually chargeable against income and the net income from the proceeds of sale after payment of all sale costs and expenses in trust for [name] during her life PROVIDED always that at any time or times instead of paying to the said [name] any such rents and profits or income accruing during her life my trustees may apply all or part of the same for or towards the personal support maintenance and education of her or her issue for the time being or such one or more to the exclusion of the others or other of such objects of this discretionary power in such manner and if more than one in such shares as my trustees shall think proper and after the death of the said [name] [gift over].

C.17.7 Trust for a person under a disability

If my said son [name] shall be living and incapable by reason of mental disorder within the meaning of the Mental Health Act 1983 of administering his property or managing his affairs at the time of my death the property hereinbefore directed to be held upon trust for him (hereinafter called "the fund") shall not vest absolutely in him but shall be retained by my Trustees and held upon the following trusts and with and subject to the following powers:

(1) My Trustees shall have power at their absolute discretion to pay or apply the whole or any part of the income of the fund to or for the benefit of [name] during his life.

(2) My Trustees shall during the life of [name] and for a period of 21 years commencing with my death accumulate any income of the fund which shall not be paid or applied for the benefit of [name] as aforesaid as an accretion to the capital of the fund but shall have power to pay or apply such accumulations during the life of [name] as if the same were income of the then current year.

(3) If [name] is still living at the expiration of the said period of 21 years my Trustees shall thereafter and throughout the remainder of

the life of [name] pay or apply all income of the fund arising after the expiration of the said period of 21 years which shall not be paid or applied to or for the benefit of [name] under the foregoing power to or for the benefit of all or any one or more of [my children and remoter issue for the time being living other than the said [name]] in such shares and proportions as my Trustees think fit.

(4) Subject to the foregoing trusts and to any or every exercise of the foregoing powers my Trustees shall hold the fund or such part thereof as shall not have been paid or applied as aforesaid and the income thereof upon trust for ......

7. Protective trusts

The basis of a protective trust is a determinable interest, given to the principal beneficiary, but determinable on, for example, bankruptcy or an attempted alienation of the property. On determination, a discretionary trust arises in favour of the principal beneficiary and others.

The term of a protective trust is normally the life of the principal beneficiary but a shorter period may be used.

Section 33 of the Trustee Act 1925 operates to imply into trusts certain terms concerning income which is directed to be held "on protective trusts" for someone's benefit. The statutory implied terms are subject to any contrary intention appearing in the will. They may, on the other hand, be expressly incorporated into the will.

Section 33 provides for the income to be held during the trust period:

"(a) Upon trust for the principal beneficiary ...... until he, whether before or after the termination of any prior interest does, or attempts to do or suffers any act or thing, or until any event happens, other than an advance under any statutory or express power, whereby, if the said income were payable during the trust period ...... he would be deprived of the right to receive the same or any part thereof ...... [and thereafter] ......

(ii) upon trust for the application thereof for the maintenance or support, or otherwise for the benefit, of all or any one or more ...... of the following persons ...... –

(a) the principal beneficiary and his or her wife or husband, if any, and his or her children or more remote issue, if any; or

(b) if there is no wife or husband or issue of the principal beneficiary in existence, the principal beneficiary and the persons
who would, if he were actually dead, be entitled to the trust
property or the income thereof or to the annuity fund, if any, or
arrears of the annuity, as the case may be;

as the trustees in their absolute discretion ...... think fit".

This section does not validate any trust which would otherwise be
invalid, such as a settlement by a man of his own property on himself
until bankruptcy.

C.17.8 Protective income trusts for woman for life – variation of statutory protective trusts

My trustees shall hold the income of my residuary estate [the fund]
upon protective trusts for the benefit of [name] during her life PRO-
VIDED that the discretionary trusts by statute implied to arise after
the failure or determination of the trust to pay such income to her
during her life shall be varied as follows:

(i) My trustees may during the period within 21 years from the date
of my death and in their discretion apply any income accrued but
unapplied in any year for the purpose of such discretionary trusts in
any subsequent year.

(ii) Notwithstanding the protective trusts hereinbefore declared and
without determining her life interest thereunder the said [name] may
by deed or deeds but only with the consent of my trustees therein
expressed (which consent my trustees shall have absolute power to
give or withhold) assign any part or parts not exceeding in total one
half of the income of the fund to any child or children or issue of the
said [name] who shall at the date of such assignment have attained
the age of [eighteen] [twenty-one] years or have married.

C.17.9 Protective income trusts for woman for life – statutory protective trusts not referred to

My trustees shall pay the income of my residuary estate [the fund]
to [name] during her life unless or until some act or event shall have
happened or shall happen whereby the said income or any part
thereof or any interest therein belonging absolutely to her would
become vested in or charged in favour of some other person and in
the event of the failure or determination during her life of the trust
last above declared in her favour my trustees shall during the

remainder of her life pay or apply such income unto or for or towards the personal support maintenance education and benefit of the said [name] [her husband] and her issue for the time being or such one or more to the exclusion of the others or other of such objects of this discretionary trust in such manner and if more than one in such shares as my trustees shall think proper with power while [name] is still living within three years after the death of any object of such discretionary trust to apply any income which accrued in his or her lifetime in or towards the discharge of any liability incurred by or on behalf of any such object which my trustees shall think fit to satisfy.

[Add clause (ii) of Precedent C.17.8, above.]

C.17.10 Statutory protective trusts, varied by allowing accumulation for a period of years after a forfeiture has occurred

I DECLARE that the income hereinbefore directed to be held upon trust for or to be paid to the said [name] for life shall not vest absolutely in him [her] but shall be held by my trustees upon the statutory protective trusts save insofar as the same are hereinafter varied for the benefit of the said [name] for the period of his [her] life PROVIDED however that in each year prior to the expiration of twenty-one years from my death during which my trustees under the said statutory trusts have a discretion as to the application of the said income my trustees shall from time to time exercise their absolute discretion to determine how much if any of the income of the then current year they will apply under the statutory trusts and the said trusts shall apply to the amount so determined and my trustees shall accumulate any income above that amount by investing the same and the resulting income thereof but my trustees shall have power at any time or times during the said period of twenty-one years to declare that any whole or part of the past accumulations shall be income of the current year and be applicable accordingly at the discretion of my trustees AND I DECLARE that after the death of the said [name] the said accumulations or the balance thereof shall be deemed to be and treated as an accretion to the capital of the property from which such accumulations arose and be one fund with such capital for all purposes and shall be held by my trustees upon trust accordingly.

Chapter 18

Interest on legacies

1. Immediate specific gifts and devises

Income and profits which derive from an immediate specific gift or devise will accrue to the beneficiary of that gift as from the testator's death. Where part of the income (or profits) is paid after the date of death but has arisen both during a period before and a period after death then, in the absence of express words excluding the appointment rules, the income must normally be apportioned according to s 2 of the Apportionment Act 1870. That section states "All rents, annuities, dividends, and other periodical payments in the nature of income ...... shall, like interest on money lent, be considered as accruing from day to day, and shall be apportionable in respect of time accordingly". Rent, profits, interest, dividends on company shares or other income accruing before the testator's death fall into the testator's residuary estate.

C.18.1 Exclusion of s 2 of the Apportionment Act 1870
I DECLARE THAT all interest dividends and other income arising from any of my property in respect of any period partly before and partly after my death shall be treated as if it had accrued wholly after my death and shall not be subject to apportionment.

The Apportionment Act does not apply to the profits of the testator's business if he was a sole proprietor or in private partnership. No apportionment is necessary in such a case as the profits are treated as accruing on the last day of the period in respect of which they are declared.

A beneficiary must normally take the gift subject to any liabilities outstanding at the testator's death. There are, however, two exceptions to this general rule. The first is where the testator has during his lifetime entered into a leasehold covenant as a landlord. In such a case, the testator's estate, rather than the beneficiary, will bear the burden of that covenant.

The second is where a testator has entered into a contract to have building work done to property devised to a beneficiary. The estate will then bear the expense of that building work – see *Re Rushbrook's Will Trusts* [1948] Ch 421.

2. Contingent or deferred specific gifts

Contingent and deferred specific gifts are governed by s 175 of the Law of Property Act 1925 which states:

"(1) A contingent or future specific devise or bequest of property, whether real or personal, and a contingent residuary devise of freehold land, and a specific or residuary devise of freehold land to trustees upon trust for persons whose interests are contingent or executory shall, subject to the statutory provisions relating to accumulations, carry the intermediate income of that property from the death of the testator, except so far as such income, or any part thereof, may be otherwise expressly disposed of.

(2) This section applies only to wills coming into operation after the commencement of this Act".

The effect of this section is that any contingent or deferred specific gift of property to which the section relates will carry the intermediate income of that property, and this income can be accumulated, but only for so long as the statutory rule against accumulations permits (see Chapter 21). For the purposes of s 175 a residuary gift is not construed as an "express disposition" of income and therefore s 175 will apply to it.

In the case of a beneficiary who is alive and contingently entitled to a specific gift, s 31 of the Trustee Act 1925 governs the destination of any intermediate income arising. During the infancy of the beneficiary the personal representatives have power to apply any part or all of the income for his maintenance, education or benefit (any surplus income being accumulated), and after the beneficiary has attained eighteen the personal representatives must pay all the income to him until he attains a vested interest, or dies, or until his interest fails. Section 31 may be excluded where the will shows a contrary intention.

C.18.2 Power to apply intermediate income to maintenance, education or benefit, and to accumulate surplus

I DECLARE that my trustees shall have power in their absolute discretion to apply any part or all of the income of any expectant or presumptive share in my residuary estate given to [any of my grandchildren] under the trusts hereinbefore contained or in any codicil hereto for or towards the maintenance education or benefit of any such [grandchild] for so long as he or she shall remain under the age of [21] years and I FURTHER DIRECT that any payments made by virtue of this provision may be made to the parent or guardian of any such [grandchild] or to the said [grandchild] personally as my trustees think fit and that my trustees may accept the receipt of any such person as a full discharge to themselves AND I FURTHER DIRECT that until any such share has vested absolutely in such grandchild my trustees shall accumulate any surplus sums therefrom not so applied at compound interest by investing the same and the resulting income thereof in any of the investments hereby authorised so as to augment the said share and subject to the trusts hereinbefore declared in respect thereof but with power to apply any such accumulations in any subsequent year for or towards the maintenance education or benefit of the [grandchild] for the time being presumptively entitled as aforesaid as if such accumulations were income arising from the original share in the then current year.

3. General and demonstrative gifts

A general gift will, subject to contrary intention, carry interest from the time it is payable. When the gift is payable depends upon the express provisions of the will or rules of law. Immediate gifts are usually payable one year after the testator's death. Interest is payable at 6 per cent per annum and is simple interest only, although the testator may state a different rate should apply.

If a testator fixes a time for payment then interest is payable from that time. Thus a gift expressed to be payable "immediately after my death" carries interest from the date of death.

Even though it may be impracticable for the personal representative to pay an immediate legacy at the end of the executor's year it will still be treated as payable from that time, and will bear interest from that time until payment.

The same rule applies to a general legacy held on trust for the first beneficiary for life with the remainder to a second beneficiary absolutely. The legacy carries interest from the end of the executor's year and the first beneficiary would not be entitled to any interest in respect of the executor's year itself.

A general legacy which is contingent or deferred carries interest from the time at which it becomes payable. For example a gift to a beneficiary on attaining the age of twenty-one becomes payable on the beneficiary's twenty-first birthday and will bear interest from that birthday until payment.

Some legacies may contain a direction that the subject matter be severed from the testator's general estate and may carry interest from the end of the executor's year even though the beneficiary's interest in the legacy is contingent or deferred. If the purpose of the severance was merely to simplify the administration of the testator's estate, then the legacy will carry interest only from the time of absolute vesting. If, on the other hand, the severed property is to be invested by the trustee and held together with any investments representing that legacy upon trust for the beneficiary until the latter attains a given age, then the legacy will carry interest as from the end of the executor's year. This is also the case where property is severed to be held for the beneficiary if he attains a certain age.

There are four exceptional rules under which a general legacy carries interest from the date of the testator's death.

(a) Satisfaction of a debt

Subject to contrary intention any legacy made in satisfaction of a debt bears interest from the date of the testator's death and not from the end of the executor's year.

(b) Legacy charged only on realty

Subject to contrary intention if a legacy is vested and charged upon realty, interest will run from the date of the testator's death. The rule does not apply to a legacy directed to be paid out of the proceeds of sale of realty devised upon trust for sale. In that case the legacy will carry interest from one year after the testator's death, on the basis that the sale should reasonably have taken place during that period.

(c) Testator's infant child

A legacy given either to the testator's own infant child, or to an infant to whom he stands *in loco parentis*, will generally carry interest from the date of the testator's death, primarily in order to provide maintenance for the child. The rule does not apply:

(i)   where the testator has made other provisions for the maintenance of the child in his will; or

(ii) where the testator gives the legacy to trustees upon trust for the child.

The rule applies to contingent gifts but only if the specified contingency is referable to the child's infancy.

The rule, when applicable, overrides the time for payment fixed by the testator in his will and the other general rules outlined above. Section 31(3) of the Trustee Act 1925 provides that interest on such a legacy should be paid at the rate of 5 per cent per annum provided the income available is sufficient. The interest may be applied for the child's maintenance either under the statutory powers of maintenance or pursuant to an order of the court. Any surplus interest is accumulated and added to the capital of the legacy.

(d)   Intention to provide for maintenance of infant

If a testator gives a legacy to any infant indicating in his will that the legacy is intended to provide for the infant's maintenance then, unless the testator has made some other provision for that child's mainte-nance in his will, the legacy carries interest from the date of the testa-tor's death. The legatee need not be the testator's own child.

In the case of a contingent legacy where the contingency has no reference to the legatee's infancy, the legacy will generally carry interest only from the time at which the contingency is satisfied. There are, however, two exceptions to the general rule:

(i)   if the testator directs that the subject matter of the legacy is to be severed from the general estate for some purpose connected with the legacy (other than administrative ease) then interest is payable from the end of the executor's year;

(ii)   unless the testator makes some other provision for the legatee's maintenance, then where the testator is the infant's parent or stands *in loco parentis* to him, or if the testator shows in his will his intention to provide for the infant's maintenance, then inter-est accrues from the date of the death of the testator.

When drafting a general legacy to an infant, express directions should be given as to the payment of interest.

4. Residuary gifts

Where any residuary gift, either of personalty or realty, is to have immediate effect, all the income or profits arising after the testator's death pass with the gift. With contingent or deferred residuary gifts, residuary bequests (of personalty) and residuary devises (of realty) are treated differently.

(a)   Contingent or deferred residuary bequests

Where a residuary bequest of personalty is contingent, any intermedi-ate income of that personalty will pass with the residuary gift unless otherwise disposed of by the will. Therefore, until the contingency is satisfied (and the gift vests), unless the will provides otherwise, any intermediate income from a residuary bequest will either be:

(i)   dealt with under s 31 of the Trustee Act 1925 (see page 178) where there is a beneficiary living who is contingently entitled; or

(ii) accumulated during the statutory accumulation period as an addition to the capital and thereafter any further income will pass as under the testator's intestacy.

Where the residuary bequest is deferred to a future date, it does not carry with it any intermediate income which should be disposed of separately under the will. Any such income not dealt with under the provisions of the will passes as on the testator's intestacy.

(b)   Contingent or deferred residuary devises

Section 175 of the Law of Property Act 1925, which applies to real property only, provides that:

"a contingent residuary devise of freehold land, and a ...... residuary devise of freehold land to trustees upon trust for persons whose interests are contingent or executory shall, subject to the statutory provisions relating to accumulations, carry the intermediate income of that property from the death of the testator, except so far as such income, or any part thereof, may be otherwise expressly disposed of".

Thus a contingent residuary devise of realty will fall within s 175, unless it is also deferred to some future date. This is so even if made to trustees upon trust for a beneficiary whose interest is contingent. Subject to contrary provision in the will, the devise will carry with it any intermediate income. The intermediate income will either be:

(i)   subject to s 31 of the Trustee Act 1925 (if there is a beneficiary living who is contingently entitled); or

(ii) accumulated during the statutory accumulation period as an addition to the capital.

Section 175 does not, apparently, cover all deferred residuary devises but does cover devises made to trustees upon trust for persons whose interests are "executory". In those circumstances a deferred residuary devise will carry intermediate income during the statutory accumulation period, subject to contrary provision in the will.

5. The rule in *Allhusen* v *Whittell*

Where a will provides for the testator's residuary estate to be settled for successive persons, the presumed intention of the testator is that each such person should enjoy the same property successively.

The testator's estate will clearly be subject to various payments in respect of legacies and other outgoings. The tenant for life is not entitled to receive income arising on the part of the estate set aside for the payments of such outgoings. This is because the income of the part set aside is not properly the income of the residuary estate. Under the rule in *Allhusen* v *Whittell* (1867) LR 4 Eq 295, any outgoings are treated as being paid partly out of the capital of the part of the estate set aside for the payment of such outgoings, and partly out of the income of that part (the income accruing from the date of the testator's death to the date of payment of the particular outgoings). The result of this is to preserve capital in the residuary estate, as less capital is required to discharge each expense.

As a simple example, let us say that a testator provides for general legacies of £11,000, which his personal representatives pay after one year. During the year from the testator's death the whole of his estate may have been earning income at the rate of, say, 10 per cent. Under the rule in *Allhusen* v *Whittell*, the £11,000 required for payment of the general legacies may be regarded as that part of the capital of the testator's estate (in this case £10,000) which, together with its own interest during the relevant period (in this case £1,000) is sufficient to discharge the outgoing (£11,000). Thus the effect of the payment on the net residuary estate is given by deducting £10,000 from the gross residuary estate.

The rule applies to contingent debts or liabilities but not to contingent legacies. In the latter case the part of property required to pay the legacy remains in residue, yielding income for the tenant for life unless and until the contingency occurs. An annuity made *inter vivos* by the testator would also be subject to the rule.

For the purpose of the rule income is calculated by means of the average rate of income yielded by the residuary estate as a whole, net of income tax, apportioned to the relevant capital funds.

C.18.3 Clause excluding the rule in *Allhusen* v *Whittell*

I DIRECT that my trustees and personal representatives shall not be bound by the rule known as the rule in Allhusen v Whittell which shall not apply to and shall be excluded from the administration of my estate and the trusts hereof.

C.18.4 Clause excluding the rule in *Allhusen* v *Whittell*, **full form**

Notwithstanding any rule of law or equity to the contrary my debts funeral and testamentary expenses [and] legacies [and the inheritance tax aforesaid] shall be paid or discharged entirely out of the capital of my estate without recourse to the income thereof.

C.18.5 Clause giving the trustees power to disregard the rule in *Allhusen* v *Whittell*

My trustees shall have power to pay my debts funeral and testamentary expenses and legacies [and the inheritance tax aforesaid] out of the capital and income of my estate in such proportions as they shall in their absolute discretion think fit notwithstanding any rule of law or equity requiring apportionment between capital and income and without being liable for any loss occasioned to any beneficiary thereby.

Note: Exclusion of the rule in *Howe* v *Earl of Dartmouth* (1802) 7 Ves 137 (see Chapter 20) requiring apportionment of income, does not exclude the rule in *Allhusen* v *Whittell*.

Chapter 19

Abatement, ademption, election, satisfaction and conversion

1. Abatement

General legacies will normally rank equally with each other, unless a direction is given that a particular legacy should have priority over another. There is no presumed priority in respect of a legacy given to the testator's widow or a charging clause in favour of a solicitor acting as executor or trustee. If a particular beneficiary claims to have priority then the onus is upon him to prove that that was the testator's intention.

If the estate, after payment of tax, funeral and testamentary expenses and priority legacies, is insufficient to discharge the general legacies in full then each general legacy is subject to abatement. This means that each legacy is reduced in proportion to the overall shortfall in moneys required to satisfy the general legacies.

Where legacies are given in satisfaction of a debt they will abate, together with other pecuniary legacies, if the legatee has elected to accept the legacy in the will which is "far in excess" of his debt – *Re Whitehead* [1913] 2 Ch 56.

This may not be the case, however, where creditors are seeking only the amount of their debts. In such cases creditors may have priority over legatees who are volunteers – *Beyfus* v *Lawley* [1903] AC 411.

A demonstrative legacy does not abate with the general legacies provided the fund from which it is to be paid is sufficient to satisfy that legacy. In so far as the fund is insufficient, the balance will rank equally with general legacies and abate accordingly.

Similarly, a specific legacy will not abate with general legacies but may be subject to abatement *pro rata* with other specific legacies where the general estate is insufficient to pay all the debts. Where specific gifts are made out of a particular fund and the balance is disposed of as residue, if there are insufficient funds in the general estate to satisfy the debts then first recourse must be had to the residue before the specific gifts abate.

For abatement of annuities see Chapter 15.2.

2. Refunds

Generally, once an executor has voluntarily paid a legacy to the legatee, the executor has no right to ask for that legacy to be refunded. In the case of residue, if the executor had notice of a debt before parting with the residuary estate to the residuary legatee then he cannot call upon the residuary legatee to refund any part of that money or property merely because there is a deficiency of assets to discharge the liabilities. If, however, the executor is given notice of the debt after making a distribution to the residuary legatee, he is entitled to demand a refund of so much of the capital so paid as is necessary to satisfy the debt. The residuary legatee cannot be forced to refund any interest paid on capital.

If a trustee makes an overpayment to a beneficiary then he is not able to seek an immediate refund but may correct matters by making a reduced payment to the overpaid beneficiary when a further payment is due at a later date.

Provided the estate was sufficient to discharge all legacies and therefore solvent at the time when one legatee is paid, that legatee cannot be compelled to refund any part of payment merely because the estate has become insolvent and another legatee remains unpaid.

3. Ademption

Where property, identifiable at some time before the testator's death, and made the subject of a specific gift in the testator's will, does not form part of the testator's estate at the time of his death, that specific gift will adeem and thereby fail.

Ademption does not affect demonstrative or general legacies, nor does it affect gifts of property referred to as existing "at the time of my death" although, naturally, such gifts may fail if there are insufficient funds or if the property referred to does not form part of the testator's estate at the time of his death.

A change in substance in the subject matter of a specific gift causes that gift to adeem but a mere change in name or form does not. For example, if the testator makes a specific legacy of ordinary shares in a particular company owned by him at the date of his will and the shares are in some way altered, due to an amalgamation or reconstruction of the company during the testator's lifetime but represent the same stock in the same company, then the gift will not adeem – see *Re Clifford* [1912] 1 Ch 29 and *Re Leeming* [1912] 1 Ch 828. If, on the other hand, the original company is acquired by another and the shareholders are given shares in the new company as payment or compensation for their shares in the old company, then the substance of the subject matter will change and the gift will then adeem – *Re Slater* [1907] 1 Ch 665.

A binding contract for the sale of property which has been made the subject of a specific gift will cause the gift to adeem even if the testator dies before completion. The beneficiary is not entitled to the purchase price payable by the purchaser although he is entitled to enjoy the property or its rents and profits until completion of the contract.

If the testator makes a specific gift of property after entering into a binding contract for the sale of that property to a third party then, in the absence of contrary intention appearing in the will, the beneficiary is presumed to be entitled to the purchase price payable by the purchaser.

4. Options to purchase and ademption

Where a testator makes a specific gift of property in his will and subsequently grants an option to purchase that property to a third party,
then the beneficiary will not be entitled to the property itself while the
option remains in force. It is open to the third party to exercise his
option at any time during the operational period of that option,
whether or not it is after the testator's death. From the testator's death
until the option is exercised or the option period expires, the beneficiary is entitled only to the rents and profits arising from the property
(Lawes v *Bennett* (1785) 1 Cox Eq Cas 167).

Where, on the other hand, property is already subject to an option
and the testator then makes a specific gift of the property, the beneficiary will stand in the place of the testator on the testator's death and,
if the option is exercised, he will be entitled to the purchase price.

Conditional contracts for the sale of real property are similarly subject to the rule in *Lawes* v *Bennett*. See, for example *Re Sweeting*
[1988] 1 All ER 1016 where it was held that the fulfilment of a conditional contract for the sale of land after the testator's death effectively
converted the land into personal property. The result is that any specific gifts of the land adeem and the proceeds of sale fall into residue.

5. Republication and ademption

In general, the republication of a will does not necessarily restore any
gift that has already adeemed. However, republication may alter the
construction of a will with regard to the subject matter of a specific
gift. This can often have the effect of saving the specific gift. See, for
example *Re Reeves* [1928] Ch 351, where a testator, by his will executed in 1921, gave "all my interest in my present house" to his
daughter. At the date of execution the testator had a five year lease
which had been granted in 1917. He then took a new twelve year
lease, and in a codicil executed in 1926 confirmed his earlier will. The
court held that the daughter was entitled to the fresh lease. The effect
of the codicil was to republish his earlier will which was re-affirmed
at the date of the codicil, not the date of the original will.

Ademption may be avoided by an express provision in the will.

C.19.1 Clause avoiding ademption

I DEVISE all my freehold land situate at [etc] to [name] absolutely
PROVIDED THAT if any part or all of the said land shall in my lifetime be sold or contracted to be sold or made subject to an option to
purchase which is exercisable either before or after my death then I
GIVE to the said [name] free of inheritance tax a sum equal in
amount to the sum received by way of sale proceeds in respect of
such land after the deduction of all expenses of such sale AND I
DIRECT that the legacy hereby given shall be subject to abatement
as if it were property specifically devised or bequeathed.

6. Election

The question of election arises very rarely in practice. If a testator
makes a gift by will to beneficiary (A) of property which actually
belongs to another person (B), and if B is also a beneficiary under the
will then B is "put to his election" as to whether he will:

(a)   take the benefit given to him under the will and give effect to
      the testator's gift to A; or
(b)   forgo the gift under the will to himself but retain his own prop-
      erty that was the subject of the gift to A; or
(c)   accept the gift under the will AND retain his own property but
      compensate A for the gift which A will not receive.

In (b) both gifts will normally fail as the testator has no interest in the
subject property to pass to A.

7. Satisfaction

(a) Satisfaction of a debt by a legacy

Where a testator makes a will containing a pecuniary legacy to someone (C) who is owed a sum equal to or in excess of the amount of that
legacy, then an equitable presumption arises that the legacy to C was
intended to discharge the testator's debt owed to him. Thus, if the testator discharges his debt to C after the date of his will, the legacy will

be adeemed. If the debt remains outstanding at the time of the testator's death then C must choose whether to accept the legacy and forgo the debt or *vice versa*. He is not entitled to both.

It should be noted that no presumption arises if the legacy given to C is for less than the amount of the debt outstanding. Similarly the presumption arises in respect of pecuniary legacies only, and not devises of land or gifts of residue.

If the debt is secured (but the legacy is unsecured) then the presumption of satisfaction will not arise. Again the presumption has no effect if the debt is due immediately and the legacy due some time in the future.

The presumption may be rebutted either by an expression of contrary intention in the will or by extrinsic evidence showing that it was the testator's intention to give a legacy in addition to the debt.

(b) Satisfaction of a legacy by another legacy

If a testator makes two general legacies to the same legatee of the same amount then, in the absence of any expressed intention, certain rebuttable presumptions arise, namely:

(i)   Where both legacies are contained in the same will or codicil it is presumed that they are intended to be substitutional, although the presumption may be rebutted by extrinsic evidence.

(ii) Where each legacy is contained in a different instrument but the motive expressed for each gift is the same then they are presumed to be substitutional. Again, extrinsic evidence may be admitted to rebut the presumption.

(iii) In other cases where each legacy is contained in a different instrument then, as a matter of construction, the legacies are *prima facie* cumulative.

(c)   Equity leans against double portions

The equitable principle against "double portions" applies to gifts from a father but not the mother (or other person standing *in loco parentis*) to his child. It is based on the imputed intention of the father to give equal shares to each of his children. A gift is treated as a "portion" if made to establish the child in life or to make permanent provision for him or her.

Not all gifts by will are "portions" but many, such as shares of residue, are – see *Re Tussaud's Estate* (1878) 9 Ch D 363.

(i) Satisfaction of a portion-debt legacy: If a testator is under a legal obligation to provide a portion for a child and if he then makes a will giving either a legacy or a share of residue to that child, then it is presumed in equity that the legacy or share of residue so provided for was intended to be given in satisfaction (or partial satisfaction) of the portion-debt. The child must elect whether or not to take the gift in the will in satisfaction of the portion-debt.

(ii) Ademption of a legacy by a portion: If a testator falls under a legal obligation to provide a portion for a child after he has made a will or codicil providing for that child to have a legacy or share of residue, then a portion provided after the making of the will is presumed to adeem the testamentary gift either in whole or in part, unless a contrary intention can be shown on the part of the testator.

These equitable doctrines relating to double portions apply only between a child and father (or other person acting *in loco parentis*), and must not be applied to benefit a stranger.

C.19.2 Provision against satisfaction and ademption

I DIRECT AND DECLARE that no child or issue of mine receiving any share interest or benefit hereunder or under the trusts hereof or under any codicil hereto shall be liable to bring into account any other sum of money or any other property or interest paid transferred or settled or covenanted to be paid transferred or settled upon him or her or them either before or after the date hereof.

8. Conversion

The doctrine of conversion arises where land is devised upon trust for sale or where money is bequeathed with a direction to purchase realty, provided the direction is mandatory and not merely a discretion or power. For example, where the will creates a trust for sale of land, equity notionally regards the land as money from the date of death of the testator. The direction may be express or implied.

The effect of conversion is to include realty in a residuary bequest of personalty, and personalty in a residuary devise of realty, irrespective of the actual time of sale, since conversion takes effect from the testator's death notwithstanding any postponement of the sale. If the sale is contingent upon a future event then conversion will not take place until that event occurs.

In the event of postponement, any immediate income passes with the proceeds of sale. If the ultimate beneficiary elects to take the land rather than the proceeds of sale then such election will have the effect of a re-conversion.

Chapter 20

Administrative provisions in a will

1. Introduction

In the absence of detailed provisions in the will, the personal representatives and trustees may rely on various statutory powers to aid them in the administration of the estate. The main body of these powers is contained in the Administration of Estates Act 1925 and is supplemented by the Trustee Act 1925 and the Trustee Investments Act 1961. For the purposes of these Acts the term "trustee" includes a personal representative. Although the statutory powers are of great use they are not ideal for all situations. Some are subject to limitations which the testator may wish to remove or extend in order to give greater freedom to the trustees. It should also be noted that trustees and personal representatives require different administrative provisions since; although they may be, and frequently are, the same people, their roles are very different (see Chapter 8). Thus the objects of the gifts in the will should be considered when the administrative provisions are drafted.

2. Appropriation of assets

Under s 41 of the Administration of Estates Act 1925 personal representatives may, with the relevant consents, appropriate assets in order to satisfy a legacy in the will either in whole or in part.

If the beneficiary is absolutely and beneficially entitled, is an adult, and has full mental capacity, then his consent alone is all that is required for such an appropriation. If the beneficiary, though absolutely and beneficially entitled, is an infant or is mentally incapable of dealing with his own affairs, then the consent of his parent, guardian or receiver, as appropriate, must be obtained.

In the case of a settled legacy the consent of the trustees of the settlement is required unless those trustees are also the personal representatives of the estate, in which case the consent of the person for the time being entitled to the income of the settlement (provided that person is of full age and has full mental capacity) is required.

Where the person entitled to the income of the settlement is not of full age and capacity and the personal representatives are the trustees of the settlement, then the personal representatives may appropriate without consents only those investments that are authorised by law or by the will.

C.20.1 Power of appropriation

I DECLARE that my trustees may appropriate any real or personal property forming part of my estate to or towards the interest or share of any person or persons in the proceeds of sale thereof and may set apart from my estate any investments as they in their absolute discretion see fit to answer any annuity hereby bequeathed PROVIDED THAT the powers conferred hereunder are in addition to any power of appropriation or partition conferred upon my trustees by statute [and FURTHER PROVIDED THAT in every case my trustees shall not be required to obtain the consent of any person to any such appropriation].

C.20.2 Appropriation where trustee beneficially interested

I DECLARE that the power of appropriation hereinbefore contained shall be exercisable by my trustees notwithstanding the fact that one or more of such trustees may be beneficially interested in any property appropriated or partitioned thereunder.

C.20.3 Power to appropriate given by reference to Statutory Will Forms 1925, Form 6
I DECLARE that Statutory Will Forms, 1925, Form No 6 is incorporated herein.

C.20.4 Power of appropriation with consent of beneficiaries of full age
I DECLARE that my trustees may at any time or times with the consent in writing of all other persons for the time being entitled to share in my estate who are of full age and capacity appropriate any part of my residuary estate in its then actual condition or state of investment in or towards satisfaction of the share of any beneficiary in my estate PROVIDED THAT my trustees shall be required only to give notice of such appropriation to the last known address of each such person and if no objection to the intended appropriation is received within [three] months of the date of posting of such notice my trustees shall assume that such consent has been given and be entitled to proceed with such appropriation without such consent in writing AND I DECLARE that the powers conferred hereunder are in addition to any powers of appropriation and partition conferred on my trustees by statute.

3. Management of land and other assets

The Settled Land Act 1925 gives a tenant for life wide-ranging powers of management in respect of settled land. The trustees of the settlement, including those where there is a trust for sale, also have powers of management under that Act during any minority.

(a) Insurance
Section 19 of the Trustee Act 1925 allows trustees to insure any trust property against fire only up to a maximum of 75 per cent of its value. Section 102(2)(e) of the Settled Land Act 1925 allows insurance of land to any value, but again limited to insurance against fire. It is usually desirable to give trustees a full power to insure all property against all perils and to such value as they think fit.

C.20.5 Power to insure

I DIRECT that my trustees may insure against any perils any land buildings chattels or other insurable property for the time being comprised in my estate to such value as they think fit notwithstanding that any person is absolutely entitled to such property with discretion to pay the premiums for such insurance out of income or capital as they consider fit PROVIDED THAT any money received by my trustees in respect of any such policy shall be applicable as if the same were proceeds of sale of the property insured.

(b) Improvement of land

The powers relating to development and improvement of settled land are set out under Sch 3 of the Settled Land Act 1925 and s 102 (2)(b) and (d) of that Act. The complexities of those provisions are such that an express power in simple form may often be more desirable.

C.20.6 Power to improve land

I DIRECT THAT my trustees may carry out any development redevelopment alteration demolition or any work of improvement of whatever nature in respect of any land building or structure wheresoever situate upon property forming part of my [residuary] estate or the proceeds of sale of which form part of the [residuary] estate and may pay the cost of the same and any incidental expenses out of the capital of my residuary estate to be held upon the same trusts as the land building or structure aforesaid.

(c) Repairs

Trustees may generally carry out repairs, paying for them out of income (ss 102(2)(b) and 13 Settled Land Act 1925). There are exceptional circumstances in which repairs may be paid for out of capital, notably if they are in the nature of permanent improvements.

It may be desirable to extend the trustees' powers to pay for repairs out of capital but care should be taken to avoid such a provision in an accumulation and maintenance trust.

C.20.7 Power to repair and pay for repairs from capital

I DIRECT THAT my trustees may repair any building structure chattel or other property forming part of my [residuary] estate or the proceeds of sale which form part of my [residuary] estate whatsoever and wheresoever situate and may pay the costs of such repairs from such of the income or capital of any part of my [residuary] estate as they think fit to be held on the same trusts as the property repaired.

(d) Leases

Except for some limited powers in respect of building, mining and forestry leases contained in s 41 of the Settled Land Act 1925, the trustees have no power to grant leases. If such powers are required, for example in respect of residential properties, an express power should be inserted in the will.

It may be useful to give an express power permitting not only the granting of leases but also the sale, purchase and mortgaging of property.

C.20.8 Power to lease, mortgage, sell or purchase

My trustees shall have power to enter into and approve any agreement lease deed or other instrument for the purposes of any sale lease mortgage charge or purchase in relation to any property wheresoever situate as if absolute and beneficial owners of my residuary estate.

(e) Foreign land

The Settled Land Act 1925 applies to land in England and Wales only. Express powers should be given to trustees in respect of any land situated elsewhere.

C.20.9 Extension of powers to foreign land

I DECLARE that any powers conferred on my trustees hereby or by statute or by the general law on trustees for sale which but for this provision apply only to land in England and Wales shall apply equally to any land or immovable property outside England and Wales.

(f) Debts
C.20.10 Power to defer payment of debts

My trustees may defer the calling in or collection of any debt or debts which may be owing to me from [name] at the date of my death for any period not exceeding [3] years provided any interest due thereon be regularly paid and I declare that they shall not be liable for any loss occasioned thereby.

4. Power to carry on a business

Where the testator runs a business as a sole trader his personal representatives have an implied power (in the absence of any express provision) to enable them to continue the business in order to sell it as a going concern. That power is limited to realising the value of the business and does not continue indefinitely. In case market conditions are unfavourable it is wise to give the personal representatives power to carry on any business for so long as they think fit, or for a long but specified period. Furthermore it should be noted that, unless otherwise provided, the personal representatives may employ only those assets already used in the business at the date of the testator's death.

It will also be noted that personal representatives running the business will be liable for any debts they incur. If the business is being carried on only for the purposes of realisation, then the personal representatives have a right to an indemnity from the estate in priority to the testator's creditors and to the beneficiaries. If, however, the personal representatives are given express authority to carry on the business, their indemnity will give them priority over the beneficiaries only, not creditors.

In the case of partnerships or limited companies the personal representatives cannot normally take over any management functions on behalf of the testator. Unless the partnership deed states otherwise, the death of one partner will terminate a partnership.

In the case of companies, reference should be made to the Articles of Association as to what is to happen upon the death of a shareholder. It is usually possible to sell the shares and may be possible to transfer the shares to a beneficiary – subject to the company's agreement to register the transfer. It is important that any relevant partnership agreement or the Articles of Association of any relevant company are made available to and considered by the draftsman preparing a will. (See also Chapter 12.)

C.20.11 Power to carry on a business

My trustees may carry on any business of which I am a proprietor or partner at the time of my death and may act either alone or in partnership for so long as my trustees shall in their absolute discretion consider expedient and my trustees shall have power to employ any of the capital of my [residuary] estate in order to carry on such business and shall be fully indemnified in respect of any liabilities arising from that business and no such trustee shall be liable to any of the beneficiaries under this my will or any codicil hereto for any loss sustained as a result of the conduct of the business by my trustees unless such loss arises from fraud or wrongdoing on the part of that trustee personally.

5. Power to borrow

The statutory powers of borrowing are contained in s 16 of the Trustee Act 1925 and s 71(1)(ii) of the Settled Land Act 1925. The former provision allows trustees to borrow and mortgage property in order to raise money for an authorised payment or application of capital money. Unsecured borrowing is not permitted. The money cannot be used to finance other investments. The latter provision is restricted to obtaining a legal mortgage in order to fund improvements authorised by statute or the settlement.

Testators will often wish to extend the trustees' powers of borrowing.

C.20.12 Power to borrow

My trustees shall have full power to borrow money upon such terms as they in their absolute discretion think fit with or without giving security and may apply any moneys so borrowed for any purpose connected with the trusts of my estate.

6. Purchase of trust property by trustees

Because of the fiduciary nature of the trustee's position he is generally prohibited from purchasing trust property, although there are some circumstances in which a court may authorise such a purchase (see

Holder v *Holder* [1968] Ch 353, and *Ex parte Lacey* (1802) 6 Ves 625).

A testator may give the trustees a power to purchase specific items of trust property from the estate, but provisions should be included in order that an appropriate purchase price may be ascertained.

C.20.13 Power to trustees to purchase trust property

I DECLARE that the said [name] shall have power to purchase [specific property] [any part of my estate not otherwise specifically disposed of whether real or personal] either by private treaty or public auction notwithstanding that the said [name] is a trustee of this my will [and in the event of a sale by private treaty the purchase price shall be that price agreed between the said [name] and my other trustees for the time being] [provided that any price agreed in respect of quoted securities shall not be less than the market price thereof at the time of the execution of the transfer] [and further provided that my trustees other than [name] shall obtain a valuation of the property by an independent surveyor or valuer [to be paid for by the said [name]] and the purchase price shall not be less than the said valuation].

7. Retention of directors' remuneration

In the absence of a contrary provision a trustee would be liable to account for all director's fees received by him, and an ordinary charging clause is not a sufficient contrary provision to give a trustee-director power to retain such remuneration.

C.20.14 Power for trustees to become directors and to retain remuneration

I declare that any one or more of my trustees may act as a director or other officer or employee of [the said Company Limited] [any company] without being liable to account to my estate or the persons beneficially interested therein for any remuneration paid to such trustee or trustees for so acting [and any trustee may become qualified as a director (if the Articles of Association of the said company so allow) by holding in his own name shares belonging to my estate provided that he executes a declaration of trust thereof in favour of my trustees generally accompanied by the certificates of such shares and also provided that he accounts to my estate for all dividends and bonuses payable in respect thereof].

8. Power to act by majority

Trustees, other than trustees of a charity, must act unanimously unless a special provision permits them to act by a majority.

C.20.15 Direction to trustees to act by majority

I declare that in all matters relating to the execution of the trusts of this my will or any codicil hereto the opinion of the majority of the trustees for the time being thereof shall be decisive.

9. Power to employ agents

Under s 23(1) of the Trustee Act 1925 a personal representative may employ an agent to do any act on his behalf connected with the trust or its administration, but he may not delegate the exercise of any discretion.

Provided that the agent has been employed in good faith the personal representatives will not be vicariously liable for their agent's acts, but the personal representatives do owe a duty of care properly to supervise the trust and the administration of the estate and to ensure that any agents they employ are suitable and reliable.

The exercise of any trusts, power or discretions vested in a trustee may be delegated to a third party by a power of attorney for a period up to but not exceeding one year – Powers of Attorney Act 1971, s 9.

C.20.16 Power to employ and pay agents

My trustees shall have power to engage and employ any agents advisers managers (whether corporate or not) or any other person or body and may pay any remuneration or other expenses or outgoings in respect of the same out of the capital or the income of my estate as they think fit and I declare that my trustees shall not be liable for any loss or damage caused to my estate or the income thereof by reason of any act or omission on the part of any such person or corporation if engaged or employed in good faith.

C.20.17 Direction to employ named solicitor

It is my wish that [name of solicitor or firm] be employed by my trustees in all matters relating to [the proving of this my will and in transacting] any legal business in the administration of the trusts hereof.

10. Power to take counsel's opinion

Legal issues may arise as to the interpretation of the will, the terms of its trusts or in relation to the estate itself. The trustees may apply to the court for directions in any such case, but this will be an expense to the estate and the trustees may prefer to rely on the opinion of a senior barrister. In estates where such difficulties are likely to arise, a power should be given to the trustees to rely on the advice of counsel without being liable for any loss. This will give some protection to trustees who do not wish to apply to court for directions. Either the trustees or the beneficiaries may still apply to the court if they think fit.

C.20.18 Power to act on counsel's opinion

My trustees shall have power to seek and act upon the advice of any Queen's Counsel [or any barrister who has been admitted for not less than 10 years] practising in the Chancery Division of the High Court of Justice in relation to any question of interpretation or administration arising under this my will or any codicil hereto or the trusts hereof and my trustees shall not be liable to any of the persons beneficially interested in respect of any act or omission done or made in accordance with such advice or opinion.

11. Appointment of new trustees

The number of executors who may take a grant in respect of any particular part of any estate is limited to four – Supreme Court Act 1981, s 114(1).

It is not usual, therefore, to appoint more than four trustees in a private trust. Where only one trustee is appointed he will be able to perform most acts of joint trustees except that a single trustee cannot give a valid receipt for capital moneys arising on the disposition of land unless the trustee is a trust corporation. The Trustee Act 1925 ss 36(1)(2) and 41 detail the circumstances in which new trustees may be appointed either by the persons nominated in the Act (s 36) or by the court (s 41).

C.20.19 Power of appointment of new trustees conferred by the Trustee Act 1925

I DECLARE that my wife shall have vested in her the statutory power of appointment of new trustees of the trusts hereof and upon her death the same shall vest in such person of full age as shall for the time being have an interest in possession in the trust property in respect whereof a new trustee is to be appointed.

C.20.20 Direction as to number of trustees

I direct that there shall at all times be [four] trustees of this my will and that any vacancy in the trusteeship hereof shall be filled as soon as may be reasonably practicable always provided that the trustees hereof for the time being shall during any vacancy have the same powers authorities and discretions and may act in all respects as if there were [four] trustees hereof.

12. Indemnity clauses

Trustee "indemnity" clauses are clauses which are intended to absolve trustees or executors from liability in the event of their own negligence or the negligence or fraud of their co-trustees or agents.

C.20.21 General indemnity clause

I DECLARE that none of my trustees shall be liable for any act or omission of his or hers or for any act or omission of any agent employed in the administration of my estate or in the execution of the trusts hereunder nor for any act or omission of any co-trustee or any co-personal representative save and except for any act or omission involving wilful fraud or dishonesty committed by the trustee or personal representative sought to be made liable.

C.20.22 Indemnity to trustees acting on counsel's opinion

No trustee hereof shall be personally liable for any act or omission done or made in accordance with the written opinion of a Queen's Counsel or other counsel qualified for at least [10 years] and practising in the Chancery Division of the High Court of Justice upon any question of procedure or interpretation of whatever nature including questions in connection with the administration of the trusts hereof.

C.20.23 Exclusion of liability for acts of attorneys

Notwithstanding any statutory provisions to the contrary none of my trustees or personal representatives who grant a power of attorney to any third party shall be liable for the acts or omissions of the donee of such power provided that the donor acts in good faith and the power so given does not endure for longer than 12 months.

C.20.24 Exclusion from duty to intervene in affairs of a private company in which trust funds are invested

Notwithstanding the fact that part or all of (my residuary estate) may be invested in any company my trustees shall not be under any duty to intervene in the affairs of that company or enquire into its management or conduct of business UNLESS my trustees have received actual notice of dishonesty on the part of the directors of any such company.

C.20.25 Receipt by or on behalf of minors

I DECLARE that where my trustees are to pay any money whether capital or income to a minor or apply it for his or her benefit under any obligation or discretion my trustees may pay the said money to any parent or guardian of that minor or to the minor himself or herself if over sixteen years of age and their respective receipts shall be good discharge to my trustees who shall not be bound to enquire as to the application of such moneys.

Note: If this clause is omitted the trustees would have only the powers conferred on them by s 31 of the Trustee Act 1925 (see page 209).

C.20.26 Clause dealing with missing beneficiaries

I DECLARE that if after employing all reasonable diligence my trustees are unable to trace any beneficiary under my estate within three years from the date when the gift to him or her becomes payable then my trustees may distribute my estate as if all such unfound beneficiaries if any had predeceased me and the interest of any such beneficiary in my estate shall wholly and irrevocably cease.

13. Charging clauses

As a general rule a professional trustee may charge for his professional work only. To ensure that the trustee will receive remuneration for all his time spent a charging clause is necessary, and may be advisable even where it is not originally intended to appoint a professional trustee, as one may be appointed during the period of the trust.

C.20.27 Charging clause in respect of professional trustee
I DECLARE that any trustee hereof who may be a solicitor or engaged in any profession or business may retain and receive out of my estate all usual professional costs and charges by way of remuneration for business transacted by him or his firm [whether such business was of a professional nature or could have been done personally] together with any out of pocket expenses incurred in the execution of such business as if any such trustee had not been one of my trustees but had been employed in the administration of my estate and the execution of the trusts hereof and I further declare that the said costs and charges shall be paid in priority to all legacies and annuities and the satisfaction of all specific gifts hereby or by any codicil hereto given.

Note: In the absence of the words in square brackets the professional trustee could charge for his professional work only – *Re Chalinder and Herington* [1907] 1 Ch 58.

C.20.28 Provision for appointment of trust corporation
I DECLARE that in exercising the power of appointment vested in them by statute my trustees may appoint a trust corporation to act alone or with another or other trustees and in the event of a trust corporation being so appointed I hereby authorise such trust corporation to charge retain and receive out of my estate such fees and remuneration [as is agreed upon between my trustees and the said trust corporation at the time of such appointment] [as is chargeable according to the scale of fees charged by such trust corporation from time to time].

14. Power of investment

In the absence of an express investment clause the Trustee
Investments Act 1961 gives trustees a power to invest in three kinds
of authorised investment:

(a) Narrow range not requiring advice
These include such items as Defence Bonds and National
Savings Certificates. Such investments may be selected without
the trustee taking any expert advice.

(b) Narrow range requiring advice
These include such items as debentures in UK companies complying with certain conditions (see (c) below), mortgages of
freehold land or leasehold land provided that the lease has more
than 60 years of its term left, and Government stock.

(c) Wider range investments
These include authorised unit trusts, shares in designated building societies and shares in UK companies complying with the
following conditions:
  • the company must be quoted on a recognised stock exchange;
  • the shares or debentures must be fully paid up or required to
    be paid up within nine months of issue;
  • the company must have a total issued and paid up share capi-
    tal of at least £1m;
  • the company must have paid a dividend on all shares ranking
    for dividend in each of the immediately preceding five years;
  • the company must be incorporated in the UK.

A trustee who wishes to invest in wider range investments must
divide the fund into two parts which must be equal at the time of the
division, and a written valuation must be obtained from a person reasonably believed by the trustees to be qualified to make it. One half of
the fund must be invested in narrow range investments, the other may
be invested in either narrow range or wider range investments. If
property is transferred from one part of the fund to another a compensating transfer must be made in the opposite direction.

If property subsequently accrues to the trust fund the trustees must
ensure that the value of each part of the fund is increased by the same
amount. But where the property which accrues relates directly to one

part of the fund (for example, a bonus share issue) it is treated as accruing only to that part of the fund and a compensating transfer is not required. A trustee is free to withdraw property for trust purposes from either part of the fund without making any compensating transfer.

Before making investments in wider and narrow range investments the trustees must obtain and consider written advice on the suitability of the investment from a person reasonably believed to be qualified in such financial matters. Such advice must be periodically obtained and considered. The advice must relate *inter alia* to the need for diversification of investments and the suitability of investments of the type proposed and of the particular investment as an example of the type.

As the powers of investment enjoyed by the trustees under the Trustee Investments Act 1961 are thus limited, trustees are often expressly given wider powers of investment.

Even the widest investment clause, however, does not authorise trustees to purchase property, be it realty or personalty, for purposes other than investment, and therefore if the testator wishes the trustees to purchase a house as a residence for a beneficiary rather than as an investment, then an express clause containing such a power must be included.

C.20.29 Wider power of investment

My trustees shall have full power to invest any trust money subject to the trusts hereof in such amounts and proportions as they see fit in any of the following:

(i) The public stocks funds or government securities of the United Kingdom

(ii) Any securities the interest or dividends on which is or shall be guaranteed by Parliament

(iii) Freehold and leasehold securities in Great Britain [but not in Ireland] PROVIDED any such leasehold securities have at least 60 years to run at the date of such investment and always provided that each such security ranks in priority as a first mortgage or a first registered charge under the Land Registration Act 1925

(iv) The bonds debentures or rentcharge stock mortgages or the preference stock of any public company wherever incorporated or carrying on business

[(v) The ordinary stock or shares or ordinary preferred or deferred or other stock or shares of any public or private company wherever incorporated or carrying on business [but not including bonds to bearer or other negotiable instruments or any documents of title negotiable by delivery with or without indorsement]]

(vi) Bonds stocks debentures or other securities of any municipal or local body or authority in any part of the world not including bonds to bearer or other negotiable instruments or any documents of title negotiable by delivery with or without indorsement

C.20.30   Wide power of investment – obligation to take advice

My trustees shall have full power to invest trust moneys in any of the following:

(a) any investment for the time being authorised by law for the investment of trust funds

(b) any investments of whatsoever nature which at the date of purchase are or on allotment will be dealt in or quoted on the London Stock Exchange or on any of the stock exchanges of New York Montreal Paris Amsterdam Zurich Tokyo or Johannesburg

PROVIDED ALWAYS that no money forming part of the trust funds shall be invested:

(i) In partly-paid-up shares except shares of banking and insurance companies incorporated in the United Kingdom

(ii) In ordinary or deferred shares or stocks of a company unless at the time of investment such company has a paid-up capital of [£500,000] or its equivalent at the rate of exchange current at the time of the investment

(c) the purchase of freehold and leasehold land situate in the United Kingdom provided that leasehold land shall be purchased only if at the date of the purchase the unexpired term exceeds sixty years

PROVIDED ALWAYS that the requirements of the Trustee Investments Act 1961 as to the division of trust funds before investing in investments specified in Part III of the First Schedule to the said Act shall not apply but the requirements of the said Act as to obtaining advice shall apply as if the investments authorised hereby were specified in Part II or III of the First Schedule to the said Act.

C.20.31   Power to purchase property as a residence for beneficiaries

(1) My trustees may invest or apply any part or all of my residuary estate and the income therefrom subject to the trusts hereof in the

purchase of any freehold or leasehold land or property for the purpose of providing a residence for any one or more of my wife and children and my trustees may invest or apply such capital and income as they think fit for the purpose of having a residence built on any land so purchased and extending repairing maintaining altering demolishing rebuilding or improving any house or buildings upon any land so purchased by my trustees or otherwise forming part of my estate for the time being ALWAYS PROVIDED THAT my trustees shall not purchase any leasehold property unless at least sixty years of the leasehold term remains unexpired at the date of purchase.

(2) My trustees shall hold any land buildings and property purchased under clause (1) hereof upon trust to sell the same with full power to postpone the sale for so long as they in their absolute discretion think fit and any capital moneys arising from the sale shall form part of my residuary estate and be subject to the trusts and provisions herein declared.

C.20.32 Power to invest in investments in which any part of the estate is invested at death of testator

My trustees shall have full power to invest the whole or any part of trust moneys in or upon any of the investments or securities in which any part of my personal estate is invested at the date of my death and any requirements of the Trustee Investments Act 1961 as to the division of trust funds before investment or as to obtaining advice shall not apply to any such investments.

C.20.33 Power to delegate investment powers

My trustees may delegate with respect to the whole or any part of [my residuary estate] any of their powers hereby or by law conferred relating to the investment management or administration of trust moneys or other trust assets to any person carrying on the business of management of investments to any extent for any period on any terms and in any manner as my trustees think fit and may pay the remuneration of such person out of the capital or income of [my residuary estate] and vest trust assets in such person as nominee for my trustees.

C.20.34 Clause authorising investment in a particular company

I direct that my trustees may invest in any stocks shares and securities of every description in [name] Company Limited and in any company which upon any reconstruction amalgamation or sale shall take over the business of the said company.

C.20.35 Clause prohibiting investments in specific country

My trustees shall not invest any part of [my residuary estate] in any stock shares debentures or other securities of any description of any company corporation government or public authority of or situated in or owning assets in [name of country].

C.20.36 Power to purchase any freehold or leasehold property

My trustees may purchase any freehold or leasehold property in England or Wales provided that any leasehold property purchased is held upon a lease [or under-lease] having not less than [50] years unexpired at the date of investment.

C.20.37 Power to lend on mortgage and related powers

My trustees shall have power to invest trust money by advancing the same on the security of a contributory mortgage [whether on freehold or leasehold property and] subject to such stipulations and for such fixed period as they shall think expedient and my trustees may accept such other security as they think fit for any part of the trust property which may be invested on real security in lieu of all or any of the properties comprised in any such security as aforesaid and release from any such security as aforesaid any of the properties therein comprised without which the trustees shall deem the remaining security or securities sufficient.

15. Power to maintain infants

Trustees and personal representatives are given statutory powers of accumulation and maintenance under s 31 of the Trustee Act 1925. Under that section they can apply any available income towards the maintenance, education or benefit of any infant beneficiary, and that power extends to beneficiaries whose interests are contingent only. Any income that is not applied under that section must be accumulated.

The statute directs trustees in the exercise of their discretion to consider various factors, namely, the age and requirements of the minor, the general circumstances of the case and, more particularly, whether any other income is available to be applied for the same power.

Where the income of more than one trust fund is available for the same purposes, the trustees must generally apply the income of each fund proportionately to satisfy the purpose, any excess income being accumulated in its respective fund.

Any income that has been accumulated may be applied during the minority of the beneficiary as if it were the income of the current years. This power thus enables the trustees to make up for any deficiency in income in current years from any unrequired income of previous years.

Once a minor beneficiary attains the age of eighteen then, if the gift remains contingent, the trustees must pay to the beneficiary the income of the trust fund until the contingency is met or the gift fails – Trustee Act 1925, s 31(1).

Any accumulations arising during the minority of the beneficiary will normally be added to the capital of the fund when the minor becomes eighteen. However, if the beneficiary has only a life interest in the fund then that beneficiary is entitled to all the accumulated income when he attains the age of majority. If, however, the beneficiary dies under the age of eighteen then the accumulations will be added to capital and devolve accordingly – Trustee Act 1925, s 31(2).

If a gift is contingent upon a beneficiary's attaining an age greater than eighteen years then, unless the statutory right to receive the income at eighteen is removed by an express provision to the contrary, the beneficiary obtains an interest in possession at eighteen for inheritance tax purposes. If the beneficiary then dies before the contingency is met the whole of the trust property will be included in his estate for the purposes of calculating inheritance tax, even though the beneficiary has no right to the capital at the time of his death.

C.20.38 Simple clause for maintenance

(1) My trustees shall have power to apply any part or all of the income of the expectant or presumptive share of any child [or grandchild] [of mine] entitled under the trusts hereof during the minority of such child [or grandchild] and subject to payment of any prior charge or interest affecting the said income as they shall in their absolute discretion think fit for or towards the maintenance education or benefit of such child or grandchild and I DIRECT that

my trustees may pay the same to any parent or guardian as for the time being of any such minor for the purposes aforesaid without being liable to enquire as to the application of the same.

(2) My trustees may exercise the power aforesaid notwithstanding the fact that there may be another fund or other funds or income available for any of the aforesaid purposes and whether or not there is any person bound by law to provide for such maintenance or education.

(3) Any income not applied towards the purposes aforesaid shall be accumulated by investing the same and the resulting income thereof in any investments authorised under the trusts hereof and by the general law and such accumulations shall be added to the property or to the share therein from which the same was derived and shall devolve therewith so as to follow the destination of such property or share but my trustees shall be entitled at any time to apply any part of such accumulations for any of the purposes aforesaid as if the same were income arising in the then current year.

16. Power to advance capital

Subject to certain statutory limitations, trustees and personal representatives have an absolute discretion to apply capital for the advancement or benefit of any person who has either a vested or a contingent interest in capital – Trustee Act 1925, s 32. The power does not extend to capital money or land under a Settled Land Act settlement.

The statutory power is wide enough to allow property to be advanced to new trustees under new trusts which may contain powers and discretions not given under the original trust instrument.

Any advance given to a contingently interested beneficiary cannot be recovered from that beneficiary's estate should he die before the contingency is met.

There are three limitations on the power, as follows:
- (a) the trustees may advance up to one-half only of the beneficiary's vested or presumptive share;
- (b) any advance made must be brought into account when the beneficiary becomes absolutely entitled;
- (c) any person with a prior interest must consent to the advance.

A testator may wish to remove or amend one or more of the statutory limitations and leave the exercise of the power to the trustees' discretion.

C.20.39 Variation of statutory power of advancement

I declare that the statutory power of advancement conferred on trustees by s 32 of the Trustee Act 1925 shall apply to the trusts hereof as if incorporated herein save that my trustees shall be permitted to advance up to [three-quarters] of the value of any beneficiary's vested or share presumed [the sum of £......].

C.20.40 Power of advancement

My trustees shall have power to raise any sum or sums out of the then presumptive contingent expectant or vested share of any [child] of mine not exceeding altogether [one third] of that share and may pay or advance the same as my trustees think fit for the advancement or benefit of such child PROVIDED THAT any person entitled to any prior interest whether vested or contingent in the money so to be paid or advanced shall first consent to such payment or advancement.

C.20.41 Extension of statutory power of advancement to tenant for life

I DECLARE that the statutory power of advancement under s 32 of the Trustee Act 1925 shall apply to the trusts hereof and I further declare that my trustees shall have a power of advancement like in all respects to the foregoing statutory power to pay or advance money out of or raised from the trust property or a share thereof in favour of any person who may be entitled to a life interest therein.

17. Duties and powers where the residuary estate is settled

Trustees must act impartially at all times and balance the interests of all the beneficiaries in the estate. They must not, for example, choose high income producing shares in preference to capital growth, as this will unfairly favour the tenant for life over the remainderman. A system of rules has developed to guide trustees through their duties.

(a) Duty to convert

In general, trustees need not convert the original trust fund even when the investments held would normally be unauthorised. Although the trustees may not increase their holding of unauthorised investments, the original investments may be held as "special range" investments. They will, however, be under a duty to convert:

(a)   if directed to do so expressly by the trust instrument, for example under a trust for sale; or

(b)   if the rule in *Howe* v *Dartmouth* (1807) 7 Ves 137 applies. This rule applies when there is a gift by will of a testator's residuary personalty upon trust for persons by way of succession. In such a case, the trustees must sell those parts of the residuary personalty which consist of the following:

- wasting assets, which are those assets whose value is bound to depreciate over the years. Leaseholds having at least 60 years to run are not wasting assets (see, however, *Re Gough* [1957] Ch 323).

- reversionary interests – for example an interest in remainder where there is a subsisting life interest. This term includes any interest in property which is not immediately available on the testator's death and which will become available only at some time in the future.

- unauthorised investments – these are investments not authorised by the Trustee Investments Act 1961 or by the testator in his will, that is, by a special investment clause.

The rule in *Howe* v *Dartmouth* does not apply:

(i)   where there is an express clause that *Howe* v *Dartmouth* shall not apply;

(ii)   where there is an apparent intention that the tenant for life shall enjoy the property in the form in which it exists at the testator's death;

(iii)   where there is an express provision that no item in the estate be sold;

(iv)   where there is a provision in the will conferring a discretion to sell assets if and when expedient, for example a power "to retain or sell or convert";

(v)   where the trustee or some other person has a discretion as to what part of the estate should be converted;

(vi)   where the will directs that the property be converted only on the death of the tenant for life;

(vii) to leasehold interests with an unexpired term of more than 60 years, since these are authorised investments under the Settled Land Act 1925, s 73(1)(xi);

(viii)to leasehold interests with an unexpired term of less than 60 years since these are treated as capital moneys under the Settled Land Act 1925.

(c) where a trust for sale is imposed under statute, for example Administration of Estates Act 1925, s 33.

C.20.42 Power to postpone conversion

My trustees shall have power to postpone the sale calling in and conversion of my residuary real and personal property or any part thereof [(except shares in companies with unlimited liability which I direct shall be sold as soon as conveniently may be after my death)] for so long as my trustees shall in their absolute discretion think fit without being liable for any loss occasioned thereby.

Note: The words in square brackets are adequate to exclude the implied statutory power to postpone sale.

(b) Apportionment of income

Various rules of apportionment have developed which govern what is to happen to the income of property which the trustees are under a duty to convert, but there is delay in converting. The rules will come into play if the testator has made no express provision regarding that intermediate income. They vary depending on the nature of the property concerned.

(i) Freehold and leasehold property: The life tenant will take the full income as from the date of death. No apportionment has to be made.

(ii) Authorised investments: The life tenant takes the whole income as from the date of death.

(iii) Wasting and unauthorised investments (other than leaseholds): The life tenant is not entitled to the actual income and an apportionment has to be made so that the life tenant receives, from the date of death until the date of sale, a minimum of 4% of the value of the

investments, and the remaining income accrues to the capital part of the fund. The value to be taken can be:

- the value of the investments one year after the testator's death, if there is no power to postpone sale and the investments are still unsold at that time;
- if investments have been sold within the year, the actual proceeds are taken as the value;
- if the will gives power to postpone sale, the value of the investments is taken as at the testator's death.

If the income earned by the unauthorised investment is less than 4%, the life tenant receives that actual income and is entitled to have it made up to 4% from future surpluses of income or, if none, then from capital when the asset is sold.

(iv) Reversionary interests: Where the trustees are under a duty to convert a reversionary interest, that interest will be producing no income and therefore until it falls into possession or is sold, there is nothing to apportion. When it eventually does fall into possession or is sold, an apportionment has to be made in order to be fair to the life tenant, and the rule governing the method of that apportionment is known as the rule in *Re Earl of Chesterfield's Trusts* (1883) 24 Ch D 643. Under this rule, a part of the amount actually received is treated as arrears of income and paid to the life tenant, and only the balance is regarded as capital. The proportion of the amount actually received which is regarded as capital and which goes to the capital of the fund for the benefit of the remainderman is:

such sum which, if invested at 4% compound interest at the testator's death with yearly rests, would, after allowing for the deduction of income tax at the basic rate for the time being in force, have produced the sum actually received.

Yearly rests are the intervals at which the interest is compounded. For example one of the assets in an estate may be a reversionary interest consisting of the right to receive £5,000 on the death of A, who is still alive when the testator dies. The interest will remain reversionary and not "fall in" until the death of A. Assuming that the *Howe* v *Dartmouth* conditions are satisfied, or that there is an express trust for sale in the will, the trustees are under a duty to convert that reversionary interest and invest the proceeds in authorised investments from which the life tenant will receive the income. However, if the trustees decide not to sell but to wait until the interest falls into possession, then the life tenant will get no income in the meantime. If A then dies (or the interest is sold) two years after the testator's death and the value of the reversionary interest was £15,000 at that time then, assuming a basic rate of income tax throughout the period of 25%, the trustees would find that £14,138.94 invested at the testator's death at 4% compound interest would, after allowing for deduction of tax at 25%, have produced £15,000 at the date this sum was actually received. The £14,138.94 would therefore be invested by the trustees as capital, the remaining £861.06 being paid to the life tenant as income for the preceding two years. To calculate the apportionment amounts, one must start with the value of the reversion when it fell in or was sold – £15,000 in this case – and then "work backwards" year by year until the date of the testator's death. With the basic rate of income tax at 25% the net income earned at 4% on each £100 of capital is £3. So the sum needed to produce the £15,000 after one year of investment can be found by applying the formula:

$$\frac{£15,000 \times 100}{103} = £14,563.11$$

Applying the formula again to this new figure, the sum needed to produce the £15,000 after two years of investment can be calculated:

$$\frac{£14,563.11 \times 100}{103} = £14,138.94$$

Alternatively, to find the sum which must be invested at compound interest to provide a given amount in a given number of years the following formula is used:

$$\text{Sum} = \text{Amount} \times \left(\frac{100}{100+R}\right)^{n} \quad \text{(where R is the rate of interest and n is the number of years).}$$

It is usual for the rule in *Howe* v *Dartmouth* and *Re Chesterfield's Trusts* to be excluded in order to avoid the administrative expense and difficulty in operating them. The usual way of excluding them is to direct that the actual income of the estate is to be treated as the income from the testator's death.

C.20.43 Clause expressly excluding the rule in *Howe* v *Dartmouth* and *Re Chesterfield's Trusts*

I DIRECT that the rule of equity known as the rule in Howe v Earl of Dartmouth and any derivative rule shall not apply in the administration of my estate and the execution of the trusts hereof.

C.20.44 Clause excluding the rule in *Howe* v *Dartmouth* – full form

I DIRECT that no reversionary or future property comprised in my estate shall be sold until it falls into possession unless it appears to my trustees in their absolute discretion that an earlier sale would be beneficial to my estate AND I FURTHER DIRECT THAT the income of all parts of my estate however constituted or invested shall as from my death be treated and applied as income and the income of all parts of my estate for the time being remaining unsold shall be applied as if the same were income of authorised investments and no reversionary or other property not producing income shall be treated as producing income.

C.20.45 Clause excluding the Apportionment Acts on the death of the testator

I direct that all interest dividends and other payments in the nature of income arising from my estate or any part thereof and received after my death in respect of a period wholly or partly before my death shall be treated as accruing wholly after my death and shall not be apportioned.

C.20.46 Clause excluding the Apportionment Acts on the death of persons entitled to a life interest or lesser interests

All interest dividends and other payments in the nature of income arising from my residuary estate or any share therein and received after the time when any person entitled to the income thereof ceases to be so entitled in respect of a period wholly or partly before such time shall be treated as accruing wholly after such time and shall not be apportioned.

(For clauses excluding the rule in *Allhusen* v *Whittell*, see Chapter 18.)

Chapter 21

Perpetuities and accumulation

1. The general perpetuity rule

It is important that any gift in a will complies with the perpetuity rule.
The rule was initially developed at common law but has been amended by the Law of Property Act 1925 and the Perpetuities and
Accumulations Act 1964. The 1964 Act is not retrospective in its
effect and applies only to gifts made on or after 16 July 1964. It
should be remembered that there are three aspects to this rule:
  (a) the rule against vesting (see below);
  (b) the rule against perpetual trusts (see page 226);
  (c) the rule against accumulations (see page 226).

2. The common law rule against vesting outside the perpetuity period

This states that any future interest in any property is void *ab initio* if
at the time of its creation (which in the case of a will is the date of
death of the testator) there is a remote possibility that the gift may
vest outside the perpetuity period.

The rule applies to future interests, that is, interests which do not give rise to a present enjoyment of the property, but it should be remembered that it does not apply to all future interests, only to those which are contingent as opposed to vested. An interest is vested for the purposes of the perpetuity rule if certain criteria are satisfied:

(a) the person or persons entitled must be ascertained;

(b) there must be no condition attached to the gift;

(c) the size of the beneficiary's interest must be known (particularly in relation to class gifts).

If there is any possibility, however remote, that a person's share of the property may vest outside the perpetuity period, the gift is void. A future interest is still vested if the above criteria are fulfilled and the person entitled to the interest is being kept out of enjoyment not because any condition is unmet for the time being, but by a prior interest which has been granted. For example, Blackacre to A for life then to B absolutely. A has a vested interest which is in possession and B has a future interest, but that future interest is vested since A must die at some time.

The rule applies to all types of proprietary interests, except charitable gifts and devises, and it is irrelevant that a gift may never vest at all. The rule is only concerned with the fact that if it is going to vest it does so within the perpetuity period.

A gift which would in normal circumstances be void for perpetuity at common law may be saved by the insertion of an express clause confirming that the gift will vest within a valid period. Such a clause must be explicit. The phrase "within the limitations prescribed by law" has in the past been held to save a gift – *Re Vaux* [1939] Ch 465, but the phrase "so far as the rules of law and equity will permit" has not – *Portman* v *Viscount Portman* [1922] 2 AC 473.

3. Period allowed by the rule

The common law perpetuity period is a life or lives in being at the date of the gift plus a period of twenty-one years after the termination of the last of those lives. The expression "life in being" includes a person *en ventre sa mère* at the date the gift comes into effect and born alive later. A testator may choose any person or persons to be the life or lives in being for the purposes of the perpetuity rule, provided that such a person is alive or *en ventre sa mère* at the date of the death of the testator (that is, the date of the gift). Such a person can expressly or implicitly be referred to in the gift, or can be a person whose life or lives have some connection with the vesting contingency although they need not be entitled to any benefit under the gift. Any number of people may be lives in being at any one time as long as it is reasonably possible to ascertain them – *Thelluson* v *Woodford* (1805) 11 Ves 112.

This is the basis of the so-called "royal lives clause", which is a period of restriction ending at the expiration of, for example, twenty years from the day of the death of the last survivor of all the lineal descendants of Queen Victoria who shall be living at the time of the testator's death – *Re Villar* [1929] 1 Ch 243. Such a clause is always valid provided that it is workable and practicable (see clause C.4.10 for an example of a royal lives clause). Where there are no lives in being, the perpetuity period is twenty-one years only (see Chapter 4.6 and 4.7).

4. Future parenthood at common law

Under the common law rule, if there is a remote possibility that the limitation would vest outside the perpetuity period then the gift is void *ab initio*. This led to some bizarre results particularly in the area of "future parenthood", as is illustrated by the case of in *Re Dawson* (1888) 39 Ch D 155, where the court said that a woman over the age of 70 may give birth to a child, although the court accepted that such an occurrence was all but physically impossible.

Legal impossibilities are recognised at common law as illustrated by the case of *In Re Gaite's Will Trusts* [1949] 1 All ER 459, where the court accepted that it was legally impossible for a person under the age of sixteen to give birth to a legitimate child.

5. Class gifts at common law

Special rules apply to gifts which are "class gifts". A class gift is a gift of property "to a class, consisting of persons who are included and comprehended under some general description and ...... it may be nonetheless a class because some of the individuals of the class are named", *per* Lord Davey in *Kingsbury* v *Walter* [1901] AC 187, 192. The object of the special rule is to facilitate the distribution of the estate or fund at the earliest possible date. Where a class gift is made, the composition of the class and the size of the share that each member of that class is to take must be described in the will.

It used to be the case that to comply with the vesting requirement it had to be possible to say at the outset, that is, at the time the instrument creating the gift took effect, that by the end of the perpetuity period one would know who all the members of the class were. If this could not be done the gift would fail, even in relation to those beneficiaries who were in being and otherwise satisfying the contingency within the period.

This general rule was modified by the rules of construction known as the "class closing rules". The rule in *Viner* v *Francis* (1789) 2 Bro CC 658 states that where there is an unconditional class gift, and there is at least one person who satisfies the class description who is alive when the instrument takes effect, the class closes at that point. All those who are born afterwards are excluded. If there is no one who satisfies the class description when the instrument takes effect, the rule does not apply and the class remains open.

The rule in *Andrews* v *Partington* (1791) 3 Bro CC 401 applies to conditional class gifts. It provides that a class can be closed when the first member becomes entitled to claim his share. The effect of this is that no one born after the class has closed can become a member of the class, but any potential members who are already born will be included, provided they ultimately satisfy the contingency. Where a class gift is preceded by a life interest, the class cannot close until the death of the tenant for life at the earliest, since only then will the interest be vested in possession. Where members of a class are to take an interest at birth, and no member exists at the time of distribution, the class will then remain open indefinitely.

The class closing rules can be excluded by a contrary intention – in *Re Edmondson's Will Trusts* [1972] 1 All ER 444 and *Re Tom's Settlement* [1987] 1 All ER 1081, the rules were held to have been excluded by express language in the deed, showing an unequivocal intention that the class was to remain open until a defined date.

6. Age reduction provisions

Where a gift is made contingent upon the beneficiary's attaining an age greater than twenty-one, then that gift is *prima facie* void at common law. However, if the age contingency is the only reason that the gift is void, then the gift will be saved by s 163(1) of the Law of Property Act 1925 which allows for the substitution of the age of twenty-one years for the offending age provided for in the gift.

7. Dependent gifts

A dependent gift is one that is expressed to take effect only if a prior gift takes effect or fails to take effect.

The prior gift will not be void merely because the second dependent gift is void, but if a gift is made to take effect subsequent to and dependent upon a prior gift which is itself void then the subsequent gift will fail at common law.

8. The unborn spouse trap

Some gifts at common law used to be caught by what was known as the "unborn spouse trap". This would involve a gift to A (a bachelor who is alive at the testator's death) for life; remainder to any wife A might marry; remainder to the children of A living at the death of the survivor of A and such wife. The gift to A and any wife he may marry is a valid gift, but there is a remote possibility that A might marry someone who is not yet born at the date of the gift. Therefore she would not be a life in being, and if she survived A by more than twenty-one years, the gift to the children would be postponed beyond the perpetuity period.

9. Powers and the perpetuity rule

In order to determine the application of the common law rule of perpetuity to powers of appointment, it is important to determine whether the power is general or special. For perpetuity purposes a power of appointment is regarded as special unless it was equivalent to absolute ownership of the property by the donee. If, therefore, a power allowed the donee to appoint anyone in the world, including himself, or was limited to a class of which the donee was a member, so that he could appoint himself, then the power would be general. It should also be noted that an unrestricted power to appoint by will only is treated as a special power for the purpose of ascertaining the validity of the power, but as a general power for ascertaining the validity of the appointment.

The common law rule could affect a power of appointment in one of two ways:

(a) by affecting the validity of the power itself. If the power was general, it was valid if it was bound to become exercisable within the perpetuity period, although the fact that it may also be exercised outside the perpetuity period was of no consequence. If, however, the power was special, it was void if there was a possibility that it would be exercised outside the perpetuity period.

(b) by affecting the validity of the appointment made under the power. Just because a power has been validly created does not mean that an appointment made under the power is also valid. The appointment itself must also comply with the perpetuity rules. In the case of a general power the perpetuity period begins at the date the instrument exercising the power comes into effect. In the case of a special power, the period begins not at the date of the appointment but at the date of the instrument creating the power, that is, the appointment is "taken back" to the instrument creating the power.

10. Vesting and the Perpetuities and Accumulations Act 1964

Section 1 of the 1964 Act provides an alternative to the common law perpetuity period of a life in being plus twenty-one years. Under s 1 the gift may expressly include a fixed perpetuity period of up to eighty years and, in certain circumstances, a fixed period will be implied.

Section 2 of the Act creates presumptions in relation to child bearing which overcame the common law difficulties which often rendered gifts void because of the possibility of further children being born, even when such births were a virtual physical impossibility.

The presumptions, which are rebuttable, are that:

   (a) a male cannot father a child until he is fourteen years old; and

   (b) a woman is capable of bearing children only between the ages of twelve and fifty-five.

In general, the Act aims towards ensuring that any gift which will in fact vest within the perpetuity period is valid.

Under the common law, the test to determine whether or not a gift would vest during the perpetuity period was made on the creation of the gift. This meant that many gifts were rendered void as they could possibly vest outside the perpetuity period. Section 3 of the Perpetuities and Accumulations Act 1964 provides that a gift will only fail if and when "it becomes established that the vesting must occur, if at all, after the end of the perpetuity period". Until such time the gift is treated as if the common law rule does not apply. Section 3 is normally referred to as the "wait and see" rule.

Section 3 applies only where:

   (a) the gift is void at common law;

   (b) the instrument creating the gift takes effect after 15 July 1964; and

   (c) s 15(4) of the Act does not apply to the gift.

For the purposes of the "wait and see" rule, a statutory category of lives in being is provided. The categories are:

"(a) the person by whom the disposition was made;

 (b)   a person to whom or in whose favour the disposition was made, that is to say –

    (i)   in the case of a disposition to a class of persons, any member or potential member of the class;

(ii) in the case of an individual disposition to a person taking only on certain conditions being satisfied, any person as to whom some of the conditions are satisfied and the remainder may in time be satisfied;

(iii) in the case of a special power of appointment exercisable in favour of members of a class, any member or potential member of the class;

(iv) in the case of a special power of appointment exercisable in favour of one person only, that person or, where the object of the power is ascertainable only on certain conditions being satisfied, any person as to whom some of the conditions are satisfied and the remainder may in time be satisfied;

(v) in the case of any power, option or other right, the person on whom the right is conferred;

(c) a person having a child or grandchild within sub-paragraphs (i) to (iv) of paragraph (b) above, or any of whose children or grandchildren, if subsequently born, would by virtue of his or her descent fall within those sub-paragraphs;

(d) any person on the failure or determination of whose prior interest the disposition is limited to take effect." – s 3(5).

As well as falling within this list the lives in being must:

(a) be alive and ascertainable at the date of the gift; and

(b) in the case of a class or description they must not be so numerous as to render it impracticable to ascertain the death of the survivor.

Where there are no lives in being, as in trusts of imperfect obligation for animals, the period is twenty-one years (see Chapter 4).

Section 4 of the Act affects gifts made after 15 July 1964 and comes into operation where a gift is void at common law because of an age contingency greater than twenty-one and is not covered by the "wait and see" rule in s 3. The section replaces s 163 of the Law of Property Act 1925 in relation to such gifts. Where the age contingency is greater than twenty-one, then that age is replaced by s 4(1) with "that age which would, if specified instead, have prevented the disposition from being so void".

The age will not necessarily be twenty-one but will vary according to the respective ages of each potential beneficiary. For example, if a gift is expressed to be "to all my children who attain the age of thirty" and if the testator's two children are aged one and two at the date of his death, then s 4(1) will substitute the age of twenty-two for the offending age in the gift to ensure that the gift will vest in all the beneficiaries within the perpetuity period. Section 4(1) is open to alternative interpretation, namely that the age contingency in the case of each child will be reduced to twenty-two and twenty-three respectively.

Subsections 4(3) and 4(4) apply only to class gifts. Where under the pre-1964 law a class gift would be void for remoteness because of the possibility that more members may be added to the class outside the perpetuity period, and it is not saved by s 3, or by the reduction in the age of vesting under s 4(1), subss 4(3) and 4(4) provide that the possible additional members will be treated as excluded from the class.

Section 5 deals with the "unborn spouse trap" of common law (see page 221) by applying a variation of the "wait and see" principle. If, for example, a gift were made to a bachelor (B) for life with a gift over to any wife B may have at his death, and a remainder to such of the children of B and his wife as survive them both, then (see page 221), the gift of remainder to the children would be void at common law.

Section 5 applies the "wait and see" principle and the gift will be saved if it vests within the perpetuity period. If, at the end of the perpetuity period, the gift has not vested then under s 5 the gift is "converted" into a gift to the children of B and his wife living at the expiry of the perpetuity period and the gift takes effect as if B's wife predeceased those children.

Section 6 of the Act overcomes the common law rule of dependent gifts (ante) and provides that a disposition will not be void for remoteness only because it is "ulterior to and dependent upon" a prior void gift. In such a case the perpetuity period is applied to the subsequent gift independently of the prior gift, and both gifts are dealt with as if distinct and unrelated.

11. The rule against perpetual trusts

The rule basically states that a gift which requires capital to be retained beyond the perpetuity period is void. This rule cannot be avoided just by giving a power to change the property and investments if the proceeds of sale are required to be re-invested and the capital fund has to be retained in perpetuity. This rule again does not apply to charitable bequests and devises.

12. Accumulation of income

The rules relating to the restriction of accumulation of income were developed to prevent the testator from inflicting compulsory "hoarding" on the beneficiaries by compelling the personal representatives or trustees by directions in the will to accumulate income.

(a) The common law rule
At common law, if the period for which an accumulation is directed may possibly exceed the common law perpetuity period the direction to accumulate is totally void.

(b) The statutory rules
For dispositions taking effect before 16 July 1964, ss 164-166 of the Law of Property Act 1925 require that the accumulation of income may not be directed for longer than one of the following periods:
  (i)   the life of the settlor;
  (ii) twenty-one years from the death of the settlor or testator;
  (iii) the minority or minorities of any person or persons living or *en ventre sa mère* at the death of the testator;
  (iv) the minority or minorities of any person or persons who under the limitations of the instrument directing the accumulation would for the time being, if of full age, be entitled to the income directed to be accumulated.
Two further periods were added by s 13 of the 1964 Act for dispositions taking effect after 15 July 1964:
  (v)   twenty-one years from the making of the disposition;

(vi) the minority or minorities of any person or persons in being at that date.

If the period for which the accumulation is directed could exceed the perpetuity period at common law the accumulation direction is void *ab initio*.

If the period for which the accumulation is directed cannot exceed the perpetuity period at common law but exceeds the relevant accumulation period, the direction to accumulate is good *pro tanto*. Only the excess over the appropriate accumulation period is void. In ascertaining the appropriate period, the courts will try to get as near as possible to the testator's intentions.

If a direction to accumulate income is void, wholly or partially, the income so released passes to the persons who would have been entitled had no such accumulation been directed.

Chapter 22

Construction of wills

1. General principles

The overriding aim of the rules of construction is to discover as nearly as possible the meaning the testator intended in any particular words. The will is to be looked at as a whole and extrinsic evidence is sometimes admissible to aid interpretation.

Generally, the court will rely only on the words written by the testator and will not seek to make more sense of those words by adding to them, altering them or by assuming they are mistaken.

2. Presumptions

(a) Ordinary meaning
In the absence of any indication to the contrary, the words used in a will are presumed to bear their "ordinary meaning".

Where one word has several possible "ordinary" meanings, the court must consider the will as a whole and any available extrinsic evidence to determine the meaning intended by the testator.

If, after having examined all the other provisions of the will and having construed those provisions with the aid of any extrinsic evidence, it is apparent that the testator intended a word or phrase to convey a meaning other than its ordinary meaning, then the word or phrase will be construed in that different sense. If this is the intention of the testator then a "definition clause", setting out the intended meaning, should be included in the will.

If a word or phrase has an ordinary meaning and a secondary meaning, and if the word or phrase as used will only make sense if construed as having its secondary meaning, then that secondary meaning will be applied.

(b) Technical or legal words and expressions

Technical or legal words and expressions will, *prima facie*, be construed in accordance with their technical meaning. Again this presumption may be expressly or impliedly rebutted by the will or the surrounding circumstances. Any secondary meaning may be applied if the technical meaning fails to make sense in the context.

(c) General intention

Once the testator's intention has been ascertained with reasonable certainty from examining both the will as a whole and any admissible extrinsic evidence, then that general intention will govern the sense not only of ambiguous words or phrases but also of clear words if subject to more than one possible interpretation. Thus the general intention which is apparent may be sufficient to rebut the presumption that a word is to bear its ordinary or technical meaning if the ordinary or technical meaning is inconsistent with the general intention of the testator.

In certain circumstances the court will rely on the general intention demonstrated by the will to imply that certain words have been omitted or mis-written. However, before the court will read words into the will it must be clear from the will itself that:

(i)   a word or words have been omitted or mis-written; and

(ii) the substance of the omission or error can be seen in the light of the intended wording.

If the court is thus satisfied it may read the will as if any omitted words were included and any error corrected and may omit any words which should not properly have been included.

Where two provisions are irreconcilable with each other then it may be possible for the court to amend the provision which is inconsistent with the testator's intention under the foregoing rules. However, if such amendment is not possible, then the latter of the two inconsistent provisions will prevail.

The court's power to supply, omit or change words when construing a will are limited to instances where the substance of the intended wording is clear. If there is any doubt about the intended meaning then the words cannot be changed by the court of construction, although it may be possible to remedy a defect by rectification.

(d) Later codicil
A gift clearly expressed in a will or codicil is not revoked by a later codicil unless the intention to revoke is as clear as the original intention to give.

(e) Presumption against intestacy
Where the construction of a will is in doubt, the court presumes that the testator did not intend to die either wholly or partly intestate. The presumption will depend upon the context of the words being construed and upon the surrounding circumstances.

An intestacy cannot be defeated merely by showing an intention on the part of the testator to make a disposition by will. The wording of the will must be sufficient to constitute a gift, either expressly or by necessary implication, in favour of a particular beneficiary. Thus the rights of those entitled upon intestacy are protected.

(f) Apparent meaning
Where the words of a will give rise to an apparent and clear meaning then they must be interpreted in accordance with that meaning even if that makes the gift invalid, and even though it is apparent that the testator himself misunderstood the legal effect of his words.

Where the wording gives rise to more than one possible interpretation then, if one interpretation would give rise to the gift's being invalid in whole or in part and the alternative possible interpretation results in a valid gift then the latter interpretation is presumed to be the intention of the testator.

When considering the testator's intention with a view to determining the validity of the gift the will must be interpreted by reference to the laws in force at the time the will was made, unless the will expressly or impliedly refers to the law existing at the testator's death.

(g) Unambiguous words

Unambiguous words must be interpreted according to their clear meaning even if it is difficult or inconvenient to carry out the testator's intention, and even if the testator is being deliberately capricious.

Where the words are ambiguous, however, it is presumed that the testator did not intend to be capricious.

(h) Accidental creation of life interest

A frequent problem of "home made" wills used to be the accidental creation of life interests in favour of spouses where the actual intention of the testator was to make an absolute gift to his or her spouse. Phrases such as "I leave everything to my wife and then to my children" *prima facie* give rise to a life interest in favour of the spouse with remainder to the children.

Section 22 of the Administration of Estates Act 1982, which affects the construction of the wills of testators dying after 31 December 1982, provides for a statutory presumption against such life interests. Thus, in the absence of a contrary intention it is presumed that if a testator devises or bequeaths property to his or her spouse in terms which, in themselves, would give an absolute interest to the spouse, but by the same instrument purports to give his issue an interest in the same property, then the gift to the spouse is absolute regardless of the purported gift to the issue.

(i) Provisions for family members ambiguous

Where a will makes provision for members of the testator's family, but is ambiguous as to its terms, the court will construe the provisions in the way which will most benefit the family generally, including as many children as possible. In the absence of contrary intention, relatives of equal degree are presumed to be equally important to the testator. The court does not, however, presume that the testator intended to benefit all of his family, or that each member should be benefited equally, and the court will not construe the will against the expressed intention.

3. Admissibility of evidence

Once proved, the will admitted to probate or annexed to a grant of letters of administration is conclusive as to the contents of the will. A court of construction is not entitled to alter the wording of the will to correct any alleged error. Neither can a court of construction admit extrinsic evidence to complete any blanks or omissions in the will.

The court of construction may consider the format and punctuation of the original will and the existence of blanks and erasures, all of which may assist in determining the testator's intention.

Where two testamentary documents have been admitted to probate the court may decide, as a matter of construction, that part or all of the earlier document has been revoked or replaced by the later document.

Extrinsic evidence is admissible to prove the existence and identity of any person described in the will.

(a) Before 1983
The common law rules apply to all wills where the testator died before 1 January 1983. In such cases direct extrinsic evidence is admissible only in the event of equivocation and to rebut equitable presumptions.

Equivocation or latent ambiguity arises where a given description may be applied to two or more different objects or people. Certain circumstantial extrinsic evidence is admissible under the "armchair principle". The "armchair principle" is an aid to construction by which the court of construction is permitted to place itself in the testator's position and consider the surrounding circumstances that existed when the will was made. If that is sufficient to identify the thing or person referred to then there is no equivocation.

If there is still equivocation, direct extrinsic evidence of any declaration of intention of the testator is admissible to prove which thing or person the testator was referring to. If there is still doubt as to the testator's intention then the gift will fail for uncertainty.

Direct extrinsic evidence of a testator's intention is admissible to rebut the equitable presumptions of the satisfaction of a debt by a legacy, the satisfaction of a legacy by a legacy, and the satisfaction of a portion-debt by a legacy (see Chapter 19).

Extrinsic evidence will also be admitted to show a contrary intention to rebut other equitable presumptions. Generally, no other extrinsic evidence is admitted.

The case of *Kell* v *Charmer* (1856) 23 Beav 195 is a good example of extrinsic evidence being admitted to identify the subject matter of a gift. The testator made a gift "to my son William the sum of i.x.x.. To my son Robert Charles the sum of o.x.x.". The court heard evidence that the testator was an antique dealer who used symbols to represent prices and that the symbols i.x.x. and o.x.x. denoted £100 and £200 respectively.

Circumstantial extrinsic evidence can only be used to ascertain the testator's intention from the words as written where there is uncertainty or ambiguity. It cannot be used to make words bear a meaning which they are incapable of bearing on the face of the will.

Where a person completely satisfies the description in a will there is a strong presumption that that person was the intended object of the particular gift and that presumption will only be rebuttable by circumstantial extrinsic evidence in exceptional cases – see, for example, *NSPCC* v *Scottish National Society for the Prevention of Cruelty to Children* [1915] AC 207.

(b) Testator who dies after 31 December 1982
The effect of s 21 of the Administration of Justice Act 1982 is to make both direct and circumstantial extrinsic evidence of the testator's intention admissible to assist in interpretation in three situations:
(i)   to construe any part of a will which is meaningless;
(ii) to construe words which appear ambiguous;
(iii) where evidence, other than evidence of the testator's intention, shows that the language used in any part of the will is ambiguous in the light of the surrounding circumstances, circumstantial extrinsic evidence of the testator's intention is admissible to

construe the testator's intended meaning. This is so whether or not it is a case of equivocation.

4. Date from which a will "speaks"

When interpreting any provision it is essential to know at what time any description is to be applied.

(a) Subject matter

Generally, a will takes effect as if executed immediately before the death of the testator in relation to the subject matter of gifts – s 24 Wills Act 1837. Thus a will "speaks from death". In the absence of a contrary intention, any description in the will of the subject matter of a gift is applied at the testator's death, whether the gift is specific or general.

Thus a gift of "all my shares in X Co Ltd", in the absence of contrary intention, will be construed as a gift of such shares in X Co Ltd as the testator holds at the date of his death. This may include shares acquired after the date of the will and exclude shares disposed of after the date of the will.

A contrary intention will be implied when the subject matter is described so particularly that it is plain an object in existence at the date of the will was intended. Express words may also exclude s 24 by stating the date at which the subject matter is to be ascertained.

However, words such as "now" or "at present" are inconclusive as to the testator's intention as, *prima facie,* the will speaks from death and the testator may have meant "now" when the will was signed or "now" when the will takes effect. In such a case the will must be considered as a whole to determine whether s 24 is to be excluded.

Where s 24 has been excluded by a contrary intention and a provision is to speak as from the date of the will then, if the will is later republished by re-execution or a later codicil, the effect is that the will will speak from the date of the codicil or re-execution, unless a contrary intention is apparent.

(b)   Objects

When determining the object of a gift, a will speaks from the date of its execution, unless a contrary intention is apparent.

When the will is republished by a later codicil or re-execution then, in the absence of contrary intention, the gift will speak from the date of the republication.

5. The falsa demonstratio doctrine

The first limb of this doctrine provides that where the description of a person or thing is partly true and partly false then provided the part which is true describes the person or thing to a high degree of certainty then the untrue part of the description will be rejected and the gift will be allowed to take effect.

The second limb provides that additional words are not rejected as false if they can be read as words of restriction. For example, in *Wrightson* v *Calvert* (1860) 1 John & H 250, a gift was made to the grandchildren of the testator living near another named person. Only two of the testator's grandchildren lived near the other person and the third grandchild was therefore not entitled to a share in the gift.

The doctrine also apparently covers descriptions which are wholly false if the context and surrounding circumstances show the testator's intention unambiguously. In such a case the whole erroneous description is rejected but the gift still takes effect. Thus in *Ellis* v *Bartrum* (1857) 25 Beav 107 the object of the gift was wrongly described as "the resident apothecary" instead of "the resident dispenser", but the gift was given effect as the intention of the testator was apparent from the circumstances.

6. Construing the same words in different parts of the same will

A word may not necessarily be used in the same sense throughout a will, but if it is used in one place with a clear and unambiguous meaning then it is presumed to have the same meaning if used ambiguously in another part of the same will, provided that meaning makes sense in the context – *Re Birks* [1900] 1 Ch 417. Such a presumption arises only where there is ambiguity. In any event, words must be construed with reference to their subject matter and may therefore bear different meanings even within the same gift – for example when relating to realty and personalty.

7. Alteration and rectification

A number of common law powers have developed allowing the court to add or omit words in some circumstances, and these have been supplemented by the Administration of Justice Act 1982. Thus, a probate court can omit words that have been included in the will without the testator's knowledge and approval – *Re Morris* [1971] P 62. Further, if it is clear to the court that certain words have been accidentally omitted and if no sensible literal construction of the words is possible as they are written, then the court may read additional words into the will in order to construe it sensibly.

Similarly a court may change a word when it is apparent from the context that the word was used incorrectly in place of another word – the most common examples being the use of the word "or" instead of "and" and *vice versa*. The court will look at the intention, or presumed intention, of the testator, but will not generally construe the words against their meaning as written if to do so would prejudice the interest of a subsequent beneficiary. For example, if a gift is made to X absolutely with a gift over to Y to take effect if X predeceases the testator "without issue or under the age of twenty-one" then, *prima facie*, the gift over will take effect if X dies under the age of twenty-one even if he leaves children. However in the absence of a contrary intention, the court will presume that the testator intended to benefit the children of the beneficiary X and will therefore read the word "or" as "and". Thus, the gift over will not take effect unless both events happen. The rule is dependent on the gift being made in fee simple or absolutely. Where the original gift is for life or entail with a similar gift over, the gift over will take effect as written as to change the word "or" to "and" would be to defeat the interests of the subsequent beneficiaries.

If a gift over is made to "X or Y" (and no contingency expressed or implied) then, if X and Y are mutually exclusive, the gift will fail for uncertainty, unless it is apparent that the gift to Y was in substitution for the gift to X if the latter should fail.

The court may change the word "or" to "and" in order to avoid inconsistency and to arrive at a reasonable construction of the whole will, the overriding principle being to give effect to the testator's intention.

The court is generally less willing to change the word "and" to "or" although it may be so construed if necessary to give sense to a sentence as a whole where one or more parts of the sentence do not make sense when construed literally. The court will look at the words of the will in context and may change the word "and" to "or" if an alternative gift is clearly intended to be substitutional. This may avoid the gift being void for uncertainty or infringing the rule against perpetuities.

Under s 20 of the Administration of Justice Act 1982 a court may order that a will be rectified in order to carry out the testator's intentions if satisfied that the will "is so expressed that it fails to carry out the testator's intentions in consequence:

(a) of a clerical error; or

(b) of a failure to understand his instructions".

An application for rectification must generally be made within six months of the grant of probate or letters of administration with the will annexed.

8. Meaning of particular words of description

(a) Personal chattels and household effects

If used in its ordinary sense and provided the article in question is not used for business purposes, then the phrase "personal chattels" will bear the meaning ascribed to it in s 55(1)(x) of the Administration of Estates Act 1925 (see page 254).

The word "furniture" has been held to include ornaments, but not books. The phrase "household effects" is wider in scope and may include books and sewing machines, for example, but has been held not to include pets or a collection of postage stamps. The word "effects" has no fixed meaning and is construed in the light of the context of the will and the surrounding circumstances. The *ejusdem generis* rule will apply and thus if a number of personal chattels are listed followed by words such as "and all other effects" the word will be restricted to such effects as are personal chattels.

A gift of "the contents" of, for example, a desk will include the contents and any *choses in action* found in the desk, but not items in a separate box, the key of which is in the desk.

(b)   Money or cash

The word "money" has many different meanings, depending on the context and circumstances in each case. However, it will normally include cash in hand (including notes) and cash at the bank, either on current account or on deposit where no notice of withdrawal is required.

The phrase "moneys due" to the testator includes a balance at a bank (except deposits requiring notice of withdrawal), stock, money receivable under a life assurance policy on the testator's life, and money payable to the testator from the estate of another deceased person provided that estate has been "got in" at the time of the testator's death. It will not include money due under a service contract which has not been completed at the time of the testator's death.

The phrase "moneys owing" includes all items included in the phrase "money due" and also money on deposit at a bank where notice of withdrawal is required. "Moneys on deposit" include National Savings Account and Certificates.

The phrase "ready money" is the rough equivalent of "moneys due", including cash. "Cash" is normally taken to mean notes and other coins and does not include promissory notes, bonds or long annuities.

(c)   Land or house

Unless an intention to the contrary is apparent from the context or circumstances, the term "land" will generally include any buildings on the land and any sale proceeds arising from the land if subject to a trust for re-investment in land. It will also include incorporeal hereditaments.

Without express provisions a devise of land does not pass mortgage debts charged on land or other charges on land.

A devise of a "house" passes with it everything belonging to the house for its enjoyment, such as a garden or orchard. The term "messuage" includes any garden, orchard and curtilage.

Where a testator gives part of his land to A and the remainder, adjoining land to B, leaving B's part land-locked, B is entitled to a necessary right of way over A's land.

(d) Shares, investments and securities

The definition of "stocks and shares" depends on the context and circumstances, but is generally taken to mean only stocks and shares in limited companies and not government securities, redeemable debentures or holdings in public limited companies. However, the phrase will be given its widest possible construction where the testator demonstrates an intention to dispose of all his personal estate and the will contains no residuary gift.

Again the scope of the term "investments" depends upon the circumstances and has been held to include money on deposit.

"Securities" may include such things as Government stock, liens for unpaid purchase money, money lent on a mortgage and promissory notes but will not generally include money at a bank on current or deposit account, stocks and shares, life assurance policies and their proceeds or debts. If money has been lent on a mortgage where the legal estate is vested in trustees and the testator is entitled only to the residue of the repayments after the discharge of other payments, then the testator's interest will not pass as a "security".

(e) Businesses and partnerships

Generally, a bequest of a business passes the whole of the business, both assets and liabilities. If the testator is not the sole proprietor of a business but is in partnership, then the disposal of his interest may be limited by the partnership deed and any bequest will be subject to those provisions. See also page 120.

(f) Miscellaneous other terms

"Probate valuation" means the valuation of items by valuers for the purpose of obtaining a grant of probate. Unless a contrary intention is shown or the context requires otherwise, any reference to a "month" is construed as a calendar month. The word "moiety", meaning half, may also be used to mean an equal share where there are two shares. "Unmarried" may mean "never having been married" or "not now married", depending on the context.

(g) Words of gift

The term "devise" is generally limited to gifts of land. Although the terms "legacy" and "bequeathed" commonly refer to personalty they may include gifts of land and interests in land in some circumstances.

Even words such as "personal property" may not be limited to personalty if the context shows that the testator intended to pass some real property. Leaseholds are regarded as personalty but may pass under a gift of realty if the context shows that that was the testator's intention. The phrase "worldly goods" may also include realty.

9. Per capita and per stirpes distribution

A gift intended to be distributed *per capita* amongst the beneficiaries results in each beneficiary's taking an equal share of the whole.

A gift distributed *per stirpes* is divided according to family or stock. Each family (or branch of the family) takes an equal share and that share is then subdivided amongst the members of each family. Thus where one branch of a family has many members, all the members may receive a small share, whereas another branch may consist of merely one beneficiary and that person may take a large share of the whole.

Unless the will demonstrates a contrary intention or gives rise to a contrary inference then it is presumed that gifts to a number of donees are to be distributed *per capita* rather than *per stirpes*.

10. Unlimited gifts of income and charges

Where rents and profits of land are demised to a beneficiary without any limitation then, unless a contrary intention appears from the will (as where the gift is of a life interest only) the devise will, *prima facie,* take effect as a gift of the land itself. Similarly, if a testator makes a bequest of all the income and other benefits of personal property then the donee is *prima facie* entitled to the capital (or corpus) itself. This is so even where the gift is made to the donee under a trust. However, the principle does not apply to charities.

An unlimited charge upon the rents and profits of land or the income of personalty may likewise be treated as a charge on the land or property itself.

11. Description by reference to locality

Where property is described by reference to the place in which it is kept, movable property, which is normally kept at the place described, but which has been temporarily removed, may be included. This is so unless a contrary intention is apparent. Property described as being in one place which is in fact in another place at the testator's death generally will not be included in the gift.

If documents are generally kept in a certain locality and a gift is made of all things in that locality, then such *choses in action* as are represented by the documents may be included in the gift. Bank of England notes at the locality will also be included. With the above exceptions, such gifts will not *prima facie* include any *choses in action* due, payable or recoverable at the described location, neither will the gift include *choses in action* represented by documents which are in the locality at the testator's death but which are not normally kept there.

12. Absolute interests made subject to restrictions

Where an absolute gift is given and further words are added to describe the testator's intention when making the gift, then the subsequent words will not generally restrict the absolute interest. Where a particular interest is given to X with an additional power for X to dispose of the property, then the gift may take effect as an absolute gift but will normally do so only if the additional power is exercised.

The rule in *Lassence* v *Tierney* (1849) 1 Mac & G 551 provides that if there is an absolute gift to a legatee in the first instance, and trusts are engrafted or imposed on that absolute interest which fail either from lapse, invalidity or any other reason, then the absolute gift takes effect so far as the trusts have failed, to the exclusion of the residuary legatee or next of kin as the case may be.

Similarly if a life interest is settled upon trust for a wife for life with remainder to her children, and if there prove to be no children or no children eligible to take an interest, then the previous absolute interest remains and takes effect unqualified.

In order to determine that there has been an absolute gift which is capable of taking effect despite subsequent restrictions or powers, the court must be satisfied firstly that the subject matter of the gift has been segregated from the remainder of the testator's estate "once and for all"; and secondly, that behind any trusts or powers attached to the gift there remains an interest vested in the legatee which may take effect in so far as the engrafted trusts fail or do not exhaust the subject matter of the gift.

13. Gifts to legatees and their children

The effect of a gift "to X and his children" will depend upon its construction. It may be a gift to X and his children concurrently, or to X and then his children in succession, or the children may even be intended to take in substitution for X. The words could be taken as words of limitation to create an entailed interest.

The court will first look to the intention of the testator as evidenced by the will as a whole. In general, such a gift takes effect in favour of both the parent and the children concurrently as joint tenants. However, the court leans towards the creation of successive interests.

14. Gifts to legatees and their issue

Before 1926 a gift of land to "X and his issue" *prima facie* created an estate tail as the word "issue" was treated as a word of limitation. However, where the context allowed, it was treated as a word of description only. Since 1926 such a gift will pass the fee simple to the donee and, where the context admits, the issue will take as joint tenants with the named legatees.

In respect of personalty such a gift will, *prima facie,* give both the named donee and the issue concurrent interests as joint tenants. Such gifts may be construed as absolute gifts to the named donee, for example where there is a gift over upon failure of issue.

Since 1925 the word "issue" no longer creates an estate entail. This means that whenever such words are construed as words of limitation the donee will take an absolute interest.

15. Gifts to benefit legatees

Where the whole of the capital or income of a fund is given to a beneficiary or to trustees for the beneficiary then, in the absence of a contrary intention, it is presumed that the testator intended to benefit that beneficiary to the full extent of the subject matter of the gift. In such circumstances the gift will be held to be a valid gift of the whole fund, even where the testator expresses the gift to be for a particular purpose and where that purpose cannot be performed or does not exhaust the whole of the fund. The statement of the intended purpose is construed as a mere statement of motive – *Re Osoba* [1979] 1 WLR 247.

Generally there must be a clear indication in the will before a beneficiary becomes entitled to an interest. However, some interests may arise by necessary implication. For example, if a gift is made to B after the death of A, then A will take a life interest by implication unless the will provides for the income of the property during A's life to form part of the residuary estate or unless a contrary intention is otherwise demonstrated by the will. The implication arises because no other provision has been made regarding the income from the testator's death until A's death. For this life interest to arise by implication,

B must be the sole person entitled on intestacy at the time the will was made and the intermediate income must not be caught by any residuary gift.

In any other case undisposed of property will pass under any residuary gift or, if there is no such gift, to the person entitled upon intestacy.

It will be noted that specific devises and bequests also carry the intermediate income to the devisees and legatees unless that income is expressly otherwise disposed of. A life estate by implication will therefore never arise in the case of specific gifts.

16. Gifts over

Where property is given to A absolutely with a gift over of that property in the event of A's death then, unless some other period is indicated by the context, the gift over will take effect if A dies before the distribution or vesting. Thus a gift over attached to an immediate gift will take effect only if A predeceases the testator, the gift over being in substitution for the gift to A.

If the gift to A is postponed to the life interests of B with a gift over to C then the gift over will *prima facie* take effect only if A dies during the life of the life tenant, B. The gift over to C will take effect upon the death of B as an alternative to the gift to A.

If the gift is made to one person indefinitely with a gift over to a second person upon the death of the first then, *prima facie,* the first donee takes a life interest only and the gift over to the second donee will take effect upon the death of the first by way of succession.

17. Contingencies relating to gifts over on death

Generally where a gift over is to take effect upon the death of a prior donee and upon the satisfaction of other contingencies, it is irrelevant whether the contingencies are satisfied or whether the prior donee dies before or after the testator's death. This will not be so if the will, on its true construction, refers only to the events occurring after the testator's death or at some specified time.

The gift will *prima facie* take effect once the prior donee has died and all the contingencies have been fulfilled. However, a gift over may be intended to be substitutional and the will may be construed to allow the gift over to take effect only if the prior donee dies within a specified period. There may be alternative gifts over.

18. Divesting

Wherever there is uncertainty the court of construction will construe divesting conditions strictly and restrictively and will favour the construction that leads to the vesting indefeasibility of the property as early as possible.

19. Failure of issue

Section 29 of the Wills Act 1837 provides that where words in a gift import either the want or failure of issue of any person in his lifetime, or at the time of that person's death or indefinitely, then, unless a contrary intention is apparent in the will, such words will be construed to mean a want or failure of issue during the lifetime or at the date of death of that person as appropriate. Examples of such words are "have no issue" or "die without issue" or "die without leaving issue".

A contrary intention may be expressed within the will or may be evident from the context generally. Section 29 will have effect only where the words may bear the construction the section imposes. If the words written must import an indefinite failure of issue then the section has no effect and the words must be construed accordingly.

20. Gifts by implication

In certain circumstances gifts and limitations may be implied from the will. There must be so strong a probability, based on the words of the will, that the testator's intention was to benefit a particular person, that a contrary intention cannot be supposed. This doctrine may be used to fill a gap where the testator obviously intended to make a gift but did not include an express provision in the will.

The court will lean against a construction which would lead to an intestacy, unless that is the only possible true construction based on the words of the will. No interest will be implied in favour of any person unless the will shows that the testator intended to provide for that person.

It may also be inferred from the testator's declared intention that the words of a gift as written should be modified or extended to give effect to that intention.

The doctrine of implication does not encompass altering or supplying words that have merely erroneously been written or omitted, neither does it include the interpretation of words in the will from the context. The doctrine is applied to cases where the court will infer an interest over and above that appearing on the face of the words of the will.

An absolute gift may arise by implication where a gift over arises on the failure of the prior interest to fulfil a condition. For example, if there is a gift to A with a gift over to B should A fail to attain twenty-five years of age then it is presumed that the gift to A was intended to be an absolute gift to A provided he reaches the age of twenty-five. The implication will be made only where the prior interest and the gift over rely on either the fulfilment or non-fulfilment of the same event.

Since the Law of Property Act 1925 came into force, there can be no estate in tail arising by implication, and if the words are such that an estate tail would have been implied before the passing of that Act, then any such gift takes effect as if it were a gift in fee simple.

21. Early vesting

In cases of doubt the presumption of early vesting may be applied to determine which of a number of possible beneficiaries was intended to be the object of a gift. The word "vest" may be construed otherwise than in accordance with its strict legal meaning if this is required by the context.

Where there is doubt as to the time of vesting, the court will favour the vesting of the gift at the earliest possible time, that is, at the date of the testator's death or the earliest moment thereafter. A gift by will cannot vest before the testator's death. It is presumed that the testator intends all gifts to vest.

The presumption of early vesting will not assist in identifying intended beneficiaries where the description in the will may apply to different beneficiaries at different times and the context does not indicate any future time at which the beneficiary is to be ascertained. In such a case the beneficiary is *prima facie* taken to be the person satisfying the description at the date of the will. Where the context shows the identity of the donee is to be identified at an unspecified future time then the first person to satisfy the description will generally be the presumed donee.

If there is an immediate gift of separate and specific amounts to each of a number of individuals in a group of children – taking as individuals and not as members of a class – then, *prima facie*, only those alive at the testator's death will take. If the gift is postponed, all are included as long as they are born before the date of distribution.

22. Inconsistent numbers

Where a testator specifies the number of donees to take, and that number is inconsistent with the number of people who actually satisfy the description in the gift then, unless it is apparent that the testator intended all persons fitting the description to take, the court will first look at the number of such persons with whom the testator was acquainted at the time the will was made. If the number corresponds with that stated in the gift then it is presumed those people only were intended to take. If the number known to the testator cannot be ascertained or does not correspond with the number stated in the will, then the court may reject the number in the will as a mistake and decide that all members satisfying the description are intended to benefit.

23. Alternative donees

Two or more alternative gifts may be made, each to take effect if a mutually exclusive event is satisfied. A contingency is generally implied if not expressed, upon which the alternative gift is dependent. This may be, for example, the death of the first donee within a given period. It is inferred that the gift to the first donee is intended to take effect if that donee survives the specific period, and the substitutional gift takes effect in favour of the second donee if the first dies within the specified period.

If the contingency of the death of one of the other donees is neither express nor implied then, if the donees are mutually exclusive, the gift will be void for uncertainty.

Whether a gift is original or substitutional is a question of construction. If there is a direct gift to the second donee then the gift is original even if dependent upon a contingency. If the second donee does not take a direct gift on the occurrence of a contingency but takes only the gift that would have been given to the first donee, then the gift is substitutional.

Where in a class gift it is provided that the issue of any deceased member shall take the share that member would have had if living, then the gift to issue is substitutional.

Chapter 23

Failure of gifts and intestacy

A gift in a will may fail for a number of reasons:
  (a) the beneficiary is an attesting witness – see Chapter 3;
  (b) lapse – see Chapter 4;
  (c) the dissolution of the testator's marriage to the beneficiary – see Chapter 6;
  (d) ademption – see Chapter 19;
  (e) the beneficiary is guilty of the murder or manslaughter of the deceased – see Chapter 4;
Other reasons, not discussed elsewhere in this book, are examined in this chapter.

1. Uncertainty

If, after considering any admissible evidence and applying the relevant rules of construction, it is impossible to identify the subject matter or the object of the gift, then the gift is void for uncertainty; see, for example, *Peck* v *Halsey* (1726) 2 PW 387; *Re Stephenson* [1897] 1 Ch 75. But also see *Re Golay's Will Trusts* [1965] 1 WLR 969 where the court allowed a gift by a testator who directed his executors to let B enjoy one of his flats during her lifetime "and to receive a reasonable income from my other property". The words "reasonable income" were held not to give rise to uncertainty since the court could, from the wording of the gift, make an objective assessment of reasonable income.

The court will use its best endeavours to give some sense to a gift if the result of holding it to be void is to create an intestacy.

There are two maxims that are sometimes used in cases of uncertainty:

(a) *certum est quod certum reddi potest;* and

(b) *ut res magis valeat quam pereat.*

The first means that unclear words which are added to a gift do not render the gift uncertain if it can be substantially ascertained from the nature of the case. The maxim will be applied where the gift is stated to be for a particular purpose even though the amount of the gift is indefinite. The court can by inquiry in such a case ascertain what sum is sufficient or necessary to answer the purpose.

The second maxim means that in cases where the words used are capable of two constructions, the construction should be adopted which tends to make the document effective and a will should be construed to give effect, as far as possible, to every word.

Where there is a power in the nature of a trust the intention to benefit the class is mandatory and the beneficiaries can compel the trustees to execute the trust if they are in default. It is essential that the beneficiaries should be known, in the sense that it is possible to draw up a definitive and complete list of all the persons within the class of beneficiaries.

Where there is a fixed trust and it is not possible to ascertain the beneficiaries at the date of the document declaring the donor's intention, the trust fails for uncertainty. The position with regard to powers is different. Where there is doubt the court may be required to assess the validity of any proposed appointment and be able to say with certainty whether a particular person is or is not within the permissible class of objects. This rule has been held to apply to discretionary trusts.

2. Disclaimer

A beneficiary is free to disclaim any gift given to him in a will. He is likely to do this where the gift is subject to conditions or is of a burdensome character. A disclaimer affects only the interests given to the donee and does not affect any other right or interest given by the will, such as a charge on the property or a trust. Where a beneficiary disclaims a gift the property devolves as if he had predeceased the testator.

If a beneficiary is given two different properties, he is entitled to disclaim one and take the other even where the two are included in the same gift, although if upon the true construction of the will the two properties are intended to be taken together or not at all he may not disclaim one and take the other. Where there is a single undivided gift, for example a gift of residue, the whole must be taken or none.

The right to disclaim is lost once the beneficiary has accepted the benefit of the gift.

Acceptance is generally inferred from the acts of the donee – acts amounting to ownership of the property given. However, the will may prescribe some specific act necessary for the beneficiary to perform to indicate acceptance.

A beneficiary who refuses to accept a gift is treated for IHT purposes as making a transfer of value (see Chapter 25). The effect of this is that if the beneficiary were to die within seven years of disclaiming, then, subject to IHT exemptions and reliefs, he would be liable to pay IHT on the disclaimed gift. However, the Inheritance Tax Act 1984, s 142, says that if a testamentary benefit is disclaimed by an instrument in writing within two years of death and the disclaimer is not made for consideration in money or money's worth, the disclaimer is not treated as a transfer of value. Likewise under Capital Gains Tax principles a disclaimer amounts to a disposal by the original beneficiary for CGT purposes. The CGTA 1979, s 49(6), however, provides that if the benefit is disclaimed by an instrument in writing within two years of death and the disclaimer is not made for consideration in money or money's worth, the disclaimer will not be treated as a disposal. The property will be treated as if left by the deceased to the person entitled once the disclaimer has taken effect.

3. The effect of failure

Where a legacy or specific devise fails, the subject matter of the gift passes under the residuary gift contained in the testator's will, provided such a clause is effectively drafted.

Where a residuary gift fails completely, the residuary estate devolves according to the rules of intestacy. If a gift of a share in the residuary estate fails, then *prima facie* that share goes on intestacy. This can be excluded if the will shows a contrary intention.

In the case of a class gift to persons who are to be ascertained at or after the testator's death, the gift will not necessarily fail if a presumptive member of the class dies in the testator's lifetime, or if such a member proves to be incapable of taking for any reason, provided in each case that at least one other member of the class can take. Similarly where there is a gift to four beneficiaries as joint tenants and three die before the testator but one survives him, the gift does not fail and the survivor takes the whole of the gift.

4. Acceleration of a subsequent interest

Acceleration of an interest occurs where a testator purports to give real or personal property to a tenant for life but the gift fails. If there is a vested gift in remainder after the tenant for life's interest, then this remainder is accelerated and takes effect immediately in possession. This may be excluded by a contrary intention. The doctrine applies even where the vested gift in remainder is vested subject to being divested. In such a situation under the doctrine of acceleration the remainder interest takes effect immediately in possession, but the remainderman's interest remains liable to be divested in accordance with the terms of the will.

The remainder is not accelerated where after the tenant for life's interest there is only a contingent gift in remainder. If, however, the gift in remainder subsequently becomes vested the remainder will be accelerated and take effect in possession.

5. Intestacy

Total intestacy occurs where the testator fails to make an effective dis-position of any of his property. A partial intestacy arises where he makes testamentary dispositions which fail to dispose of part or some interest in all or part of the property of which he is competent to dis-pose by will. It is beyond the scope of this book to discuss the rules on intestacy in detail and therefore only an outline of the law on the subject is included.

Section 33(1) of the Administration of Estates Act 1925 subjects all property in respect of which the testator dies intestate to a trust for sale. The realty is held upon trust to sell the same and the personal estate is held upon trust to call in, sell and convert into money such part as may not consist of money. The personal representatives are given a power to postpone such sale and conversion for such a period as they think fit. Reversionary interests, however, must not be sold before they fall into possession unless there is a "special reason" for doing so, and the testator's personal chattels must not be sold unless the proceeds of sale are required to pay the debts or there is a "special reason" for selling them. From the fund produced by the sale the per-sonal representatives must pay all funeral testamentary and other administration expenses, the testator's debts and liabilities, and, in the case of a partial intestacy, any legacies given in the will. What is left after these payments is the testator's net estate to which the beneficia-ries under the intestacy rules are entitled.

(a) The rights of the surviving spouse on intestacy
The spouse's entitlement depends on whether or not there are any other close relatives surviving the intestate. If the intestate left a sur-viving spouse but no issue, parents or brothers or sisters of the whole blood or their issue, the personal representatives will hold the whole of the estate on trust for sale for the spouse absolutely. The remoter relatives such as grandparents or uncles and aunts have no rights to share in the estate. Since the Family Law Reform Act 1987 came into effect on 4 April 1988, references to any relationship between two persons are construed without regard to whether the person was legiti-mate or illegitimate – s 18.

Where the intestate leaves a surviving spouse and issue, the spouse receives:

(i)   the deceased's personal chattels absolutely. The term "personal chattels" is defined in s 55(1)(x) of the Administration of Estates Act 1925;

(ii) a statutory legacy of £75,000 tax free absolutely;

(iii) interest on the statutory legacy at 6% per annum from the death of the deceased to the date of payment;

(iv) a life interest in half of the residue.

Where the intestate leaves a spouse but no issue, but one or more parent or brothers and sisters or their issue, the surviving spouse receives:

(i)   the personal chattels absolutely;

(ii) a statutory legacy of £125,000 tax free absolutely;

(iii) interest on the statutory legacy at 6% per annum as before;

(iv) one half of the residue absolutely.

The remainder of the estate in both situations devolves to the issue or parents or siblings (as appropriate) on statutory trusts.

The spouse is allowed, by s 47A of the Administration of Estates Act 1925 ("AEA") to elect to "capitalise" her life interest, that is, to receive a capital sum in lieu. The spouse must exercise this right within twelve months of the grant of representation being issued.

If the intestate and the surviving spouse were joint tenants of the matrimonial home, it would automatically vest in the surviving spouse by means of *jus accrescendi*. If, however, the intestate were the sole owner of the home or if it were held under a tenancy in common, then the property would become part of the deceased's undisposed of estate. The surviving spouse can in such a case acquire the matrimonial home under the provisions of Sch II of the Intestates Estates Act 1952 and s 41 of the AEA 1925.

In the case of a partial intestacy, s 49(1)(aa) of the AEA 1925 provides that if a surviving spouse has benefited under the will, such a benefit must be brought into account against the statutory legacy only.

(b)   The rights of the issue on intestacy

The issue take an appropriate share in the statutory trusts – AEA 1925, s 47. Under this section the property is held equally for the children of the intestate who are either alive or *en ventre sa mère* at the date of the intestate's death. Such children who satisfy this requirement have a contingent interest unless and until they attain eighteen years of age or marry under that age. If an unmarried infant child dies the effect is as though the child had never existed.

Where a child predeceases the intestate and leaves issue alive at the date of the intestate's death, those grandchildren or their issue take *per stirpes* the share the parent would have taken provided they attain the age of eighteen or marry under that age.

There are two hotchpot provisions (see below) which are applicable to children:

(i) s 47(1)(iii) AEA 1925 applies only to money or property which the deceased's child received during the deceased's lifetime, by way of advancement. Advancement means a substantial payment to a child to set him up in life. There is a presumption of advancement if the payment is of so substantial an amount as to represent permanent provision for the child. Such an advancement must be brought into account;

(ii) s 49(1)(a) AEA 1925 applies only to cases of partial intestacy. Any gifts made by will to the deceased's issue must be brought into account unless the provision is excluded by a contrary intention.

(c) The rights of others on intestacy

Other relatives who take on the statutory trusts must fulfil the same requirements as must the issue, that is, they must be living at the intestate's death and reach the age of eighteen or marry earlier. Other relatives are not subject to hotchpot.

It should, however, be noted that in the recent Law Commission Report, Law Com No 187 (1989) it was recommended that there should be several amendments to the intestacy rules, namely:

(i) a surviving spouse should in all cases receive the whole estate;

(ii) the statutory hotchpot rule affecting issue should be repealed;

(iii) the statutory hotchpot rule affecting issue and spouses on partial intestacy should be repealed;

(iv) a spouse should benefit under the intestacy rules only if he survives the intestate for fourteen days.

6. Hotchpot clauses

A hotchpot clause is required for the purpose of equalising the benefits that beneficiaries of equal rank may receive by taking into account gifts from the testator during his lifetime and the provisions in his will.

C.23.1   Declaration that testamentary provisions to wife and children are in addition to *inter vivos* gifts and settlements
I DECLARE that the provisions contained in this my will and in any codicil hereto in favour of my wife [and children] [and issue] are in addition to any gifts settlements and provisions made in [her] [or their] favour during my lifetime [including the provisions contained in the settlement made by me on [date]].

C.23.2   Declaration that provisions contained in the will in favour of testator's children are in substitution for the provisions of any marriage settlement and not in addition
(1) I DECLARE that any child [and issue] of mine entitled to a share in my residuary estate under this my will or any codicil hereto who also becomes entitled under [any marriage settlement made by me] [the marriage settlement made by me on the ...... day of ......] (whether by appointment or default of appointment) to a share in the property thereby settled SHALL bring into hotchpot and account the value of the share under the settlement upon the division of my residuary estate AND I DECLARE that the value of any share under the settlement shall be taken to be the net value as at the date such share under the settlement becomes actually payable.
(2) I FURTHER DECLARE that should my residuary estate become divisible before the property settled by [the] [any] marriage settlement as aforesaid becomes divisible then my residuary estate shall be distributed without deferment ALWAYS PROVIDED THAT any child [and issue] of mine who is liable to bring into hotchpot his or her share in the property subject to the said settlement shall not be entitled to receive his or her share in any residuary estate unless and until he or she assigns to my trustees all his or her shares in the said settlement and upon the said share becoming payable my trustees shall receive the same and distribute it in accordance with the provisions hereof relating to my residuary estate.
(3) I FURTHER DECLARE that where any child of mine is entitled

to a life interest in my residuary estate under this my will or any codicil hereto and any other person or persons is entitled to take such share by substitution then any share in the property settlement as aforesaid which is to be brought into hotchpot by the said child shall be brought into account against such child and also against all other persons interested in such share in my residuary estate.

C.23.3 Declaration of specified amounts to be brought into hotchpot

I DECLARE that each of my children hereinafter named shall bring into hotchpot and account on the division of my residuary estate the respective sums hereinafter stated in respect of money or property given or transferred to each of them during my lifetime namely:
(a) My son [name] shall bring into account the sum of [£1000]
(b) My daughter [name] shall bring into account the sum of [£2000]

C.23.4 Hotchpot provision in respect of future gifts

I DECLARE that every gift of money or property made by me to any child of mine after the date of this my will and every sum of money or property settled by me for the benefit of any such child after the date hereof SHALL be brought into hotchpot and account by any such child upon the division of my residuary estate unless within six months of the making of such gift settlement or agreement I shall in writing signed by me declare to the contrary and I DIRECT that any property as aforesaid shall be valued as at the time of making any such settlement or agreement.

7. Accruer clauses

Clauses in a will which divest and dispose of the share of a donee dying before a particular time or event, in the absence of evidence to the contrary, refer only to that donee's original share and do not extend to shares which have accrued under another such clause so as to pass them a second time. For example, the testator leaves a gift to A, B, C, D, E and F to be paid to them at twenty-one, with a direction that if any die under the age of twenty-one, the share is to devolve to the others. A and B die under the age of twenty-one and predecease the testator. A dies first, then B. B's original share goes to the survivors, but the share which has accrued to B on the death of A will not pass to the survivors – see *Rickett* v *Guillemard* (1841) 12 Sim 88.

In the absence of an express or inferred intention to the contrary, conditions which apply to the original share are not applicable to the accrued share under such a clause, although they may be held to be applicable to prevent the accruing shares from being void under the rule against perpetuities.

The original shares may not be equal but, in the absence of a contrary provision, an accruing share will be divided and accrue to each survivor equally.

There are several situations, however, when the accrued share will devolve with the original share:

(a) where there is express direction to that effect;

(b) where there is a gift of residue the presumption against an intestacy may allow the accrued share to devolve with the original share;

(c) where the testator, although he speaks of individual shares, treats the fund as an aggregate – see *Re Lybbe* [1954] 1 WLR 573.

C.23.5 Accruer of shares

I DECLARE that if the foregoing trusts shall fail in relation to any share by reason of the failure of any person to attain a vested interest therein then the said shares and any shares which may accrue thereto either under the provisions of this my will or otherwise shall be held on trust by my trustees subject to the trusts powers and provisions hereinbefore expressed and such trusts powers and provisions as may be implied by statute as an accretion to the other share or shares (and equally if more than one) the trusts whereof shall not at the date of such accruer have failed as aforesaid and upon the trusts and subject to the powers and provisions as hereinbefore provided in so far as the same shall be capable of taking effect.

C.23.6 Accruer where share given to child

I DECLARE THAT if any child of mine shall survive me and die without leaving issue living or en ventre at the time of his or her death then the share of such child together with any share or part of any share which may have accrued to him or her under this provision shall be held by my trustees as an accretion to the other share or shares (and equally if more than one) the trusts whereof shall not at the date of such accruer have failed and upon the trusts and subject to the powers and provisions hereinbefore contained in so far as the same are applicable at the date of such accruer and capable of taking effect.

Chapter 24

Family provision

1. Introduction

When drafting a will the provisions of the Inheritance (Provision for Family and Dependants) Act 1975 must be borne in mind, since the concept of complete testamentary freedom has been eroded, at least to some extent, by this Act. The Act gives the court limited powers to order financial provision from the net estate of the deceased for the benefit of certain categories of applicant.

In order to bring a successful application four conditions must be met:

(a) the deceased must have died domiciled in England and Wales after 31 March 1976;

(b) the application must be made within a prescribed time limit;

(c) the applicant must fall into one of the five possible categories of applicant;

(d) the will (or intestacy) must not have made reasonable provision for the applicant.

If these conditions are met the court may make an order of financial provision for the applicant.

2. Time limit for applications

Applications should usually be made within six months of the date of the general grant of representation – s 4. The court has a discretion to extend this time limit. The cases of *Re Salmon* [1981] Ch 167 and *Re Dennis* [1981] 2 All ER 140 outlined the guidelines the court should take into account in the exercise of its discretion:

(a)   the discretion is to be exercised judicially;

(b)   the onus is upon the applicant to make out a substantial case for the court to exercise its jurisdiction;

(c)   the court should consider how promptly and in what circumstances the applicant applied for an extension and warned the defendant of the proposed application;

(d)   the court should see whether negotiations have started within the time limit;

(e)   the court is to look at whether the estate has been distributed before the claim has been notified;

(f)   the court should consider whether a refusal to extend the time would leave the applicant without redress against anyone, including his own solicitors for negligence.

The personal representatives can distribute after the expiry of six months from the date of grant without incurring any personal liability – s 20.

3. Who may apply

The following persons may apply to the court for an order under the Act:

(a)   The deceased's spouse

Such an applicant must show that there was a marriage subsisting at the time of the deceased's death. A judicially separated spouse, a party to a voidable marriage which was not annulled before death, and a wife of a polygamous marriage come within this category. A person also comes within this category where the marriage was void but the applicant entered into it in good faith, unless, during the deceased's lifetime, the marriage was annulled or dissolved or the applicant entered into a later marriage.

The Act provides that a court may bar a claim under the Act when making a decree of judicial separation – s 15.

(b)   A former spouse

This means a person whose marriage with the deceased was dissolved or annulled during the deceased's lifetime by a decree of divorce or nullity made in the courts of England and Wales. Persons whose marriages were dissolved abroad, or in Scotland or Northern Ireland, do not come within this category, but may have a claim under category *(e)*. Section 15 of the Act provides that a former spouse may be barred from applying for financial provision by a court order made with the agreement of both parties on the granting of a decree of divorce or nullity.

(c)   A child of the family

A child of the family includes an illegitimate, legitimated or adopted child and a child *en ventre sa mère* at the deceased's death. Any application is looked at on its merits, but able-bodied adults are unlikely to be favoured – see for example *Re Coventry* [1980] Ch 461, but cf *Re Christie* [1979] Ch 168.

(d)   A child treated as a child of the family

A person (not being a child of the deceased) treated by the deceased as a child of the family in connection with a marriage to which the deceased was a party may make a claim. The relevant "treatment" is the deceased's behaviour towards the applicant and such treatment must stem from that marriage.

(e)   Other people

Any person (not being a person included in the foregoing paragraphs) who immediately before the death of the deceased was being maintained wholly or partly by the deceased, may also claim.

Section 1(3) provides that "a person shall be treated as being maintained by the deceased, either wholly or partly ...... if the deceased, otherwise than for full valuable consideration, was making a substantial contribution in money or money's worth towards the reasonable needs of that person". The definition of "a substantial contribution" is ambiguous, but in *Jelley* v *Iliffe* [1981] Fam 128 the court said that the provision of rent-free accommodation was sufficient. Any claim under category *(e)* must be brought within s 1(3).

The applicant must show that the deceased was making a substantial contribution towards his reasonable needs and that the contribution was not made for full valuable consideration. This is a question of fact in each case, and the provision of services may be sufficient to constitute valuable consideration. Section 1(1)(e) expressly provides that the applicant must have been maintained "immediately before the death" of the deceased. This need not be literally interpreted where the deceased had been maintaining the applicant but had been unable to do so in the few weeks before his death when the applicant was taken into hospital. Megarry VC said in *Re Beaumont* [1980] Ch 444 that the court must look at "the settled basis or ...... arrangement between the parties".

The right of action under the 1975 Act has been held to be personal to the applicant so that if both parties to the marriage die, the right to claim against the deceased's spouse's estate no longer exists - see *Re Bramwell* [1988] 2 FLR 263.

4. Reasonable financial provision

The Act sets out two standards of provision, one applicable to the surviving spouse and one applicable in all other cases.

(a) The surviving spouse standard

Reasonable financial provision in this case is "such financial provision as it would be reasonable in all the circumstances ...... for a husband or wife [not including a judicially separated spouse] to receive, whether or not that provision is required for his or her maintenance" (s 1(2)(a)).

Under s 14 the court has a discretion to apply the surviving spouse standard to a former spouse where a decree of judicial separation, nullity or divorce has been made within twelve months of the death of the deceased and no order for financial provision has been made (or refused) in the matrimonial proceedings – s 14. In *Re Farrow* [1988] 1 FLR 205 a former spouse was awarded a lump sum payment to take account of the fact that for some seven years she was without periodical payments as financial provision was not finalised for such a time.

(b)   The ordinary standard

In all cases where the "surviving spouse" standard is not applied, "reasonable provision" means "such financial provision as it would be reasonable in all the circumstances of the case for the applicant to receive for his maintenance" – s 1(2)(b). Buckley LJ, in *Re Coventry* [1980] Ch 461, said that it could be regarded as "such financial provision as would be reasonable in all the circumstances of the case to enable the applicant to maintain himself in a manner suitable to those circumstances".

The court must decide objectively whether the provision made for an applicant is reasonable in all the circumstances – including circumstances not known to the testator. The court will consider any reasons expressed by the testator – either in the will or outside it – explaining why any particular provision was (or was not) made.

5. The guidelines

Once the court decides that reasonable provision has not been made for the applicant in the will, then it must consider whether or not to exercise its discretion to make an order and, if so, decide what order to make. The court is helped by two sets of guidelines, general and particular.

(a)   The general guidelines

By s 3(1) the court must have regard to:
  (i)   the financial resources and the needs of the applicant, any other applicant and the beneficiaries and the needs of all persons with a claim on the estate;
  (ii) any obligations and responsibilities of the deceased towards the applicant or towards any beneficiary;

(iii) the size and nature of the estate. The ability to make adequate provisions for all applicants may be very limited where the estate is small;

(iv) any physical or mental disability of any applicant or beneficiary;

(v) any other matter including the conduct of the applicant or any other person which the court may consider relevant.

(b)   The particular guidelines

Section 3(2) sets out additional guidelines which are appropriate to particular categories of applicant; these guidelines are to be used in conjunction with, but without prejudice to, the general guidelines.

The surviving spouse: in cases concerning a surviving spouse, the court must consider:

(i)   the age of the applicant and the duration of the marriage;

(ii) the contributions made by the applicant to the welfare of the family of the deceased, including any contributions made by looking after the home or caring for the family; and

(iii) the provision the applicant might reasonably have expected to receive if on the day on which the deceased died the marriage, instead of ending in death, had ended by a decree of divorce. However that does not mean that the same provision should be made by the court as if there had been a divorce on the day of the death – *Re Besterman* [1984] Ch 458; *Moody* v *Stevenson* [1991] The Independent 17 September.

The former spouse: guidelines (i) and (ii) immediately above apply to an application by a former spouse, but (iii) is not relevant unless the court has exercised its discretion to apply the surviving spouse standard.

A child of the deceased: Where the applicant is a child of the deceased the court must consider the manner in which the applicant was being, or might expect to be, educated or trained.

A person treated by the deceased as a child of the family: If the applicant is a child the court must consider his or her education and training, as for a child of the deceased, and:

(i)   whether the deceased had assumed any responsibility for the applicant's maintenance, and, if so, the extent to which and the basis upon which the deceased assumed that responsibility and the length of time for which the deceased discharged that responsibility; and

(ii) whether, in assuming and discharging that responsibility, the deceased did so knowing that the applicant was not his own child; and

(iii) the liability of any other person to maintain the applicant.

A person maintained by the deceased: Where an applicant has actually been maintained by the deceased immediately before the deceased's death, the court considers the extent of and the reasons for the assumed responsibility for the maintenance of the applicant, and the length of time for which the deceased discharged that responsibility.

6. Property available for financial provision

(a) The net estate

Section 25 defines the "net estate" as comprising:

(i)   "all property of which the deceased had power to dispose by his will (otherwise than by virtue of a special power of appointment) less the amount of the funeral, testamentary and administration expenses, debts and liabilities including any [inheritance tax] payable out of his estate on death";

(ii) "any property in respect of which the deceased held a general power of appointment (not being a power exercisable by will) which has not been exercised";

(iii) "any property nominated by the deceased to any person under a statutory nomination or received by a person as a result of a *donatio mortis causa* less any inheritance tax payable in respect thereof and borne by the nominee or donee";

(iv) "the deceased's severable share of a joint tenancy, in so far as the court deems fit";

(v) "any property in respect of which the court exercises its anti-avoidance powers and orders it to be available".

(b) Joint property
Section 9 provides that the court may, for the purpose of facilitating the making of financial provision, order that the deceased's severable share in any property held by the deceased under a joint tenancy immediately before his death (or the value thereof immediately before his death) shall be treated as part of the deceased's net estate to such extent as appears just in all the circumstances (and after deducting any inheritance tax payable).

Any application under s 9 must be made within six months of the date of the grant.

Section 9(4) expressly provides that for the purposes of that section there may be a joint tenancy of a *chose in action*.

7. Orders which the court may make

The types of order available to the court are set out in s 2(1) as follows:

(a) Periodical payments
An order for periodical payments may direct a specified part of the net estate to be set aside or appropriated for making periodical payments for the term specified from the income – s 2(3). Only that needed to produce the income at the date of the order can be set aside. In the case of a former spouse an order ceases to have effect on that person's remarriage – s 19(2). In any other case, the court must decide the date of termination when it makes the order.

The amount of the payments may be expressed as a specified sum to be paid at regular intervals; or may be the income of the whole or a proportion of the net estate; or may be the whole of the income from a specific part of the net estate; or may be determined in any other way the court thinks fit.

During the term of the order an application for its variation may be made by the original recipient, a former applicant, a beneficiary of the estate or the personal representatives of the estate.

On an application for variation the court will consider all the circumstances of the case and any change in the circumstances that existed at the time of the original order – s 6(7). However, only property already set aside for the purposes of paying periodical payments (relevant property) can be the subject of the variation. The court cannot increase the amount of relevant property set aside.

(b) Lump sum payment
A lump sum order cannot generally be varied but, where it is made payable by instalments, the number, amount and dates for payments of those instalments may be the subject of an application for variation – s 7.

(c) Transfer of property
The court may order the transfer of a particular asset to an applicant, which may be preferable to a sale. Once made, the order cannot be varied.

(d) Settlement of property
This type of order is useful in respect of minors or persons under a disability; an order for the settlement of property cannot subsequently be varied.

(e) Acquisition of property for transfer or settlement
The court has power to order the acquisition of a specified property using the assets of the net estate. That property may either be transferred to or settled on an applicant. Again, the order cannot be varied.

(f) Variation of marriage settlements
The court may vary any ante-nuptual or post-nuptual settlement in order to benefit the surviving spouse of the marriage or any person who was treated by the deceased as a child of that marriage. Once the order has been made varying the settlement, that order cannot itself be varied.

8. Interim payments

An interim order in favour of an applicant may be made if it appears to the court that:
- (a) the applicant is in immediate need of financial assistance but it is not yet possible to determine what order (if any) should be made; and
- (b) the property forming part of the deceased's net estate is or can be made available to meet the needs of the applicant.

9. Anti-avoidance provisions

Sections 10 and 11 of the Act enable the court to prevent *inter vivos* dispositions reducing the deceased's net estate for the purpose of evading the Act.

Section 10 covers dispositions made:
- (a) after 31 March 1976 and less than six years before the date of the death of the deceased; and
- (b) with the intention of defeating an application under the Act; and
- (c) for less than full valuable consideration.

A "disposition" for this purpose includes any conveyance of property or payment of money (including insurance premiums) but not a statutory nomination, *donatio mortis causa* or appointment.

Section 11 of the Act covers a contract where it was:
- (a) entered into after 31 March 1976; and
- (b) the deceased agreed to leave money or other property by will or agreed that money or other property would be paid or transferred to any person from his estate; and
- (c) the deceased made the contract with the intention of defeating an application under the Act; and
- (d) full valuable consideration was not given or promised.

There is no time limit to the operation of s 11.

The court may order the donee of a disposition under s 10 to provide such sum of money or other property as it may specify, subject to the following limitations:
- (a) if the donee was given money, he cannot be ordered to provide

more than was paid to him by the deceased less any inheritance tax borne by him;

(b) if the donee was given property, he cannot be ordered to provide more than the value of the property at the date of death of the deceased (or the date of the disposal of the property if disposed of before the deceased's death) less any inheritance tax borne by him in respect of the property.

Where the testator has entered into a contract caught under s 11 and, before the date of the application, the personal representatives have not transferred money or property to the donee in accordance with the provisions of the contract, the court may order them to make no payment, or no further payment, or a reduced payment – s 11(2)(ii).

If, before the date of the application, the personal representatives of the deceased have already transferred money or property to the donee in accordance with the provisions of the contract, then the court may order the donee to provide such sum of money or other property as it thinks fit – s 11(2)(i).

The court can make orders only to the extent that the property transferred under the contract exceeds the value of any consideration given. The valuation is to be made at the date of the hearing – s 11(3).

Where a donee has died the court has the same powers against the donee's personal representatives until the property has been distributed by those personal representatives. At that time the court's power ceases – s 12(4). Orders to provide property may also be made (subject to some limitations) against trustees to whom property has been transferred by the deceased with the intention of defeating an application – subss 13(1) and (3).

10. Tax implications

Where the court orders that a disposition of the deceased's estate be altered, such an alteration is deemed to take place at the date of death of the deceased for tax purposes.

Chapter 25

Taxation

PART I: INHERITANCE TAX

1. The charge to tax

Inheritance tax ("IHT") is charged not only on the assets in an estate at the time of a person's death, but also upon transfers of value made *inter vivos.*

The tax is charged by applying different rates to set "bands". From 6 April 1992 the first £147,000 worth of transfers, whether *inter vivos* or on death, fall within the "nil-rate band". Although chargeable to tax, not exempt, the nil-rate band is taxed at 0%. When assessing the tax on a transfer, transfers that have been made in the preceding seven years are taken into account, being added together to give a cumulative total. Transfers over and above the cumulative total of £147,000 are taxed at differing flat rates. *Inter vivos* transfers are taxed at 20% and death transfers are taxed at 40%.

2. Transfers of value

Section 3(1) of the Inheritance Tax Act (IHTA) 1984 states:

"A transfer of value is a disposition made by a person (the transferor) as a result of which the value of the estate immediately after the disposition is less than it would be but for the disposition."

The word "disposition" is not expressly defined but the term includes a disposition involving "associated operations" – s 272. An "operation" can include an omission – s 268(1). The term "associated operations" means:

"any two or more operations of any kind, being –

(a) operations which affect the same property, or one of which affects some property and the other or others of which affect property which represents, whether directly or indirectly, that property, or income arising from that property, or any property representing accumulations of any such income, or

(b) any two operations of which one is effected with reference to the other, or with a view to enabling the other to be effected or facilitating its being effected, and any further operation having a like relation to any of those two, and so on,

whether those operations are effected by the same person or different persons, and whether or not they are simultaneous" – s 268(1).

It is clearly necessary for IHT purposes to determine the reduction in value caused to the transferor's estate by each disposition. Section 5(1) provides, "a person's estate is the aggregate of all the property to which he is beneficially entitled."

Under s 5(2), property over which the transferor has a power of appointment or disposition by will is also included in the term "estate". "Property" includes all rights and interests of any description – s 272.

In the case of settled property a beneficiary entitled to an interest in possession in settled property is treated for IHT purposes as if beneficially entitled to the property in which he has the interest.

3. Transfers which are not transfers of value

Not all dispositions are transfers of value and some dispositions are deemed not to be transfers of value even though the transferor's estate is reduced. IHT is chargeable on transfers of value only.

(a) Transfers for full value

"A disposition is not a transfer of value if it is shown that it was not intended, and was not made in a transaction intended, to confer any gratuitous benefit on any person and either –

(a) that it was made in a transaction at arm's length between persons not connected with each other, or

(b) that it was such as might be expected to be made in a transaction at arm's length between persons not connected with each other" – s 10(1) IHTA 1984.

If a transferee provides full value to the transferor then there can be no transfer of value as there has been no net reduction in the transferor's estate. However, s 10(1) applies to sales of unquoted shares or debentures only if it can be shown that the sale price was freely negotiated or was equivalent to a price that could have been expected to be freely negotiated at the time of sale.

(b) Maintenance

Dispositions made by a party to a marriage in favour of the other party or a child (including an adopted child or step-child) of either party are not treated as transfers of value if they are for the maintenance of that other party or for the maintenance, education or training of the child until the end of the year in which the child attains eighteen or ceases full-time education or training. Similarly such dispositions are not treated as transfers of value in the case of a former marriage provided the disposition is made on the occasion of the dissolution or annulment of the marriage.

(c) Retirement benefit schemes

A disposition is not a transfer of value if:

(i) it is a contribution to an approved retirement benefits scheme which provides benefits in respect of service as an employee of the person; or

(ii) it is made so as to provide benefits on or after retirement for any person not unconnected with him who is or has been his employee, or to provide benefits on or after the death of such a person for his widow or dependants, and does not result in the recipient receiving benefits which, having regard to their form and amount, are greater than what could be provided under an approved scheme [for the purposes of this paragraph, the right to occupy a dwelling rent-free or at a rent which is less than might be expected to be obtained in a transaction at arm's length between persons not connected with each other is to be regarded as a pension equal to the rent or additional rent that could have been obtained]; or

(iii) it is a contribution under approved personal pension arrangements within the meaning of Chapter IV Part XIV of the Taxes Act 1988 entered into by an employee of the person making a disposition – s 12(2).

(d) Agricultural tenancies

Section 16 provides that a grant of an agricultural tenancy for agricultural purposes in the UK, the Channel Islands or the Isle of Man is not treated as a transfer of value provided it is made for full consideration in money or money's worth.

4. Transfers chargeable to IHT

IHT is charged on lifetime transfers if chargeable and on potentially exempt transfers if they are made within the seven years preceding the transferor's death. IHT is also charged on the estate at death. Thus, on a transferor's death, the starting point for tax assessment will be the transferor's cumulative total of chargeable gifts during the preceding seven years, together with the value of the transferor's estate immediately before death. Generally, the value of the estate will be reduced by taking into account any liabilities outstanding at the transferor's death – s 5(3).

By s 160 IHTA 1984 "the value at any time of any property shall for the purposes of this Act be the price which the property might reasonably be expected to fetch if sold in the open market at that time; but that price shall not be assumed to be reduced on the ground that the whole property is to be placed on the market at one and the same time."

The value of property can be substantially reduced by imposing conditions as to its disposal and thereby avoiding tax by artificial restrictions. Section 163 provides that where, by a contract made at any time, the right to dispose of any property has been excluded or restricted, then for the purposes of determining the value of the property for the first chargeable transfer after that time, the exclusion or restriction will reduce the value of the property only to the extent that consideration in money or money's worth was given for it. In determining the value transferred, expenses incurred by the transferor in making the transfer are to be left out of account – s 164.

(a)   Potentially exempt transfers (PETs)
The provisions relating to PETs are contained in s 3A IHTA 1984 (as amended by Sch 19 para 1 Finance Act 1986).

If the following conditions are satisfied, transfers of value may be "potentially exempt" from IHT. If the transferor survives for seven years following the date of the gift then it will become completely exempt. If the transferor does not survive for the requisite seven years then the gift will be charged to tax on his death – although the tax is reduced if the transferor survives between three and seven years.

In order to be a PET a gift must be:
(i)   made on or after 18 March 1986;
(ii) by an individual;
(iii) to another individual or into an interest in possession settlement (below) or into an accumulation and maintenance trust (below) or into a mentally disabled persons trust (below).

The gift must be by an individual out of his own free assets. Termination of an interest in possession in a trust does not qualify.

If the transferor dies within seven years of making a PET, then the transfer will be liable to tax at the death rate, but only a percentage of the tax will be payable if the transferor survives more than three years after the transfer but less than seven years. The following scale applies, showing the percentage of the chargeable tax actually payable on death:

100% if the death occurs within three years of the transfer;
80% if the death occurs within four years but after three years;
60% if the death occurs within five years but after four years;
40% if the death occurs within six years but after five years;

20% if the death occurs within seven years but after six years.

Once a PET has been made for seven years it becomes fully exempt and is no longer included in the individual's cumulative total of life-time gifts – s 7(4) IHTA 1984 as amended by Sch 19 para 2(4) Finance Act 1986.

If the transferor dies within seven years, the above scale of tapering relief is applied to the tax. The gift, however, is cumulated with other transfers made in the seven years preceding the PET. As the PET is no longer exempt it will affect any other chargeable gifts made after the PET by increasing the cumulative total on which the charge to tax is based, therefore increasing the IHT payable in respect of the subsequent gifts. Similarly, the cumulative total applicable when calculating IHT on the death estate will also be raised by the PET which was made within seven years of death.

(b)   Chargeable transfers made inter vivos

As previously mentioned, the value of lifetime gifts is determined by the amount of the reduction of the value of the donor's estate, not the gain to the donee's estate. The gift element of a sale at an undervalue is therefore taxable. Where sales are made to connected persons, the onus is on the taxpayer to show that there is no gratuitous element. Because the tax is primarily payable by the donor of a gift, the tax itself will also reduce the value of the estate. Thus, unless the donee agrees with the donor that the former will pay any tax chargeable, the amount of any gift is "grossed up" to represent the reduction in value, inclusive of the tax. Tax is charged on the grossed up amount – resulting in more tax being payable than would have been on the gift itself.

(c)   Transfers made on death (or within three years of death)

Transfers made on death are charged at the death rate. Transfers made within three years of death are charged at the full lifetime rate. In each case, the cumulative total for the seven years preceding the date of the gift is applied to determine the starting point.

Take, for example, a series of gifts by T who dies on 2 January 1995, assuming that the current tax rates apply throughout the period:

Date of gift	Amount (gross) and donee	Tax at time of gift	Tax on death
1 July 1986	£80,000 to R, an individual	PET - No IHT	T survived more than 7 years after gift, therefore no IHT
2 August 1988	£100,000 to X Co. Ltd.	IHT at lifetime rate. No PET because donee is not an individual. Nil rate band. No tax payable.	Recalculate on death. No change in cumulative total. Nil rate band. No IHT.
1 January 1990	£130,000 to P, an individual	PET. No IHT	Existing cumulative total of £100,000. T survived only 5 years after transfer. Liable to tax at 40% of death rate, taking into account remainder of nil rate band and annual exemptions
5 March 1992	£70,000 into a discretionary settlement	Existing total of £100,000. IHT at lifetime rate taking into account remainder of nil rate band and exemptions	Recalculate on death based on adjusted cumulated total of £230,000
2 January 1995	T dies leaving estate of £120,000	— —	IHT at death rate based on cumulative total of £300,000

5. Excluded property

Where property is "excluded" property it will not form part of an individual's estate on death for IHT purposes, neither will an *inter vivos* transfer of excluded property be either chargeable or a PET. However, where an *inter vivos* transfer of excluded property gives rise to a reduction in the value of the donor's non-excluded property, then that reduction will be treated as a PET or a chargeable transfer, as appropriate – s 3(2) IHTA 1984.

The most common examples of excluded property are:

(a) most property situated outside the UK and owned by a person whose domicile is outside the UK – s 6(1) IHTA 1984;

(b) settled property situated outside the UK where the settlor was domiciled outside the UK at the date of the settlement;

(c) reversionary interests on settled property provided that:

   (i) the interest is vested neither in the settlor nor his wife; and

   (ii) the interest has not been acquired for money or money's worth; and

   (iii) the interest is not expectant on a lease for life at a nominal rent.

6. Reservation of benefit – Finance Act 1986, s 102 and Sch 20

Where a donor purportedly disposes of property but retains some form of benefit from the property for himself then it will be treated as part of his estate on death for IHT purposes. If the benefit is released before the donor's death then the gift will be treated as a transfer of the whole as from the time of the release.

Thus it is important that the donee of any gift takes full possession of the property and enjoys it so that the donor is excluded or virtually excluded from the benefit and enjoyment of the property. The term "virtually excluded" is statutory but open to judicial interpretation.

However, if the gift is of land or personalty and, after the gift, the donor provides full consideration in money or money's worth for any benefit enjoyed after the date of the gift, then the donor will not be treated as having retained a benefit.

Further, where land is the subject of the gift, any occupation by the donor of all or part of that land may be disregarded if it arises as the result of unforeseen changes in the donor's circumstances – old age, infirmity or otherwise – which render the donor incapable of maintaining himself, provided the donee is a relative of the donor or of his spouse.

Lifetime exemptions and reliefs may be applied in general to lifetime gifts which fall foul of the reservation of benefit rules, except that the annual exemption cannot be claimed, neither can the exemption regarding usual expenditure out of income (see below).

7. Exemptions and reliefs

Where a transfer, whether *inter vivos* or on death, is exempt from IHT it will not be included in the individual's cumulative total. Where PETs become chargeable due to the death of the donor within seven years, the appropriate lifetime exemption may be applied to the transfer.

(a) Reliefs and exemptions in respect of lifetime transfers only

(i) Annual exemption: Under s 19 of the IHTA 1984 an individual may make *inter vivos* transfers of up to £3,000 in any tax year without liability to tax. The value of the transfer is not grossed up (see above). The exemption may be carried forward for one year only in so far as it is not used. PETs are ignored for the purposes of the exemption but, if the PETs become chargeable, the annual exemptions will be taken into account when re-assessing the IHT payable on those transfers at the donor's death. The exemption will be applied to non-PET transfers in priority to PETs that become chargeable subsequently, regardless of the date order of the transfers. Both parties to a marriage have full individual exemptions.

(ii) Small gifts: Under s 20, outright gifts of up to £250 to any one person are exempt from tax.

(iii) Normal expenditure out of income: Under s 21 lifetime gifts paid by a donor out of income which form part of the donor's usual expenditure are exempt provided the donor is left with sufficient income to maintain his usual standard of living.

The most common application of this exemption is the payment by the donor of premiums for a life policy taken out on his own life for the benefit of another, or others, such as his children. The premium payments – although gifts to the donee – will be exempt and the policy proceeds will pass directly to the children without forming part of the donor's estate and without being liable to IHT.

The exemption may also cover regular allowances made to the donor's children during his lifetime.

(iv) Gifts made in consideration of marriage: Section 22 provides family members with an opportunity to divest themselves of substantial amounts of wealth in favour of a couple who are marrying. The following one-off gifts are exempt:
- gifts of up to £5,000 by a parent of the bride or groom (s 22(1)(a));
- gifts of up to £2,500 by a grandparent of the bride or groom or by a remoter lineal ancestor (s 22(1)(b) and 22(2)(b));
- gifts of £2,500 between the prospective bride and groom and *vice versa* (s 22(1)(b) and 22(2)(c)); and
- any other gift to the bride or groom up to the value of £1,000 (s 22(1)(c)).

(v) Dispositions for the maintenance of the family: Section 11 exempts payments made by a party to a marriage for the maintenance, education or training of a child of either party, including a step-child or an adopted child.

(b) Exemptions and reliefs applicable to both lifetime transfers and death transfers

(i) Transfers between spouses: All transfers between spouses are exempt from IHT provided the gift has immediate effect – s 18. Such gifts will include gifts settled on a spouse for life. The only limit on such gifts arises where one spouse is domiciled in the UK and the other is not. In such a case s 18(2) limits the amount of the spouse exemption to £55,000 in total. On death the last seven years of marriage are taken into account regardless of when the separate domiciles were acquired.

(ii) Gifts to political parties: Section 24 of the IHTA 1984, as amended by the Finance Act 1988, makes all gifts to political parties wholly exempt from IHT (see Chapter 4).

(iii) Gifts to charities and national institutions: Gifts to charities are totally exempt from IHT whenever made and regardless of amount – s 23. Similarly, gifts to certain named institutions, including certain museums, the National Trust, government departments, local authorities and universities in the UK, are also exempt under s 25.

(iv) Reliefs for businesses: Where "relevant business property" is transferred – *inter vivos* or on death – business property relief may be applicable in accordance with ss 104 to 106 of the IHTA 1984. The relief operates by reducing the market value of the property transferred by a given percentage when assessing the IHT chargeable. The Act sets out what constitutes "relevant" business property. For example, relief is available to a partner in a business, or an individual with more than 50% of the votes in a company, in respect of assets such as land, buildings, plant and machinery, owned by the transferor but used for the business; such assets attract 50% relief from IHT.

The transfer of the whole or part of an unincorporated business, including that of a sole trader or partnership will generally attract 100% relief against IHT.

The transfer of a holding of greater than 25% of the shares of an unquoted company is also free from IHT. Shareholdings of 25% or less of shares in unquoted companies and in companies whose shares are traded on the Unlisted Securities Market are subject to 50% relief.

(v) Agricultural property relief: Provided the transferor of agricultural land has himself occupied the land for agricultural purposes for at least two years preceding the transfer, then 100% relief is available on the value of that property, whether transferred *inter vivos* or on death.

If the transferor has owned the land for at least seven years before the transfer but it has been occupied for agricultural purposes by someone else for all or part of that time, then 50% relief is available.

Agricultural land includes farm buildings. The relief applies only to the land and not to business assets – although business relief may apply to farm machinery and the like. It must be noted that business relief and agricultural relief cannot both be applied to the same property.

The provisions as to agricultural relief are contained in ss 116-117 of the IHTA 1984.

(c) Reliefs and exemptions applicable only on death

(i) Death on active service: Under s 154 IHTA 1984 no IHT is chargeable on the death of a person from a wound inflicted or a disease contracted whilst a member of the armed forces if that person was on active service at the time or on service of a warlike nature or involving the same risks; see *Barty-King* v *Ministry of Defence* [1979] 2 All ER 80.

(ii) Quick succession relief (s 141): This relief is designed to mitigate the effect of double charge to IHT where property passes through two estates due to the death of a donee shortly after the death of the original donor. The relief is based on a sliding scale depending on the time between the two deaths. A percentage of the tax charged on the property on the first occasion is deducted from the amount payable on the same property on the subsequent death. The percentage deductions are as follows:

100% if the donee dies within one year of the previous transfer;
80% if the death of the donee is between 1 and 2 years of the transfer;
60% if the death of the donee is between 2 and 3 years of the transfer;
40% if the death of the donee is between 3 and 4 years of the transfer;
20% if the death of the donee occurs more than 4 years after the transfer
(s 141 (3)(a)-(e)).

8. General tax planning

The structure of IHT and its interaction with capital gains tax (CGT) can lead to dilemmas in tax planning. *Inter vivos* gifts may often be PETs and, if the donor survives for seven years after the transfer, all IHT can be saved. However, the gift is likely to be subject to CGT. On the other hand, if an individual retains his wealth until death then IHT will be payable at the death rate on his estate.

As a general rule, more wealthy individuals should seek to take advantage of PETs as early as possible. Even if the transferor fails to survive the full seven year period some tax will be saved if he survives for three years or more, and lifetime exemptions and reliefs may help to reduce the liability further. CGT will necessarily be a concern and, if possible, gifts of CGT, exempt assets should be made (see below).

Secondly, wealthy individuals should take advantage of the nil rate band, currently £147,000. If possible that amount should be retained until death and then disposed of to children or other beneficiaries not entitled to any exemption. Any amount over and above that may be given to the deceased's spouse and will be spouse exempt. The spouse will have the advantage of his or her own nil rate band when disposing of the property, as well as possible PETs and lifetime exemptions and reliefs.

In order to take advantage of his spouse's nil rate band, a wealthy individual should ensure that *inter vivos* gifts are made to his spouse to take the spouse's estate up to £147,000, so that he may then leave that property by will directly to any children or other non-exempt beneficiaries. This will cater for the possibility of the spouse's predeceasing the transferor.

Care should be taken not to make any gifts to the spouse conditional upon the spouse's making a gift to another person. Section 268 contains anti-avoidance provisions against "associated operations". The provisions are complex but the Inland Revenue will generally not treat a gift to the spouse followed by a gift to children as an "associated operation" unless there is some form of condition imposed on the first gift.

One problem likely to arise, especially in larger estates, is that the value of the house itself, together with sufficient capital to live on, will be a sizeable sum taxable on the death of the surviving spouse, and it may be that no planning can prevent the "bunching" of assets in the hands of the surviving spouse.

Provision can be made to assist children in paying IHT while at the same time giving them a lump sum not liable to IHT. This can be achieved by means of a joint lives policy. Premiums should be paid out of income under the normal expenditure rule (above). The policy will mature on the death of the last surviving spouse with the proceeds passing directly to the children.

Discretionary trusts and accumulation and maintenance trusts may also be of use, the former providing flexibility, the latter being especially useful where intended beneficiaries are young children. One disadvantage with a discretionary trust is that the trust fund is liable to IHT payable at the time the grant of probate is taken out. It may be useful to leave an amount equal to the nil rate band on a discretionary trust, with the remainder to the spouse.

The family home is usually best retained until death, as problems may arise if the property is disposed of but a benefit (in the form of a right of occupation) retained. To avoid the reservation of benefit provisions the donor would have to lease back the property at full market rent on terms appropriate to a transaction at arm's length. Such arrangements may still fall foul of the rule – see *Nichols* v *IRC* [1975] 2 All ER 120.

Where IHT relief is available, for example in respect of business assets or agricultural land, it is desirable if possible to use those reliefs by passing qualifying property as specific gifts directly to non-exempt beneficiaries, such as the testator's children.

Finally, to facilitate the making of PETs by a surviving spouse it is preferable that he or she should be given an absolute interest in property rather than a mere life interest. If the property is to be left on trust then provision can be made for advancement of capital to the surviving spouse so that PETs can be made.

9. Rearranging succession provisions after the testator's death

Under the rule in *Saunders* v *Vautier* (1841) 4 Beav 115 it is open to beneficiaries to vary the effect of the testator's will or the intestacy rules as if rewriting the provisions. In the normal course of events this would not alter the IHT position of the deceased but would give rise both to transfers of value between beneficiaries liable to IHT and disposals liable to CGT on any increase in value from the date of death to the date of disposal.

These consequences are avoided by s 142 IHTA 1984 and s 49(6) Capital Gains Tax Act (CGTA) 1979, which provide that any variations made within two years of the date of death of the deceased will be treated for the purposes of IHT and CGT as if the variations had been made by the deceased himself. The provisions cover the deceased's severable share in joint property to which he was beneficially entitled as a joint tenant immediately before his death.

Variations of a will can be made only if the following conditions are fulfilled:

(a) any variation must be made in writing and within two years of the deceased's death;

(b) the Inland Revenue must be notified within six months of execution of the variation;

(c) any person giving up a benefit must consent to the variation. If the beneficiary is a minor or under a disability making him unable to consent then the court must consent to the variation on the beneficiary's behalf;

(d) there can only be one variation in respect of a person's death – see *Russell* v *IRC* [1988] 2 All ER 405.

Beneficiaries are permitted to "exchange" their respective interests under the will or intestacy rules, but if there is any other form of consideration in money in respect of such a variation or disclaimer then the statutory provisions will not apply and the transfer or disposition will be liable to tax in the usual way.

PART II: CAPITAL GAINS TAX

10. Introduction

The provisions in relation to Capital Gains Tax are mostly contained in the Capital Gains Tax Act 1979 as amended by subsequent Finance Acts. The tax is payable on chargeable gains accruing to a person on the disposal of assets in each year of assessment – CGTA 1979, s 1(1). The gain is calculated net of allowable losses in the same year.

The amount of gain is assessed by deducting from the disposal price the original acquisition cost, which is notionally increased to allow for inflation by means of an "indexation allowance" equivalent to the change in the Retail Price Index during the years in which the asset was held. There is no charge to CGT on gains accruing before April 1982 and any assets held since before that time are treated as if acquired at their market value on 31 March 1982. The indexation allowance is applied from that date onwards.

11. Rates of tax

Every person is allowed a net chargeable gain of up to £5,800 in any year of assessment exempt of tax. Since 6 April 1990 each party in a married couple has a full individual allowance.

Trustees and personal representatives pay CGT at a flat rate of 25% on the net gain over and above any exempt amount. Other individuals pay CGT at income tax rates. For the purposes of calculating CGT a person's net gains are added to his taxable income (for income tax purposes) in the year of assessment. Thus CGT of 20% will be charged upon gains of up to £2,000 over each individual's allowance, based upon the total of income and gains. Gains falling above the 20% band and below the higher rate threshold of £23,700 will be charged at 25%. Gains forming part of a total of over £23,700 will be charged at the 40% higher rate.

If the taxable income was less than £23,700 but more than £2,000 above the individual's allowance, and the total including capital gains is more than £23,700, the first part of the gain up to £23,700 is charged at 25% and the amount over and above that figure is subject to CGT at 40%.

12. Disposal of assets

CGT is charged on the disposal of an asset and "disposal" includes any transfer of the beneficial title by one party to another whether gratuitous or for value.

"Assets" are defined by s 19(1) CGTA 1979:

"All forms of property shall be assets for the purposes of this Act, whether situated in the United Kingdom or not, including –

(a) options, debts and incorporeal property generally, and

(b) any currency other than sterling, and

(c) any form of property created by the person disposing of it, or otherwise coming to be owned without being acquired."

The chargeable gain is generally calculated as the difference between the sale price and the acquisition cost as adjusted by the indexation allowance. Also deducted is expenditure on improvements and other allowance costs.

However, where the sale is not for full market value or where the transfer is by way of a gift or settlement, the chargeable gain is calculated with reference to the market value of the asset at the time of the gift and there is deemed to be a disposal at the price on that date. Conversely, the deemed disposal price is used as the acquisition cost when calculating the gains on the asset in the hands of the donee.

The Inland Revenue takes care to ensure that sales made at an undervalue are treated as gifts of the difference between the sale price and the market value, in which case the market value is deemed to be the consideration on disposal. This is especially true in the case of disposals between "connected persons". Disposals between connected persons are presumed not to be at arm's length and the onus is placed upon the taxpayer to prove that transactions were based on the full market value. "Connected persons" are defined by s 63 CGTA 1979 and include spouses and other relatives and partners.

13. Effect of death

Since 30 March 1971 death is no longer treated as a deemed disposal by the deceased to his personal representatives and there is therefore no charge to capital gains tax by reason of a person's death – s 49(1) CGTA 1979. For the purposes of CGT, however, the personal representatives are deemed to have acquired the deceased's assets at the date of his death at full market value. This gives rise to an "uplift" which may save a considerable amount of tax if assets are retained until death. If assets are transferred by the personal representatives to the beneficiaries then there is no disposal on the transfer for CGT purposes and the beneficiaries are deemed to acquire the assets at the market value at the date of the deceased's death – s 49(4).

Similarly, property passing under a *donatio mortis causa,* a nomination or the right of survivorship in the case of joint property will not be subject to CGT as there is no deemed disposal, but the recipient is deemed to have acquired the property at the market value at the time of the deceased's death.

Where personal representatives sell estate property the chargeable gain is calculated by deducting from the sale price the deemed acquisition cost as adjusted by the indexation allowance. Losses in the same year of assessment can be set off against the gains and any excess losses may be carried forward to the following year.

The personal representatives can take advantage of the deceased's £5,800 exemption for the year of assessment in which the deceased died and have a similar exemption in the next two years. However, after that period no further exemption is available and gains are charged at the full 25% rate.

14. Exemptions and reliefs

(a) Annual exemption

It has already been seen that individuals have an annual exemption of £5,800 in each year of assessment to set off against total net gains and that personal representatives have the same exemption for the year of assessment which includes the date of death and for the following two years. Trustees have an annual exemption of £2,750.

(b) Money

Money held in sterling is not an asset for CGT purposes and is not therefore subject to CGT.

(c) Chattels disposed of for £6,000 or less

If the amount or value of the consideration for an article or a set of articles is equal to or less than £6,000 at the time of disposal then, provided the asset being disposed of is tangible, movable property, no CGT is payable on any gain accruing on the disposal.

(d) Private dwelling houses

This is one of the most important exemptions in practice and is contained in ss 101 and 102 CGTA 1979. A person's only or main residence may be disposed of, and the whole of any gain arising is exempt from CGT. The exemption includes the garden and grounds of up to 0.5 hectare. The Commissioners of Income Taxes have a discretion to exclude a greater amount of grounds from tax if that area is appropriate to the particular house having regard to the size and character of the dwelling house. Provided the dwelling house is covered by the exemption a gain made on the disposal of part of the grounds or garden will also be exempt from CGT where the house itself is retained. If a dwelling house is to be sold separately from part of its grounds, the grounds should always be sold first to take advantage of the exemption in respect of both disposals.

(i) Qualifying residence: For relief to be available, the dwelling-house in question must have been the individual's only or main residence throughout the period of ownership, except that the last three years of ownership may be disregarded. While it is usually apparent whether particular property has been used as the main dwelling house of the individual, or forms part of it, this will not always be the case.

In *Batey* v *Wakefield* [1982] 1 All ER 61, the applicant built a dwelling house for himself and his family. He notified the Inland Revenue that the house was to be his main residence. He then built a bungalow in the grounds of the house as quarters for a housekeeper and caretaker. The bungalow had a separate access and was separately rated. At a later date the applicant disposed of the bungalow and a little surrounding land as he no longer required them for their original purpose. He claimed that the disposal was exempt from CGT as the property formed part of his main residence. The Court of Appeal upheld his claim, concluding that a dwelling house could include several dwellings not physically connected. The applicant was clearly assisted by the fact that the separate building was used to accommodate staff required for the enjoyment of the other building – the dwelling house itself.

Where a dwelling house has been occupied as a main residence for part only of the individual's ownership (after March 1982) then only a corresponding proportion of any gain will be exempt. The taxpayer is entitled to have a total of three years disregarded in respect of periods of absence – and longer periods if the absence was necessitated by employment – provided the house was the main residence of the taxpayer both before and after each such period of absence.

Similarly only a proportion of the exemption may be claimed if part of the property was not being "resided in" by the taxpayer – for example, if part was being let out. However, under s 80 of the Finance Act 1980 (as amended by subsequent Finance Acts) the part let will be exempt under s 101 provided:

(a) the relief on the part of the property which is let does not exceed the amount of relief due in respect of the part occupied by the taxpayer; and

(b) the maximum relief permissible in respect of the part let must not exceed £40,000.

(ii) Nomination of main residence: Where a taxpayer has more than one residence he may nominate which is to be the main residence for CGT purposes. Spouses who live together may nominate only one residence between them.

However, for periods of occupation up to and including 6 April 1988 a further exemption may be claimed in respect of property owned by the taxpayer and occupied rent-free by a dependent relative of his. This exemption, contained in s 105 CGTA 1979, was abolished by the Finance Act 1988 for all periods after 6 April 1988.

(iii) Trustees: Section 104 CGTA 1979 extends the private residence exemption to trustees disposing of a dwellinghouse which has been the only or main residence of a person entitled to occupy it under the terms of the settlement during the trustee's period of ownership.

The exemption clearly applies to life tenants but would not normally apply to beneficiaries under a trust for sale, as their interests are in the proceeds of sale rather than the property itself. However, the Inland Revenue makes a concession in the case of residences occupied with the trustees' permission by an individual entitled under the settlement to the whole income either of the residence or of the proceeds of sale. In such cases the Inland Revenue allows the exemption to be claimed.

(e) Other exempt property
Statutory provisions exempt from CGT on a disposal certain other property, for example private motor cars; National Savings Certificates and Government stocks; shares in Personal Equity Plans which have been held for the minimum qualifying period; gifts of historic houses and chattels of outstanding scenic, historic or scientific interest – see s 147 CGTA 1979.

(f) Business "retirement" relief
This relief is available to sole traders, members of partnerships and members of "family" companies. It is available to an individual attaining 55 years of age or retiring below that age due to ill-health.

In such circumstances any disposal (by sale or gift) of business assets owned by the individual for at least one year immediately preceding the disposal will attract the relief. The individual's gains on the disposal are exempt up to a limit of £15,000 for each year of ownership in respect of the first ten years of ownership (£150,000). If the business has been owned by the individual for ten years or more and if the individual's gain exceeds £150,000 then 50% of the gain between £150,000 and £600,000 is also exempt – s 100 Finance Act 1991.

The relief is only available for disposals of part of the business or business assets.

(g) Charities
Disposals to charities and by charities are exempt from CGT – s 145.

(h) Spouses
Disposals between spouses do not attract CGT but the spouse receiving the property is deemed to receive it at the same acquisition cost as the actual acquisition cost of the donor – s 44. Thus the exemption cannot be used to "uplift" the acquisition cost. Naturally, if the "donee" spouse receives the property by reason of the death of the other then there is the usual "uplift" on death.

(i) Hold over relief

Since the Finance Act 1989 the application of hold over relief has been restricted. The relief operates by allowing a transferee to elect not to pay CGT at the time of receiving a gift but instead to "hold over" or defer payment of the tax. The effect is that the transferee is deemed to acquire the property at the acquisition cost of the transferor and will therefore be liable for tax on the whole gain from the date when the transferor acquired the property to the time of disposal by the transferee. If the transferee makes a disposal by way of a gift, the subsequent transferee may also elect to hold over the gain. If this continues until a transferee dies then the uplift on death will mean that the tax never becomes payable.

The relief is now available only in the following situations:
(i)   gifts of business assets (including unquoted shares in trading companies) between individuals or into and out of trusts;
(ii) gifts of heritage property and gifts to heritage maintenance funds;
(iii) gifts to political parties;
(iv) gifts on which there is an immediate charge to IHT (that is, gifts that are not PETS) or on which there would be an immediate charge but for the nil rate band or the annual exemption.

Thus gifts into a discretionary trust would qualify for hold over relief as they are not eligible for PET status. So too would gifts on the determination of a discretionary trust.

15. Basic tax planning

The tax implications of the retention or disposal of assets must be looked at as a whole, taking both IHT and CGT into consideration. It is often a balancing exercise. One advantage of retaining assets which have substantially increased in value since acquisition is the "uplift" on death which exempts such property from CGT on gains during the deceased's lifetime. Assets can then be passed to beneficiaries by will or on intestacy.

If lifetime gifts are to be made then gifts of money may be made free of CGT. It is advisable otherwise to make gifts of items exempt from CGT or subject to reliefs and, if possible, to give assets which are likely to appreciate in value but which have yet to do so.

PART III: SETTLEMENTS

16. Liability to Capital Gains Tax

(a) Definition of settled property
Settled property is defined for the purposes of CGT by CGTA 1979, s 51 as "any property held in trust other than property to which s 46 applies".

Section 46 applies to assets held by a person or persons as nominee for another, or as bare trustee for another or others, or as trustee for someone who would be absolutely entitled as against the trustee but for infancy or other disability. In cases to which s 46 applies the settlement provisions are disregarded and the CGTA 1979 is applied as if the property concerned were vested in the beneficiaries themselves.

(b) The entry charge
Whereas a settlement is created *inter vivos,* there is a deemed disposal by the settlor/donor to the trustee which will give rise to a charge to CGT in the usual way. If the settlement is created on death, by will or intestacy, there is no CGT and the acquisition values are uplifted so that the trustees are deemed to acquire the settled assets at their market value as at the settlor's death.

(c) Charge on sale by trustees
A sale of settled assets by trustees gives rise to a charge to CGT on the gain, taken to be the difference between the consideration on sale and the acquisition cost (or deemed acquisition cost), taking into account the indexation allowance and allowable costs. The first £2,750 of net gains are exempt in each year of assessment. CGT is then charged at 25%, except in the case of accumulation and mainte-

nance trusts and discretionary trusts which are subject to tax at 35% (see post).

(d)   Charge when beneficiary becomes absolutely entitled
There is no charge to CGT where a limited interest under a settlement comes to an end and no beneficiary becomes beneficially entitled as against the trustees. If the end of the interest is caused by the death of the person enjoying it then this may give rise to an uplift under s 49 CGTA 1979.

When a beneficiary becomes absolutely entitled due to the death of the person enjoying the limited interest then there will be a death uplift and no charge to CGT, and the beneficiary will be deemed to acquire the property at the market value at the date of becoming absolutely entitled.

However, if a beneficiary becomes absolutely entitled to any part of the settled property as against the trustees in any way other than the death of the person with the prior limited interest, then there is a deemed disposal of that part of the property from the trustees to the beneficiary and CGT will be chargeable on any gain in value (s 54 CGTA 1979).

Similarly, in the case of a discretionary trust, then the death of any discretionary beneficiaries will not give rise to a charge to CGT but there will be a charge under s 54 when the discretionary trust itself is terminated and someone becomes absolutely entitled to the fund.

17.   Liability to Inheritance Tax

(a)   Introduction
As for CGT, property held by a nominee or a bare trustee is treated for IHT purposes as belonging to the person for whom it is held.

Where there is a settlement, IHT liability depends upon whether or not there is a beneficial interest in possession. For example, a settlement of property on "A for life and then for B absolutely" gives to A an interest in possession as life tenant. Conversely, the usual discretionary trust will not create an interest in possession, neither will a contingent gift until the contingency is satisfied.

However, such demarcation is not always as clear-cut (see *Pearson v IRC* [1980] 2 All ER 479 and *Moore v IRC* [1984] 1 All ER 1108).

(b) Person beneficially entitled to an interest in possession

If the settlement is created during the settlor's lifetime then it should be a PET in favour of the trustees which will not be chargeable to any IHT provided the settlor survives seven years from the creation of the settlement.

If the settlement is created by will, IHT will be charged on the death estate in any event and there is no further charge to IHT when the property is vested in the trustees of the settlement by the personal representatives. Generally the person entitled to the interest in possession is treated for IHT purposes as if he were entitled to the capital of the fund in which he has the interest in possession.

Thus, unless he gives away his beneficial interest (and, of course, such a gift may qualify as a PET) IHT will be chargeable on his death at the death rate on the capital value of the trust fund, which will be aggregated with his own estate.

For this reason settlements creating successive interests in possession should be avoided as IHT will be chargeable on the whole capital value of the fund on each successive termination of the interest in possession.

(c) No person beneficially entitled to an interest in possession

Where trusts do not involve interests in possession (for example, the standard discretionary trust), IHT is payable on the creation of the settlement as the payment to the trustees does not qualify as a PET.

Thereafter IHT is charged on the settled fund every ten years at 30% of the lifetime rate. The settlor's cumulative total immediately before the creation of the settlement is used as the starting point for the charge.

Where property is taken out of the settled fund during the ten year period between charges, a proportionate charge to IHT is made. For example, if property is paid out to a beneficiary one year after the last charge to tax was made, then a charge is made of one-tenth of the full tax on that property that would have been payable had the property remained in the settlement for a complete ten year period.

Of course, if the settlor's cumulative total immediately before the creation of the settlement is very low or nil then a small discretionary trust is likely to fall consistently within the nil rate band. IHT will be avoided where the settlor's cumulative total, together with the total amount settled, adds up to less than or equal to the nil rate band limit, provided the value of the fund does not increase by so much more than the index-linked IHT threshold so as to take the value of the settled fund above the nil rate band limit.

The periodic charge may be a significant disadvantage of the discretionary settlement. One advantage, however, is that there is no charge to IHT on the death of any of the discretionary beneficiaries.

(d) The accumulation and maintenance trust

The accumulation and maintenance trust enjoys a privileged status and is extremely useful when providing for young beneficiaries. There are certain conditions to be fulfilled in order to qualify for the tax privileges, namely:

(i)   The trust must make provision that one or more of the beneficiaries will become entitled to the settled property or to an interest in possession in the settled property on or before attaining a specified age not exceeding 25 years. (NB: s 31 Trustee Act 1925 provides that a person with a contingent interest in capital becomes entitled to the income therefrom on reaching eighteen, thus acquiring an "interest in possession" at that time despite his interest in the capital remaining contingent. Thus, a gift of capital contingent upon attaining an age greater than 25 will satisfy this condition – see *Inglewood* v *IRC* [1983] 1 WLR 866.)

(ii) Before the beneficiary or beneficiaries become beneficially entitled to the settled property (or an interest in possession in the settled property) there must be no interest in possession in the settled property. Thus s 31 of the Trustee Act 1925 should be specifically excluded to ensure that the accumulation and maintenance reliefs are not lost by the creation of an interest in possession under the statutory provision when the beneficiary becomes eighteen. The trustees should be directed to accumulate income until the beneficiary becomes beneficially entitled to the fund, usually at 25.

(iii) The trustees must be given power to apply the income of the fund at their discretion for the maintenance, education or benefit of the beneficiaries and any income not so used must be accumulated.

(iv) Either no more than 25 years must have passed since the creation of the settlement or all persons who are or have been beneficiaries must be or must have been grandchildren of a common grandparent.

The initial *inter vivos* creation of an accumulation and maintenance trust will be a PET and the usual rules will apply. The property settled on death will have already been subject to IHT as part of the death estate and no further charge to IHT is made on the transfer of the property to the trustees.

During the existence of the trust it is exempt from IHT and there is no periodic charge. Advances made to the beneficiary out of the capital of the fund do not attract IHT. There is also no charge to IHT when the beneficiary becomes entitled to an interest in possession in the settled property.

Appendix A

Precedents – full forms of will

A.1 Standard will – full form (long)

THIS IS the last will and testament of me [AB of ......]

1. I hereby revoke all former testamentary dispositions made by me.
2. (i) I APPOINT [CD of ......] and [EF of ......] to be executors and trustees of this my will (hereinafter termed "my trustees" which expression where the context admits shall include the trustees for the time being hereof)

   (ii) If the said [CD] and [EF] shall both fail to survive me or if the survivor or survivors of them shall decline to act as my trustee or if the appointment shall fail for any other reason then I APPOINT the partners at the date of my death in the firm of [YZ and Co] solicitors of ...... or the firm which at that date has succeeded to and carries on its practice to be the executors and trustees hereof and I DIRECT that no more than two of the said partners shall prove my will and act initially in its trusts.

   (iii) [Professional charging clause, see C.20.27]
3. [Gift of personal chattels to wife and two sons, see C.11.6]
4. I give the following specific legacies

   (i) [Gift of stamp collection, see C.11.22]

   (ii) [Gift of stock, see C.11.18]
5. I give the following pecuniary legacies payable on my death:-

   (i) [Immediate legacy to wife, see C.11.28]

   (ii) [Simple legacy to individual, see C.11.29]

   (iii) To each of my trustees [not being a professional trustee] who shall prove this my will and act in the trusts hereof I give the sum of [£1,000].

6. (a) I give the following annuities:
    (i) [Simple annuity, see C.15.1]
    (ii) [Annuity excluding rule in *Re Pettit*, see C.15.3]
  (b) [Provision for the setting aside of parts of estate as annuity funds, see C.15.8]

7. [Specific gift of freehold property, see C.13.2]

8. [Residuary gift to trustees upon trust for sale with power to postpone sale, see C.16.7]

9. [Clause excluding rule in *Howe* v *Earl of Dartmouth*, see C.20.43]

10. [Direction to pay debts, funeral and testamentary expenses and thereafter hold net estate on trusts provided for, see C.16.8]

11. [Trust for testator's children with substitutional provisions, see C.16.14]

12. [Exclusion of hotchpot, see C.11.50]

13. [Power of appropriation, see C.20.1]

14. [Power to insure, see C.20.5]

15. [Power to lease, mortgage, sell or purchase, see C.20.8]

16. [Power to defer payment of debts, see C.20.10]

17. [Power to carry on business, see C.20.11]

18. [Power to borrow, see C.20.12]

19. [Direction to act by majority, see C.20.15]

20. [Power to act on counsel's opinion, see C.20.18]

21. [General indemnity to trustees, see C.20.21]

22. [Provision for receipts of minors, see C.20.25]

23. [Wide power of investment, see C.20.29]

24. [Power to purchase house as residence for beneficiary, see C.20.31]

25. [Clause for maintenance of child, see C.20.38]

26. [Power of advancement, see C.20.40]

27. I DECLARE that any powers conferred on my trustees by the provisions of this my will and any codicil hereto shall be construed as being in addition to and not in substitution for any power discretion or trust which in the absence of the powers herein contained or any of them would be vested in my trustees by any law or statute.

[Testimonium and attestation clause, see C.3.1]

A.2 Will disposing of foreign property

THIS IS the last will and testament of [BC of ......]

1. I hereby revoke all former testamentary dispositions made by me and I declare that I am domiciled in England and Wales and that this my will is

to take effect and be construed in accordance with English law and I further declare that all sums of money payable hereunder are payable in pounds sterling.

2. (i) I APPOINT [XY of ....] and [VW of ......] to be executors and trustees of this my will to act in respect of all my real and personal estate situate being or arising in the United Kingdom or in any other country except [France]

(ii) I declare that the expression "my English Trustees" shall where the context admits be construed to mean and include the trustee or trustees for the time being of all my real and personal estate not situate being or arising in [France]

3. I appoint [P Trust Company Limited] whose registered office is situate at ...... to be the executor[s] and trustee[s] of this my will for the purpose of dealing with all my real and personal estate situate being and arising in [France] hereinafter termed "my foreign trustees" which expression shall include where the context admits the trustees for the time being of all my real and personal estate situate being or arising in [France]

4. I declare that my English trustees may receive from my foreign trustees the income and proceeds of sale and all real and personal estate devised and bequeathed to my foreign trustees and may deal with the same where it is passed to them pursuant to the directions of this my will or any codicil hereto.

5. I give the following free of all inheritance tax and foreign death duties:-

(i) [Specific gift, see C.11.9]

(ii) [Gifts, as in clause C.11.18]

6. I give the following general legacies free of all inheritance tax and foreign death duties

(i) [Legacy, see C.11.28]

(ii) [Legacy, see C.11.29]

(iii) [Legacy, see C.11.34]

7. (a) I bequeath the following annuities free of all inheritance tax and foreign death duties

(i) [Clause giving annuity, see C.15.1]

(ii) [Clause giving annuity, see C.15.1]

(b) My English trustees ...... [continue as clause C.15.8 substituting the words "my English trustees" for the words "my trustees"]

8. I give devise and bequeath all my real and personal estate whatsoever and being within the jurisdiction of the [French] courts together with all debts and choses in action recoverable or enforceable in such courts to my foreign trustees.

9. (i) My foreign trustees shall sell call in and convert into money all my

real and personal estate so given devised and bequeathed to them and shall collect realize and recover the debts and choses in action as aforesaid

(ii) From the proceeds of such sale calling in conversion and collection my foreign trustees shall retain such sums as they in their absolute discretion consider necessary to pay debts due from my estate to persons resident in the [French] jurisdiction and to pay any taxes duties and other payments due under that jurisdiction and also to exercise any of the powers hereinafter conferred upon them to pay any commission hereinafter directed to be paid AND SHALL THEREAFTER transfer the net proceeds of such sale calling in collection and conversion to my English trustees to be held by them upon the trusts hereinafter declared as to the capital of my residuary estate.

(iii) Out of the income arising from any part or all of my real and personal property in [France] for the time being unconverted my foreign trustees shall retain such sums as are required in respect of the commission hereinafter directed to be paid in respect of income and also such sums as required in respect of any other payments due therefrom AND SHALL THEREAFTER transfer the balance of the said income to my English trustees to be held by them upon the trusts hereinafter declared in respect of the income of my residuary estate.

(iv) I DECLARE that the receipt of my English trustees or any two of them shall be a good and complete discharge for all moneys paid to them by my foreign trustees.

10.(i) I give devise and bequeath all my real and personal estate not otherwise hereby disposed of (and excluding my real and personal estate hereinbefore given to my foreign trustees) to my English trustees upon trust to sell call in and convert the same into money

(ii) My English trustees shall pay thereout my debts testamentary and funeral expenses and all legacies and annuities hereinbefore provided for and shall thereafter stand possessed of the residue together with my ready money and together with the net proceeds of the sale calling in and conversion of my real and personal estate in [France] when so transferred to them as aforesaid by my foreign trustees and of any part or parts of my said real and personal property for the time being unconverted upon the following trusts:-

(a) upon trust to pay the income thereof to my said wife during her life.

(b) Subject as aforesaid ...... [continue as per C.5.3]

11. I declare that both my English trustees and foreign trustees shall have full power to postpone the sale calling in and conversion of all or any part of my real or personal property of whatever nature which is vested in each of them respectively as they shall in their absolute discretion think fit

without being liable for any loss occasioned thereby.

12. I declare that my English trustees shall have the following additional powers:-

(i) [Wider power of investment, see C.20.29]

(ii) [Power of appropriation, see C.20.4]

(iii) [Power to insure, see C.20.5]

(iv) [Power to purchase property as residence for beneficiaries, see C.20.31]

(v) To release or compound any debt owing to me and to allow further time for payment of any debt with or without taking security or further security therefor.

(vi) To pay compromise or submit to arbitration any claims against my estate of any nature whatsoever and to enter into give execute and do all necessary agreements investments releases and acts in relation to the same without being liable for any loss occasioned thereby.

(vii) [Charging Clause, see C.20.27]

13. [General indemnity to trustees as per C.20.21]

14. I declare that my foreign trustees shall have the following additional powers:-

(i) To give a full and valid receipt and discharge in writing in respect of the purchase money of any property sold or for any moneys securities or other personal property or effects paid transferred or delivered to them under the trusts hereof.

(ii) In respect of any undivided share or interest in any foreign property whether real or personal held by me at the date of my death my foreign trustees shall have power to concur with any other person or persons entitled to or having power over the other share or shares interest or interests in any such property in dealing with the said property under the trusts hereof and to partition or concur in partitioning the same or any part thereof in such manner as my foreign trustees think fit and for that purpose to agree to the apportionment of any purchase money rent expenses outgoings or other matter and to pay or receive money or equality of exchange or partition [whether or not any one or more of the said trustees may be entitled to or interested in any other such share or interest either in his own right or in a fiduciary capacity].

(iii) to carry out or enter into any arrangement reasonable for the settlement and adjustment with any partner or partners of mine or co-owner or co-owners with me of any business or property in [France] who survive me of all rights and liabilities in respect of such business or property without being liable for any loss occasioned thereby.

[Testimonium and attestation clause, see C.3.1]

A.3 Mutual wills of husband and wife

This is the last will and testament of me [name] of [address]

1. I hereby revoke all former testamentary dispositions made by me.
2. I appoint my husband [wife] [name] and [X of ......] to be the executors and trustees hereof (hereinafter referred to as my trustees which where the context admits shall include the trustees for the time being hereof)
3. Whereas my husband [wife] and I have agreed with one accord to execute like wills in similar terms and whereas we have further agreed that each such respective will shall not be altered or revoked either during our joint lives or by the survivor of us so in reliance upon the said agreement I HEREBY GIVE all my property whatsoever and wheresoever situate [including any property over which I may have a general power of appointment or disposition by will] to my trustees UPON TRUST to sell call in and convert the same into money with power to postpone the said sale calling in and conversion thereof for so long as they shall in their absolute discretion think fit without being liable for loss and to hold the proceeds of such sale calling in and conversion and my ready money upon the following trusts:-

    (a) UPON TRUST to pay thereout my debts and funeral and testamentary expenses and subject thereto upon trust for my husband [wife] during her lifetime.

    (b) Upon the death of my husband [wife] or if he [she] shall die before me or if the foregoing trust fails for any reason IN TRUST ...... [continue as in clause C.5.3]
4. [Charging clause, see C.20.27]
5. My trustees shall have full and unfettered powers including but not limited to powers of investment advancement borrowing leasing mortgaging selling and purchasing property for whatsoever purpose they see fit as if beneficially entitled to the property held by them.
6. [General indemnity, see C.20.21]

[Testimonium and attestation clause, see C.3.1]

A.4 Will disposing of a business

This is the last will and testament of me ......

1. I hereby revoke all former testamentary dispositions made by me.
2. [Appointment of executors and trustees, see C.8.3]
3. [Gift of business to trustees, see C.12.2]
4. [Power to carry on business without interference, see C.12.5]

5. [Provision of salary for trustees managing business, see C.12.7]
6. [Provision allowing trustees to exercise powers whether or not they have an interest in the business, see C.12.8]
7. [Indemnity for trustees running business, see C.12.9]
8. (i) Subject as aforesaid ...... [continue as in clause C.16.7 giving residuary estate to trustees upon trust for sale]
(ii) Direction to trustees to pay debts and interest from residue [see C.16.8]
(iii) Trust for testator's children [see clause C.16.14]
[Testimonium and attestation clause, see C.3.1]

A.5 Codicil on second marriage; rewriting will and substituting second wife as beneficiary; providing for children of second marriage

1. [Commencement and provisions as in clause C.7.2]
2. [Testimonium and attestation clause, see C.3.1]

A.6 Will of widow exercising power of appointment given by will of husband

This is the last will and testament of me [name] of ......
1. I hereby revoke all former testamentary dispositions made by me.
2. I appoint [name] of ...... and [name] of ...... to be the executors and trustees hereof (those being the trustees of my late husband's will)
3. [Specific gifts and pecuniary legacies, see clauses C.11.18 and C.11.29]
4. In exercise of a power of appointment vested in me by the will of my late husband dated the [date] over and in respect of the proceeds of sale and conversion of his residuary estate both real and personal and the investments for the time being representing the same in favour of the children and issue of our marriage I HEREBY DIRECT AND APPOINT that the trustees of the will of my said husband shall stand possessed of my husband's residuary estate as from the date of my death upon the following trusts:-
(a) As to one half thereof upon trust for my son [name] absolutely.
(b) As to one half upon trust to pay the income thereof to my daughter [name] during her life and after her death to hold the capital and income for all or any children or child of my said daughter who attain or attains the age of eighteen years and if more than one in equal shares.
5. I give to my trustees as aforesaid all my real and personal property not

otherwise disposed of hereunder upon trust to sell call in and convert the same with full power to postpone the said sale calling in and conversion for so long as they shall in their absolute discretion think fit without being liable for any loss occasioned thereby and I DIRECT that my trustees shall pay out of the net proceeds of sale and conversion all my debts funeral and testamentary expenses and all taxes payable upon my estate and shall thereafter hold the balance of my estate upon the trusts of my late husband's residuary estate as if an accretion to that estate.

[Testimonium and attestation clause, see C.3.1]

A.7 Will in favour of named children – provision of residence

This is the last will and testament of me [name] of ......

1. I hereby revoke all former testamentary dispositions made by me.
2. (a) [Appointment of executors and trustees, see C.8.5]
   (b) [Professional charging clause, see C.20.27]
3. [Specific gifts, see C.11.18]
4. [Legacy, see C.11.29]
5. [Gift to trustees upon trust for sale as per C.16.7]
6. My trustees shall hold the net proceeds of such sale and conversion as hereinbefore provided together with my ready money upon the following trusts:-

(a) Upon trust to pay thereout all my debts funeral and testamentary expenses and all taxes payable on my estate and all legacies and gifts herein provided for.

(b) Upon trust to invest the residue in accordance with the provisions hereof and with the general law save as modified hereby and to stand possessed of the same and such investments and any property for the time being unsold [hereinafter together termed "my residuary estate"] upon the trusts herein declared.

(c) In addition to the powers granted to my trustees hereby and by general law my trustees may in their absolute discretion postpone the sale of any real property forming part of my residuary estate and the furniture effects and contents thereof for so long as my children [name 1] [name 2] and [name 3] or any of them reside therein until the youngest survivor of them shall attain the age of [twenty-one] years.

(d) Upon my youngest surviving child attaining the age of [twenty-one] or at such time as no one or more of my said children continue to use the said property as a residence whichever be the sooner my trustees shall sell the same together with its contents and effects as soon as they in their absolute discretion think it desirable and shall hold the net proceeds of sale as part of my residuary estate.

(e) My trustees shall have full power to apply the remainder of my residuary estate and the income therefrom at their absolute discretion and in so far as may be necessary to pay for the outgoings of any property retained by them as a residence for my child or children as aforesaid and to pay for the upkeep thereof and the upkeep repair and replacement of any furniture contents and effects thereof and in the maintenance of my said children or any one or more of them while under the age of 21 years.

(f) All my residuary estate not so applied or disposed of under the foregoing provisions shall be held for my said [three] children or the survivors or survivor of those who attain the age of twenty-one years in equal shares.

(g) My trustees shall have full power to purchase property for the purpose of providing a residence for one or more of my said children while my youngest surviving child is under the age of twenty-one and may sell or dispose of any such property and purchase replacement property at any time or times as they in their absolute discretion think fit without being liable for any loss occasioned thereby and any property purchased in pursuance of this power shall be held upon trusts the same in all respects as if the said purchased property had formed part of my estate upon my death.

7. [General power of appropriation, see C.20.1]
8. [Power to insure, see C.20.5]
9 [Power to lease, mortgage, sell or purchase, see C.20.8]
10. [Power to borrow, see C.20.12]
11. [Wider power of investment, see C.20.29]
12. [General indemnity, see C.20.21]
[Testimonium and attestation clause, see C.3.1]

A.8 Simple will giving all property to another of full age absolutely

This is the last will and testament of me [name] of ......
1. I hereby revoke all former testamentary dispositions made by me.
2. I give all my real and personal property whatsoever and wheresover situate (including any property over which I may have a power of appointment or disposition by will) to [name] absolutely and I appoint him [her] to be the sole executor of this my will.
[Testimonium and attestation clause, see C.3.1]

A.9 Codicil following divorce

I [name] of ...... declare this to be the [first] codicil to my will made on the [date].
WHEREAS:-
1. By my said will dated [date] I have made various bequests and provisions in favour of my former wife [name].
2. The marriage between myself and the said [name] was dissolved by a decree absolute of divorce pronounced in the Family Division of the High Court of Justice on the [date].
Now I hereby revoke all bequests made to my wife in my will and declare that for all purposes in connection with my will and its provisions my will shall take effect as if my wife had died immediately prior to my death.
I hereby confirm my will as modified by this codicil.
[Testimonium and attestation clause, see C.3.3]

A.10 Codicil reviving former will previously revoked

I [name] of ...... declare this to be the [second] codicil to my will made on the [date].
Whereas by my last will dated [date] I revoked my previous will dated [date] and all other testamentary dispositions preceding my said last will.
Now I hereby revoke my said last will dated [date] and hereby revive and confirm the will dated [date of earlier will].
[Testimonium and attestation clause, see C.3.3]

A.11 Will giving all property to a minor

This is the last will and testament of me [name] of ......
1. I hereby revoke all former testamentary dispositions made by me.
2. [Appointment of executors, see C.8.3]
3. [Gift of all real and personal property to trustees upon trust for sale, see C.16.7]
4. My trustees shall hold the proceeds of sale and conversion and all unsold property together with my ready money upon the following trusts:-
   (a) to pay my debts and testamentary and funeral expenses
   (b) subject thereto for my daughter [name] absolutely PROVIDED THAT if my said daughter shall die in my lifetime or after my death but under

the age of eighteen years then the same shall be held upon trust for [name] absolutely.

5. [Wider power of investment, see C.20.29]
6. [Power of maintenance, see C.20.38]
7. [Power of advancement, see C.20.40]
[Testimonium and attestation clause, see C.3.1]

A.12 Will to wife with survivorship clause and substituted gift

This is the last will and testament of me [name] of ......

1. I hereby revoke all former testamentary dispositions made by me.
2.(a) I appoint my wife [name] and [name] of ...... to be the executors and trustees hereof (hereinafter referred to as my trustees which expression shall where the context admits include the trustees for the time being hereof)

(b) If my said wife shall die in my lifetime or after my death without having proved my will then I appoint [name] of ...... to act as executor and trustee in her stead.

3. Provided my said wife shall survive me for a period of 28 full days I give to her absolutely all my real and personal property whatsoever and wheresoever situate (including any property over which I may have a general power of appointment or disposition by will) subject to and after the payment of my debts and funeral and testamentary expenses and all taxes payable in respect of my estate and subject also to any specific gifts and the payment of any legacies given hereby and in any codicil hereto.

4. If my wife shall fail to survive me for 28 full days as aforesaid and only in that event then clauses 5 to 10 hereof shall have effect.

5. [Specific gift, see C.11.22]
6. [Legacy, see C.11.29]
7. [Gift of real and personal estate to trustees upon trust for sale, see C.16.7]
8. [Trust to pay debts and taxes etc and invest residue, see C.16.8]
9. [Trust for children with further substitutional gift, see C.16.14]
10. If my said wife shall fail to survive me by the said 28 days then the income of my residuary estate accruing from the date of my death until the death of my wife shall be accumulated and shall form part of the capital of my residuary estate.

[Testimonium and attestation clause, see C.3.1]

A.13 Will providing for settled legacy upon trust for improvident cousin, his wife and children

This is the last will and testament of me [name] of ......

1. I hereby revoke all former testamentary dispositions made by me.

2. I appoint [name] of ...... and [name] of ...... to be the general executors and trustees hereof (hereinafter referred to as my general trustees which expression shall where the context admits include the trustee for the time being hereof in relation to all my estate save for the legacy provided for in clause 3 hereof.)

3. I GIVE to [name] of ...... and [name] ...... (hereinafter referred to as "my special trustees" which expression shall include the trustees for the time being of this legacy) the sum of [fifty thousand] pounds free of inheritance tax to be held upon the following trusts:-

(a) Upon trust to invest the same in their name in any investments authorised by the general law with full power to vary and transpose the said investments without being liable for any loss occasioned thereby.

(b) Upon trust during the life of my cousin [name] of ...... to pay and apply the whole or such part of the capital and income thereof and of the investments representing the same as they in their absolute discretion think fit for the maintenance support or other benefit of my said cousin or of any wife or child of his and my special trustees shall have full power in their absolute discretion to pay the rent or other expenses of a house for him or them or any one of them and subject to any such application of capital and income any unapplied income of the trust legacy shall fall into and form part of the income of my residuary estate.

(c) After the death of my said cousin upon trust during the lifetime of any widow he may leave to exercise like powers as under paragraph (b) hereof in favour of such widow and of all or any children or child of my said cousin living for the time being ALWAYS PROVIDED that if any widow of my said cousin shall not be born or en ventre at the date of my death then the trust shall endure only during so much of the period of eighty years commencing on my death as she shall be living.

(d) Subject as aforesaid upon trust to divide the said trust legacy and any investments representing the same or so much thereof as shall not have been paid or applied under any trust or power herein before contained among the children if any of my said cousin who shall attain the age of [eighteen] years and if more than one then in equal shares absolutely.

(e) If there be no child of my said cousin who attains the age of [eighteen] years then the trust legacy and investments representing the same subject to the deduction of any money paid or applied under the trusts and powers as aforesaid shall fall into and form part of my residuary estate.

4. I HEREBY DECLARE that the perpetuity period in respect of the said trust legacy for all purposes shall be eighty years from the date of my death.

5. I GIVE to my general trustees all my real and personal property whatsoever and wheresoever situate (including any property over which I may have a general power of appointment or disposition by will) UPON trust for sale to sell call in and convert the same into money with full power to postpone such sale calling in and conversion for so long as they shall in their absolute discretion consider fit and to pay from the proceeds of sale and conversion my debts and funeral and testamentary expenses and all taxes payable by my estate and to pay to my special trustees thereout the specific legacy of [fifty thousand] pounds hereinbefore provided for and to pay all other legacies given hereunder or in any codicil hereto and thereafter to pay the balance of such proceeds to [charity] for its charitable purposes and I DIRECT THAT the receipt of the treasurer or the proper officer for the time being thereof shall be a sufficient discharge to my trustees.

[Testimonium and attestation clause, see C.3.1]

A.14 Will including deferred legacies

This is the last will of me [name] of ......

1. I hereby revoke all former testamentary dispositions made by me.
2. [Appointment of executors and trustees, see C.8.3]
3. [Immediate legacies, see C.11.28 and C.11.29]
4. [Gift of residue to trustees upon trust for sale with full power to postpone sale, see C.16.7]
5. [Trust to pay debts etc and invest residue, see C.16.8]
6. [Exclusion of the rule in *Howe* v *Earl of Dartmouth*, see C.20.43]
7. [Exclusion of apportionment rules, see C.18.3]
8. [Wider power of investment, see C.20.29]
9. [Professional charging clause, see C.20.27]
10. My trustees shall stand possessed of all proceeds of sale and conversion and any investments representing the same and all parts of my estate remaining unsold and any ready money (hereinafter called my residuary estate) and of the annual income thereof subject as aforesaid upon the following trusts:-
(a) UPON TRUST to pay the income thereof to [name of life tenant] during his life.
(b) After the death of [life tenant] my trustees shall hold my residuary estate upon trust to pay the following legacies free of all taxes which may be

payable on the death of the said [life tenant] to such of the following legatees as shall be then living namely:

    (i) Legacy, see C.11.29

    (ii) Legacy, see C.11.29

    (iii) Legacy, see C.11.29

(c) After the death of the said [life tenant] and subject to the legacies as aforesaid my trustees shall hold the balance of my residuary estate and the income thereof UPON TRUST for [continue, see C.16.14]

[Testimonium and attestation clause, see C.3.1]

A.15 Will providing for discretionary trust of income during perpetuity period with division of capital at the end of period between surviving beneficiaries

THIS IS the last will and testament of me [name] of ......

1. I hereby revoke all former testamentary dispositions made by me.

2. (i) [Appointment of executors and trustees, see C.8.5]

    (ii)[Professional charging clause, see C.20.27]

3. [Specific legacies, see C.11.18]

4. [General legacies, see C.11.29]

5. [Residuary gift to trustees upon trust for sale with power to postpone sale, see C.16.7]

6. [Direction to pay debts, funeral and testamentary expenses and thereafter hold net estate on trusts provided for, see C.16.8]

7. [Clause excluding rule in *Howe* v *Earl of Dartmouth*, see C.20.43]

8. [Clause excluding apportionment rules, see C.18.3]

9. [Wider power of investment, see C.20.29]

10. I hereby declare that the perpetuity period applicable hereto for all the purposes of the Perpetuities and Accumulations Act 1964 shall be eighty years from the date of my death.

11. The term "beneficiaries" shall for the purposes of this my will mean my children living at my death and my grandchildren and remoter issue whenever born PROVIDED THAT the expression "living" shall include any child en ventre sa mère who is later born alive and "beneficiary" shall have a corresponding meaning.

12. (i) during the said perpetuity period my trustees SHALL PAY OR APPLY the income of my residuary estate to or for the maintenance or education or otherwise for the benefit of all or any one or more of the beneficiaries for the time being living to the exclusion of any other or others in such shares and proportions and generally in such manner as

my trustees shall in their absolute discretion see fit PROVIDED THAT any such income not so applied thereafter shall be accumulated and shall form part of the capital of my residuary estate.

(ii) My trustees shall have the power to pay income to and accept the receipt of the parent or guardian of any beneficiary hereunder where that beneficiary is for the time being a minor.

13. UPON the expiration of the perpetuity period my trustees shall hold the capital and income of my residuary estate UPON TRUST to divide the same between such beneficiaries as shall then be living such beneficiaries to take through all degrees according to their stocks in equal shares if more than one the share which his or her or their parent would have taken if then living ALWAYS PROVIDED THAT no beneficiary shall take whose parent is alive and capable of taking.

[Testimonium and attestation clause, see C.3.1]

A.16 Will providing for maintenance of wife who suffers from a mental disorder

THIS IS the last will and testament of me [name] of ......

1. I hereby revoke all former testamentary dispositions made by me.
2. [Appointment of executors and trustees, see C.8.3]
3. [Legacies, see C.11.29]
4. (i) I GIVE all my real and personal property whatsoever and wheresoever situate (including any property over which I may have at my death a power of appointment or disposition by will) to my trustees upon trust to pay and satisfy any legacies made herein or in any codicil hereto and to pay my debts and funeral and testamentary expenses and to stand possessed of the residue during the lifetime of my wife [name] and to receive the income thereof and pay and apply the same in such shares and proportions and generally in such manner as my trustees shall in their absolute discretion think fit for the maintenance of my said wife and my children [and remoter issue] for the time being living or for the education or other benefit of all or any of them.

(ii) I DECLARE that my trustees shall have absolute discretion as to the application of the said income between my said wife children [and issue] and may pay or apply income to or for the benefit of any one or more of them to the exclusion of the other or others ALWAYS PROVIDED THAT the whole of the income shall be so paid or applied in each year AND I REQUEST without imposing any legal obligation on my trustees that they have regard principally to the needs and interests of my said wife.

5. Notwithstanding any other provision of this my will my trustees may in their absolute discretion at any time or times during the lifetime of my said wife raise and pay for the maintenance of my said wife any part or parts or whole of the capital of the said residue.

6. After the death of my said wife my trustees shall stand possessed of the said residue or such part thereof (if any) as remains together with the income therefrom UPON TRUST to divide the same between such of my children [and remoter issue] as shall be then living such beneficiaries to take through all degrees according to their stocks in equal shares if more than one the share which his or her or their parent would have taken if then living ALWAYS PROVIDED THAT no beneficiary shall take whose parent is alive and capable of taking.

7. [Wider power of investment, see C.20.29]

8. [General indemnity clause, see C.20.21]

9. [Power to accept receipts by or on behalf of minors, see C.20.25]

[Testimonium and attestation clause, see C.3.1]

Appendix B

Statutory will forms

Section 179 of the Law of Property Act 1925 provides that the Lord Chancellor may publish forms which a testator may refer to in his will. The forms are not incorporated, however, unless the testator refers to them in his will. The forms may be modified.

The Statutory Will Forms 1925 (SR & O 1925 No. 780)

1. The forms hereinafter contained may be cited as the Statutory Will Forms, 1925, and are divided into two groups called Part I and Part II respectively.
2. The forms in Part I may be incorporated in a will by a general reference to that Part, and the forms in Part I and Part II or any of them may be incorporated in a will in manner indicated in the Schedule hereto or in any other manner indicating an intention to incorporate them, and in the case of Forms in Part II also indicating what property or disposition is to be affected thereby.
3. (1) In any form when incorporated in a will-
   (i) The provisions thereof shall have effect subject to the express provisions of the will;
   (ii) "Disposition" means a devise, bequest, and a testamentary appointment, whether in exercise of a general or special power and includes a disposition under the statutory power to dispose of entailed interests by will: "dispose of" has a corresponding meaning; and references to a testator's property include property which he disposes of in exercise of a power;
   (iii) "The trustees" means the trustees appointed by the testator either

generally or for a specific purpose, as the case may require, and the persons who by appointment by the court or otherwise become the trustees, and include his personal representatives, when acting as his trustees;

(iv) "Authorised investments" mean investments authorised by the will creating the trust, for the investment of any money subject to the trusts of the will, or by the law;

(v) Other words and expressions have the same meanings as in the Law of Property Act, 1925.

The Schedule is as follows:

INCORPORATION OF ALL THE FORMS IN PART I
All the forms in Part I of the Statutory Will Forms, 1925, are incorporated in my will [subject to the following modifications, namely*].
* Here insert the modifications (if any).

INCORPORATION OF SPECIFIED FORMS FROM PART I
The following forms contained in Part I of the Statutory Will Forms, 1925, shall be incorporated in my will:
[Specify those of the following forms which it is desired to incorporate.]
Form 1 (Confirmation of Settlements).
Form 2 (Meaning of "Personal chattels").
Form 3 (Inventories and provisions respecting chattels).
Form 4 (Legacies to charities).
Form 5 (Directions respecting annuities).
Form 6 (Power of appropriation).
[Subject to the following modifications, namely*].
* Here insert the modifications (if any).

INCORPORATION OF SPECIFIED FORMS FROM PART II

Form 7: Trusts of a settled legacy
Form 7 of the Statutory Will Forms, 1925, is incorporated in my will, and shall apply to the following legacies* [subject to the following modifications†].
* Here insert the legacies of money or investments to be settled.
† Here insert the modifications (if any).

Form 8: Administration trusts
Form 8 of the Statutory Will Forms, 1925, is incorporated in my will, and shall apply to * [subject to the following modifications†].

* Here insert description of property to be held upon administration trusts.
† Here insert the modifications (if any).

Form 9: Trusts for spouse for life with power to appoint to issue and gift over to them

Form 9 of the Statutory Will Forms, 1925, is incorporated in my will, and shall apply to* [subject to the following modifications†].

* Here insert description of property to be held on trusts for spouse for life with power to appoint to issue and gift over to them.
† Here insert the modifications (if any).

Form 10: Trusts for spouse and issue without a power of appointment

Form 10 of the Statutory Will Forms, 1925, is incorporated in my will, and shall apply to * [subject to the following modifications†].

* Here insert description of property to be held on trusts for spouse and issue without power of appointment.
† Here insert the modifications (if any).

PART I : FORMS WHICH MAY BE APPLIED EITHER GENERALLY OR BY SPECIFIC REFERENCE

B.1 Statutory Will Forms, 1925, Form 1: Confirmation of settlements

I confirm every settlement of property made by me which is subsisting at my death, and subject to any express provision to the contrary in my will, the provisions made by my will for the benefit of persons beneficially interested under any such settlement, shall be in addition to, and not in satisfaction of, those made, or covenanted to be made by me in such settlement.

B.2 Statutory Will Forms, 1925, Form 2: Meaning of "personal chattels"

(1) "Personal chattels" shall mean "carriages, horses, stable furniture and effects (not used for business purposes), motor cars and accessories (not used for business purposes), garden effects, domestic animals, plate, plated articles, linen, china, glass, books, pictures, prints, furniture, jewellery, articles of household or personal use or ornament (including wearing apparel), also musical and scientific instruments and apparatus, wines, liquors and consumable stores, but shall not include any chattels used at my death for business purposes, nor money or securities for money."

(2) But a general disposition of personal chattels shall take effect subject to any specific disposition.

B.3 Statutory Will Forms, 1925, Form 3: Inventories and provisions respecting chattels

(1) An inventory of chattels given by my will, otherwise than by way of

absolute gift, shall be made in duplicate, one part shall be retained by the trustees and the other part shall be delivered to the person of full age for the time being entitled to the use or possession of the chattels, in this clause called the "usufructuary".

(2) A receipt shall be signed by the usufructuary, at the foot of the inventory retained by the trustees.

(3) The inventory delivered to the usufructuary shall, if he so requires, be signed at the foot thereof by the trustees.

(4) On any change of the right to the use or possession of the chattels, a new receipt shall be signed by the usufructuary at the foot of the inventory retained by the trustees.

(5) Where, by reason of the exercise of any power to sell, exchange, purchase, alter the fashion of, or otherwise deal with the chattels, or of any destruction or loss of any chattel, the inventories become inaccurate, the inventories shall be altered and re-signed, or new inventories shall, if convenient, be made and signed.

(6) The trustees may, at their discretion, exclude from an inventory, any chattels which, by reason of their trifling value or wearing out nature, they may consider ought to be so excluded.

(7) Where the chattels have been delivered to the usufructuary and a receipt is given therefor, the trustees, so long as the usufructuary remains entitled to the use of the chattels, shall not be liable in any way -

(a) for any unauthorised disposition thereof or dealing therewith,

(b) to see to the insurance (so far as the same are capable of being insured) repair, or safe custody of the chattels, unless and until required, in writing, to insure the chattels or to take any proceedings in reference thereto, by some person beneficially interested in the chattels or by his guardian, committee or receiver, and unless also due provision be made, to the satisfaction of the trustees, for the payment of the costs of insurance or of any proceedings required to be taken.

(8) Where there is no person of full age and capacity entitled to the use of the chattels, the trustees may, during the period of disability, make such arrangements for the safe custody, repair, insurance and use of the chattels as, having regard to the circumstances of the case, they may in their absolute discretion, think expedient.

B.4 Statutory Will Forms, 1925, Form 4: Legacies to charities

The receipt of the treasurer or other proper officer of a charitable benevolent or philanthropic institution, society or body of persons (corporate or incorporate), to which a legacy is given by my will shall be a complete discharge of my personal representatives.

B.5 Statutory Will Forms, 1925, Form 5: Directions respecting annuities

The following provisions shall have effect in regard to any annuities or annuity given by my will -

(1) The trustees may, and (if so requested by or on behalf of any person beneficially interested in the property affected), shall, as soon as may be after any annuity commences to accrue, set apart in their names or under their control authorised investments to provide a fund the income whereof will be sufficient, in the opinion of the trustees, to produce an annual sum equal to the amount of the annuities for the time being payable under my will.

(2) The income or, if necessary, the capital of the fund so appropriated, shall be applied in payment of every subsisting annuity.

(3) Until a fund shall be so appropriated, my residuary estate shall stand charged with the payment of every subsisting annuity, but, after appropriation, the said estate shall be thereby discharged therefrom.

(4) The appropriated fund, or, where more than one annuity is bequeathed, such parts thereof as, in the opinion of the trustees, may not be required to answer any subsisting annuity, shall, on the cesser of an annuity, fall into my residuary personal estate.

(5) Accordingly, as each annuity ceases, the trustees may treat as part of my residuary personal estate, the whole or a corresponding part of the appropriated fund, as the case may require, retaining only such part thereof (if any) as may, from time to time, in their opinion, be sufficient to produce, by the income thereof, an annual sum equal to the amount of any subsisting annuities.

(6) Any surplus income of the appropriated fund shall be applied in the same manner as the income of my residuary personal estate.

(7) The trustees may, at their discretion, vary any of the investments for the time being representing the appropriated fund for other authorised investments.

(8) In this clause "annuity" includes any periodical payment (not being a rentcharge) for life or other terminable interest.

B.6 Statutory Will Forms, 1925, Form 6: Power of appropriation

(1) The power of appropriation conferred by the Administration of Estates Act, 1925, shall be exercisable by the trustees, without any of the consents made requisite by that Act.

(2) So far as practicable, the trustees shall give one month's notice, at least, of an intended appropriation, to the persons whose consent would, but for this clause, be required under that Act; but a purchaser shall not be concerned to see or inquire whether any such notices have been given.

(3) In this clause "trustees" includes my personal representatives.

PART II: FORMS WHICH CAN ONLY BE APPLIED BY SPECIFIC REFERENCE

B.7 Statutory Will Forms, 1925, Form 7: Trusts of a settled legacy
Any legacy of money or investments to which this clause is applied shall be subject to the following provisions:-
(1) The trustees shall stand possessed of the legacy upon trust to invest the same in their names or under their control in any authorised investments, with power, at the like discretion, to vary the investments thereof for others of a like nature.
(2) The trustees shall stand possessed of the legacy, and of the investments representing the same and all statutory accumulations, if any, of income thereof, hereinafter included in the description of such legacy upon trust to pay the income thereof to the legatee during the life of the legatee.
(3) After the death of the legatee, the capital and the income of the legacy shall be held–
In trust for all or any one or more exclusively of the other or others, of the issue of the legatee, whether children or remoter descendants, at such time, and if more than one in such shares, with such provisions for maintenance, education, advancement, and otherwise, at the discretion of any person or persons, and with such gifts over, and generally in such manner, for the benefit of such issue, or some or one of them, as the legatee shall, by deed, revocable or irrevocable, or by will appoint; but so that, under any appointment, a child shall not, otherwise than by way of advancement, take a vested interest, except upon attaining the age of twenty-one years or upon marriage.
And in default of and until and subject to any such appointment –
In trust for all or any the children or child of the legatee, who attain the age of twenty-one years, or marry under that age, and if more than one in equal shares.
(4) Any child of the legatee, who, or whose issue, takes any part of the legacy under any appointment by the legatee, shall not, in the absence of any direction by the legatee to the contrary, take any share in the unappointed part without bringing the share or shares appointed to him or his issue into hotchpot and accounting for the same accordingly.
(5) If the legatee shall not have any child who, under the trusts in default of appointment hereinbefore contained, attains a vested interest in the legacy, then, subject to the trusts and powers hereinbefore expressed in favour of the legatee and his issue, the legacy and the income thereof and

all statutory accumulations, if any, of income shall fall into and form part of my residuary personal estate.

(6) The legatee may, notwithstanding any of the trusts hereinbefore expressed concerning his legacy, from time to time or at any time by deed, revocable or irrevocable, or by will, appoint to or for the benefit of any spouse who may survive the legatee, during the residue of the life of such spouse or for any less period (and subject or not to any conditions, and with such gifts over, and discretionary or other trusts for the benefit of the spouse and issue of the legatee, as the legatee may think fit), all or any part of the annual income of the legacy of the legatee, or of so much thereof as shall not, before the death of the legatee, have been paid or applied under any power affecting the same,

And, upon any such appointment, the trusts and powers limited to take effect after the death of the legatee, shall take effect subject to the interest limited by any such appointment:

Provided that the powers last aforesaid, to appoint by deed, shall not be exercisable by a woman while under coverture.

B.8 Statutory Will Forms, 1925, Form 8: Administration trusts

Any property disposed of by my will (otherwise than in exercise of a special power) to which this clause is applied shall be subject to the following provisions:-

(1) The property shall be held-
  (a) as to the real property, if any, including chattels real, upon trust to sell the same and
  (b) as to the personal property, if any, upon trust to call in, sell and convert into money such part thereof as may not consist of money.

(2) The trustees shall have power to postpone such sale and conversion for such a period as they, without being liable to account may think proper.

(3) A reversionary interest shall not be sold, until it falls into possession, unless the trustees see special reason for sale.

(4) The trustees shall out of the net money to arise from the sale and conversion of the property (after payment of costs) and out of any ready money of mine, included in the disposition, pay or provide for
  (a) my funeral and testamentary expenses;
  (b) my debts, except charges on other property of mine so far as those charges are discharged out of the property primarily charged therewith under the Administration of Estates Act 1925;
  (c) the duties, payable out of capital on my death, and not charged on or primarily payable out of other property;
  (d) any other liabilities properly payable out of the property or the pro-

ceeds of sale thereof;

(e) the legacies (including money directed to be paid by my will), and annuities bequeathed by me, but so that all legacies and annuities, and the duty on all legacies and annuities bequeathed free of duty, shall be paid primarily out of personal property, if any, included in the disposition.

(5) The trustees may invest, in their names or under their control, the residue of the said money, or so much thereof as may not have been distributed, in any authorised investments, with power, at their discretion, to vary such investments for others of a like nature.

(6) The income (including net rents and profits of real property and chattels real, after payment of rates, taxes, costs of insurance and of repairs and other outgoings properly attributable to income) of so much of the property as is not required for the administration purposes aforesaid, shall, however the property is invested, as from my death, be treated and applied as income; and for that purpose any necessary apportionment may be made between capital and income.

(7) Provided that-
   (a) statutory accumulations of income made during a minority, or pending a contingency, or accumulations made under an express trust for accumulation, may be added to capital;
   (b) income may be applied in effecting and maintaining a leasehold sinking fund policy, or may be set aside and invested for providing a fund to answer any liabilities which in the opinion of the trustees ought to be borne by income;
   (c) the trustees may in their discretion adjust, in such manner as they think fit, having regard to the circumstances of the case, the incidence, as between capital and income, of the payments made in due course of administration.

B.9 Statutory Will Forms, 1925, Form 9: Trusts for spouse for life with power to appoint to issue and gift over to them

Any property disposed of by my will (otherwise than in exercise of a special power) to which this clause is applied shall be subject to the following provisions:-

(1) The property (including the investments for the time being representing the same) shall be held upon trust to pay the income thereof to my spouse for life.

(2) After the death of my spouse, the capital and income of the property shall be held -
   (i) In trust for all or any one or more, exclusively of the other or others,

of my issue, whether children or remoter descendants, at such time, and if more than one in equal shares, with such provisions for maintenance, education, advancement and otherwise, at the discretion of any person or persons, and with such gifts over, and generally in such manner, for the benefit of such issue, or some or one of them, as my spouse shall, by deed, revocable or irrevocable, or by will, appoint; but so that, under any appointment, a child shall not, otherwise than by way of advancement, take a vested interest, except upon attaining the age of twenty-one years or upon marriage.

(ii) And in default of and until and subject to any such appointment in trust, in equal shares if more than one, for all or any of my children or child who survive me and attain the age of twenty-one years or marry under that age, and for all or any of the issue living at my death who attain the age of twenty-one years or marry under that age of any child of mine who predeceases me, such issue to take through all degrees, according to their stocks, in equal shares if more than one, the share or shares which his or their parent would have taken if living at my death, and so that no issue shall take whose parent is living at my death and so capable of taking.

(3) Any person who, or whose issue, takes any part of the property, under any appointment by my spouse, shall not, in the absence of any direction by my spouse to the contrary, take any share in the unappointed part, without bringing the shares appointed to such person or his issue into hotchpot, and accounting for the same accordingly.

B.10 Statutory Will Forms, 1925, Form 10: Trusts for spouse and issue, without a power of appointment

Any property disposed of by my will (otherwise than in exercise of a special power) to which this clause is applied shall be subject to the following provisions:-

(1) The property (including the investments for the time being representing the same) shall be held upon trust to pay the income thereof to my spouse for life.

(2) After the death of my spouse the capital and income of the property shall be held in trust, in equal shares if more than one, for all or any of my children or child who survive me and attain the age of twenty-one years or marry under that age, and for all or any of the issue living at my death, who attain the age of twenty-one years or marry under that age, of any child of mine who predeceases me, such issue to take through all degrees, according to their stocks, in equal shares, if more than one, the share or shares which his or their parent would have taken if living at my

death; and so that no issue shall take whose parent is living at my death and so capable of taking.

Index

page